PRACTICE - ASSESS - DIAGNOSE

180 Days of READING for Sixth Grade

Author
Margot Kinberg, Ph.D.

Contributing Author

Christine Dugan, M.A.Ed.

Publishing Credits

Dona Herweck Rice, *Editor-in-Chief*; Robin Erickson, *Production Director;* Lee Aucoin, *Creative Director;* Timothy J. Bradley, *Illustration Manager*; Sara Johnson, M.S.Ed., *Senior Editor*; Aubrie Nielsen, M.S.Ed., *Editor*; Leah Quillian, *Assistant Editor;* Grace Alba, *Designer;* David Saracino, *Illustrator*; Howard McWilliam, *Illustrator*; Jennifer King-Harvey, *Illustrator;* Stephanie Reid, *Photo Editor*; Corinne Burton, M.A.Ed., *Publisher*

Image Credits

Cover, Howard McWilliam; p. 54 [SF22640] Corbis; p. 138 [LC-USZ62-11564], p. 150 [LC-USZ62-105310] The Library of Congress; p. 174 Wikimedia; p. 186 [NARA mn57875] galleryget.com; p. 198 NASA; all other photos Shutterstock

Standards

Shell Education
5482 Argosy Avenue
Huntington Beach, CA 92649-1030
www.tcmpub.com/shell-education

ISBN 978-1-4258-0927-0

TABLE OF CONTENTS

INTRODUCTION AND RESEARCH

The Need for Practice

In order to be successful in today's reading classroom, students must deeply understand both concepts and procedures so that they can discuss and demonstrate their understanding. Demonstrating understanding is a process that must be continually practiced in order for students to be successful. According to Marzano, "practice has always been, and always will be, a necessary ingredient to learning procedural knowledge at a level at which students execute it independently" (2010, 83). Practice is especially important to help students apply reading comprehension strategies and word-study skills.

Understanding Assessment

In addition to providing opportunities for frequent practice, teachers must be able to assess students' comprehension and word-study skills. This is important so that teachers can adequately address students' misconceptions, build on their current understanding, and challenge them appropriately. Assessment is a long-term process that often involves careful analysis of student responses from a lesson discussion, a project, a practice sheet, or a test. When analyzing the data, it is important for teachers to reflect on how their teaching practices may have influenced students' responses and to identify those areas where additional instruction may be required. In short, the data gathered from assessments should be used to inform instruction: slow down, speed up, or reteach. This type of assessment is called *formative assessment*.

HOW TO USE THIS BOOK

180 Days of Reading for Sixth Grade offers teachers and parents a full page of daily reading comprehension and word-study practice activities for each day of the school year.

Easy to Use and Standards Based

These activities reinforce grade-level skills across a variety of reading concepts. The questions are provided as a full practice page, making them easy to prepare and implement as part of a classroom morning routine, at the beginning of each reading lesson, or as homework.

Every sixth-grade practice page provides questions that are tied to a reading or writing standard. Students are given the opportunity for regular practice in reading comprehension and word study, allowing them to build confidence through these quick standards-based activities.

Question	College and Career Readiness Standards
	Days 1–3
1–2	**Reading Anchor Standard 1:** *Read closely to determine what the text says explicitly and to make logical inferences from it.*
3–5	**Reading Anchor Standard 4:** *Interpret words and phrases as they are used in a text, including determining technical, connotative, and figurative meanings, and analyze how specific word choices shape meaning or tone.*
	Day 4
1–2	**Reading Anchor Standard 10:** *Read and comprehend complex literary and informational texts independently and proficiently.*
3–6	**Reading Anchor Standard 1:** *Read closely to determine what the text says explicitly and to make logical inferences from it* **or** **Reading Anchor Standard 6:** *Assess how point of view or purpose shapes the content and style of a text.*
7–8	**Reading Anchor Standard 2:** *Determine central ideas or themes of a text and analyze their development; summarize the key supporting details and ideas.*
	Day 5
	Writing Anchor Standard 4: *Produce clear and coherent writing in which the development, organization, and style are appropriate to task, purpose, and audience.*

HOW TO USE THIS BOOK *(cont.)*

Using the Practice Pages

Practice pages provide instruction and assessment opportunities for each day of the school year. The activities are organized into weekly themes, and teachers may wish to prepare packets of each week's practice pages for students. Days 1, 2, and 3 follow a consistent format, with a short piece of text and five corresponding items. As outlined on page 4, every item is aligned to a reading standard.

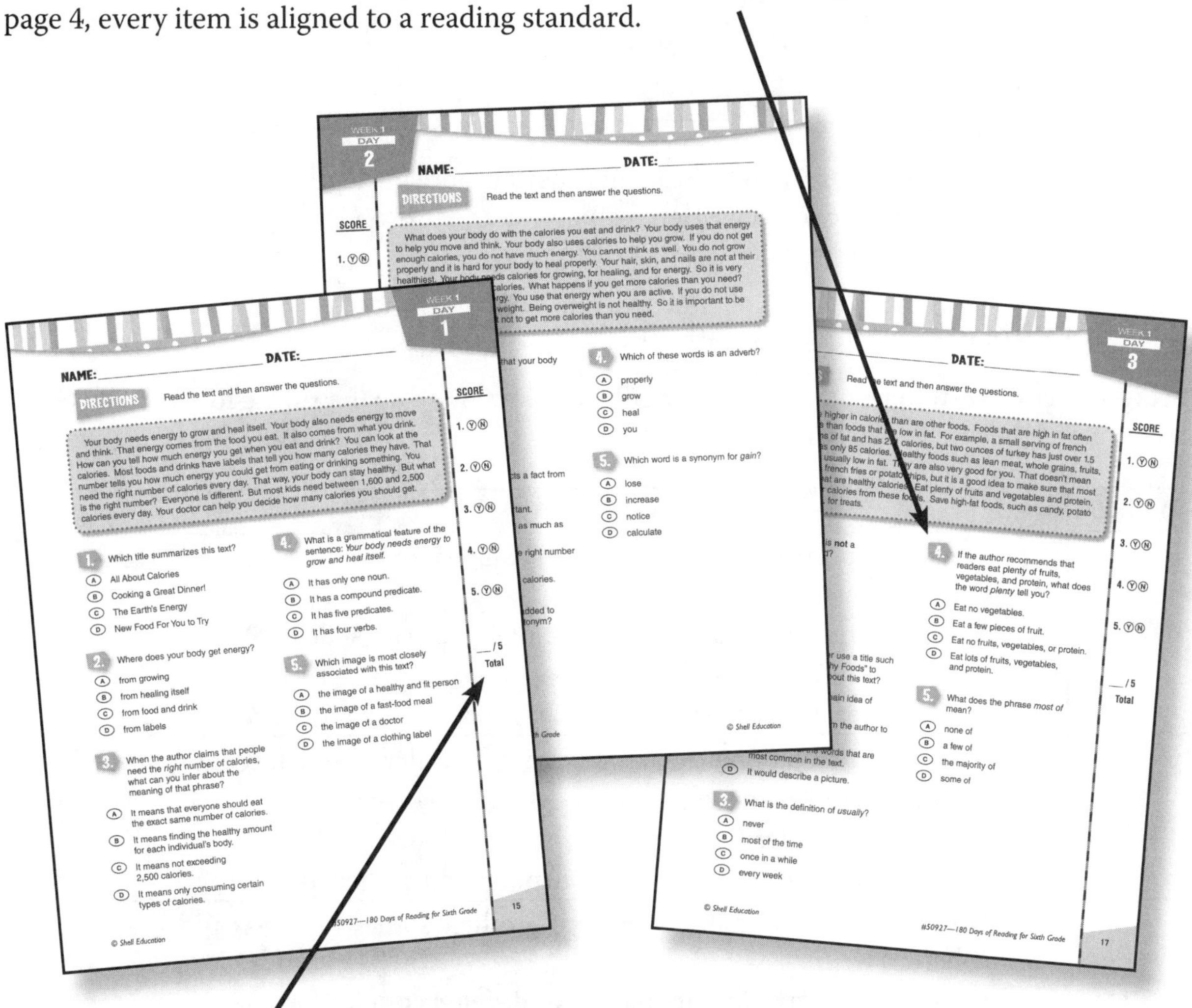
WEEK 1 DAY 2

NAME: DATE:

DIRECTIONS Read the text and then answer the questions.

SCORE

1. Ⓨ Ⓝ

What does your body do with the calories you eat and drink? Your body uses that energy to help you move and think. Your body also uses calories to help you grow. If you do not get enough calories, you do not have much energy. You cannot think as well. You do not grow properly and it is hard for your body to heal properly. Your hair, skin, and nails are not at their healthiest. Your body needs calories for growing, for healing, and for energy. So it is very ... calories. What happens if you get more calories than you need? ...rgy. You use that energy when you are active. If you do not use ... weight. Being overweight is not healthy. So it is important to be ... not to get more calories than you need.

4. Which of these words is an adverb?

- Ⓐ properly
- Ⓑ grow
- Ⓒ heal
- Ⓓ you

5. Which word is a synonym for *gain*?

- Ⓐ lose
- Ⓑ increase
- Ⓒ notice
- Ⓓ calculate

© Shell Education

WEEK 1 DAY 1

NAME: DATE:

DIRECTIONS Read the text and then answer the questions.

Your body needs energy to grow and heal itself. Your body also needs energy to move and think. That energy comes from the food you eat. It also comes from what you drink. How can you tell how much energy you get when you eat and drink? You can look at the calories. Most foods and drinks have labels that tell you how many calories they have. That number tells you how much energy you could get from eating or drinking something. You need the right number of calories every day. That way, your body can stay healthy. But what is the right number? Everyone is different. But most kids need between 1,600 and 2,500 calories every day. Your doctor can help you decide how many calories you should get.

1. Which title summarizes this text?
   - Ⓐ All About Calories
   - Ⓑ Cooking a Great Dinner!
   - Ⓒ The Earth's Energy
   - Ⓓ New Food For You to Try

2. Where does your body get energy?
   - Ⓐ from growing
   - Ⓑ from healing itself
   - Ⓒ from food and drink
   - Ⓓ from labels

3. When the author claims that people need the *right* number of calories, what can you infer about the meaning of that phrase?
   - Ⓐ It means that everyone should eat the exact same number of calories.
   - Ⓑ It means finding the healthy amount for each individual's body.
   - Ⓒ It means not exceeding 2,500 calories.
   - Ⓓ It means only consuming certain types of calories.

4. What is a grammatical feature of the sentence: *Your body needs energy to grow and heal itself.*
   - Ⓐ It has only one noun.
   - Ⓑ It has a compound predicate.
   - Ⓒ It has five predicates.
   - Ⓓ It has four verbs.

5. Which image is most closely associated with this text?
   - Ⓐ the image of a healthy and fit person
   - Ⓑ the image of a fast-food meal
   - Ⓒ the image of a doctor
   - Ⓓ the image of a clothing label

SCORE

1. Ⓨ Ⓝ
2. Ⓨ Ⓝ
3. Ⓨ Ⓝ
4. Ⓨ Ⓝ
5. Ⓨ Ⓝ

___ / 5 Total

© Shell Education #50927—180 Days of Reading for Sixth Grade 15

WEEK 1 DAY 3

DATE:

Read the text and then answer the questions.

4. If the author recommends that readers eat plenty of fruits, vegetables, and protein, what does the word *plenty* tell you?
   - Ⓐ Eat no vegetables.
   - Ⓑ Eat a few pieces of fruit.
   - Ⓒ Eat no fruits, vegetables, or protein.
   - Ⓓ Eat lots of fruits, vegetables, and protein.

5. What does the phrase *most of* mean?
   - Ⓐ none of
   - Ⓑ a few of
   - Ⓒ the majority of
   - Ⓓ some of

3. What is the definition of *usually*?
   - Ⓐ never
   - Ⓑ most of the time
   - Ⓒ once in a while
   - Ⓓ every week

SCORE

1. Ⓨ Ⓝ
2. Ⓨ Ⓝ
3. Ⓨ Ⓝ
4. Ⓨ Ⓝ
5. Ⓨ Ⓝ

___ / 5 Total

© Shell Education #50927—180 Days of Reading for Sixth Grade 17

Using the Scoring Guide

Use the scoring guide along the side of each practice page to check answers and see at a glance which skills may need more reinforcement.

Fill in the appropriate circle for each problem to indicate correct (Y) or incorrect (N) responses. You might wish to indicate only incorrect responses to focus on those skills. (For example, if students consistently miss items 2 and 4, they may need additional help with those concepts as outlined in the table on page 4.) Use the answer key at the back of the book to score the problems, or you may call out answers to have students self-score or peer-score their work.

HOW TO USE THIS BOOK *(cont.)*

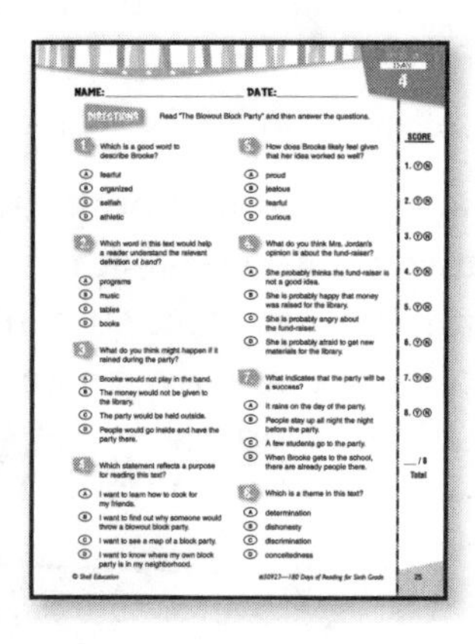

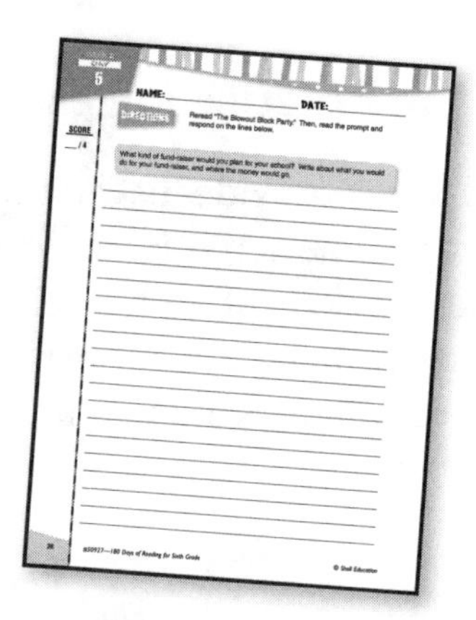

A longer text is used for Days 4 and 5. Students answer more in-depth comprehension questions on Day 4 and complete a written response to the text on Day 5. This longer text can also be used for fluency practice (see page 7).

Writing Rubric

Score students' written response using the rubric below. Display the rubric for students to reference as they write (G6_writing_rubric.pdf).

Points	Criteria
4	• Uses an appropriate organizational sequence to produce very clear and coherent writing • Uses descriptive language that develops or clarifies ideas • Engages the reader • Uses a style very appropriate to task, purpose, and audience
3	• Uses an organizational sequence to produce clear and coherent writing • Uses descriptive language that develops or clarifies ideas • Engages the reader • Uses a style appropriate to task, purpose, and audience
2	• Uses an organizational sequence to produce somewhat clear and coherent writing • Uses some descriptive language that develops or clarifies ideas • Engages the reader in some way • Uses a style somewhat appropriate to task, purpose, and audience
1	• Does not use an organized sequence; the writing is not clear or coherent • Uses little descriptive language to develop or clarify ideas • Does not engage the reader • Does not use a style appropriate to task, purpose, or audience
0	Offers no writing or does not respond to the assignment presented

HOW TO USE THIS BOOK *(cont.)*

Developing Students' Fluency Skills

What Is Fluency?

According to the National Reading Panel Report, there are five critical factors that are vital to effective reading instruction: phonemic awareness, phonics, fluency, vocabulary, and comprehension (2000). Rasinski (2006) defines fluency as "the ability to accurately and effortlessly decode the written words and then to give meaning to those words through appropriate phrasing and oral expression of the words." Wolf (2005) notes that the goal of developing fluency is comprehension rather than the ability to read rapidly. Becoming a fluent reader is a skill that develops gradually and requires practice. Reading text repeatedly with a different purpose each time supports the development of fluency in young children (Rasinski 2003).

Assessing Fluency

Fluent readers read accurately, with expression, and at a good pace. A Fluency Rubric along with detailed instructions for scoring and keeping oral reading records is included in the digital resources (G6_fluency.pdf).

The table below lists fluency norms by grade level (Rasinski 2003):

Student Fluency Norms Based On Words Correct Per Minute (WCPM)			
Grade	**Fall**	**Winter**	**Spring**
1	—	—	60 wcpm
2	53	78	94
3	79	93	114
4	99	112	118
5	105	118	128
6	115	132	145

HOW TO USE THIS BOOK *(cont.)*

Diagnostic Assessment

Teachers can use the practice pages as diagnostic assessments. The data analysis tools included with the book enable teachers or parents to quickly score students' work and monitor their progress. Teachers and parents can see at a glance which reading concepts or skills students may need to target in order to develop proficiency.

After students complete a practice page, grade each page using the answer key (pages 231–237). Then, complete the Practice Page Item Analysis for the appropriate day (pages 10–11) for the whole class, or the Student Item Analysis (pages 12–13) for individual students. These charts are also provided in the digital resources (filenames: G6_practicepage_analysis.pdf, G6_student_analysis.pdf). Teachers can input data into the electronic files directly on the computer, or they can print the pages and analyze students' work using paper and pencil.

To complete the Practice Page Item Analyses:

- Write or type students' names in the far-left column. Depending on the number of students, more than one copy of the form may be needed, or you may need to add rows.
- The item numbers are included across the top of the charts. Each item correlates with the matching question number from the practice page.
- For each student, record an *X* in the column if the student has the item incorrect. If the item is correct, leave the item blank.
- Count the *X*s in each row and column and fill in the correct boxes.

To complete the Student Item Analyses:

- Write or type the student's name on the top row. This form tracks the ongoing progress of each student, so one copy per student is necessary.
- The item numbers are included across the top of the chart. Each item correlates with the matching question number from the practice page.
- For each day, record an *X* in the column if the student has the item incorrect. If the item is correct, leave the item blank.
- Count the *X*s in each row and column and fill in the correct boxes.

HOW TO USE THIS BOOK *(cont.)*

Using the Results to Differentiate Instruction

Once results are gathered and analyzed, teachers can use the results to inform the way they differentiate instruction. The data can help determine which concepts are the most difficult for students and which need additional instructional support and continued practice. Depending on how often the practice pages are scored, results can be considered for instructional support on a daily or weekly basis.

Whole-Class Support

The results of the diagnostic analysis may show that the entire class is struggling with a particular concept or group of concepts. If these concepts have been taught in the past, this indicates that further instruction or reteaching is necessary. If these concepts have not been taught in the past, this data is a great preassessment and demonstrates that students do not have a working knowledge of the concepts. Thus, careful planning for the length of the unit(s) or lesson(s) must be considered, and extra frontloading may be required.

Small-Group or Individual Support

The results of the diagnostic analysis may show that an individual or small group of students is struggling with a particular concept or group of concepts. If these concepts have been taught in the past, this indicates that further instruction or reteaching is necessary. Consider pulling aside these students while others are working independently to instruct further on the concept(s). Teachers can also use the results to help identify individuals or groups of proficient students who are ready for enrichment or above-grade-level instruction. These students may benefit from independent learning contracts or more challenging activities. Students may also benefit from extra practice using games or computer-based resources.

Digital Resources

Reference page 239 for information about accessing the digital resources and an overview of the contents.

PRACTICE PAGE ITEM ANALYSIS DAYS 1–3

Directions: Record an *X* in cells to indicate where students have missed questions. Add up the totals. You can view the following: (1) which items were missed per student; (2) the total correct score for each student; and (3) the total number of students who missed each item.

Week: ____ Day: ____ Item #	1	2	3	4	5	# correct
Student Name						
Sample Student		X			X	3/5
# of students missing each question						

PRACTICE PAGE ITEM ANALYSIS DAYS 4–5

Directions: Record an *X* in cells to indicate where students have missed questions. Add up the totals. You can view the following: (1) which items were missed per student; (2) the total correct score for each student; and (3) the total number of students who missed each item.

Week: _____ Day: _____ Item #	1	2	3	4	5	6	7	8	# correct	Written Response
Student Name										
Sample Student		X			X	X			5/8	3
# of students missing each question										
										Written Response Average:

STUDENT ITEM ANALYSIS DAYS 1–3

Directions: Record an *X* in cells to indicate where the student has missed questions. Add up the totals. You can view the following: (1) which items the student missed; (2) the total correct score per day; and (3) the total number of times each item was missed.

Student Name: Sample Student

Item		1	2	3	4	5	# correct
Week	Day						
1	1		X			X	3/5
Total							

STUDENT ITEM ANALYSIS DAYS 4–5

Directions: Record an *X* in cells to indicate where the student has missed questions. Add up the totals. You can view the following: (1) which items the student missed; (2) the total correct score per day; and (3) the total number of times each item was missed.

Student Name: Sample Student										
	Day 4									**Day 5**
Item	**1**	**2**	**3**	**4**	**5**	**6**	**7**	**8**	**# correct**	**Written Response**
Week										
1		X			X	X			5/8	3
Total										
										Written Response Average:

STANDARDS CORRELATIONS

Shell Education is committed to producing educational materials that are research and standards based. In this effort, we have correlated all of our products to the academic standards of all 50 United States, the District of Columbia, the Department of Defense Dependent Schools, and all Canadian provinces.

How To Find Standards Correlations

To print a customized correlation report of this product for your state, visit our website at **www.tcmpub.com/shell-education** and follow the on-screen directions. If you require assistance in printing correlation reports, please contact Customer Service at 1-877-777-3450.

Purpose and Intent of Standards

Legislation mandates that all states adopt academic standards that identify the skills students will learn in kindergarten through grade twelve. Many states also have standards for Pre-K. This same legislation sets requirements to ensure the standards are detailed and comprehensive.

Standards are designed to focus instruction and guide adoption of curricula. Standards are statements that describe the criteria necessary for students to meet specific academic goals. They define the knowledge, skills, and content students should acquire at each level. Standards are also used to develop standardized tests to evaluate students' academic progress. Teachers are required to demonstrate how their lessons meet state standards. State standards are used in the development of all of our products, so educators can be assured they meet the academic requirements of each state.

College and Career Readiness

The activities in this book are aligned to the college and career readiness (CCR) standards. The chart on page 4 lists each standard that is addressed in this product.

TESOL and WIDA Standards

The activities in this book promote English language development for English language learners.

NAME: ____________________ **DATE:** ____________

DIRECTIONS Read the text and then answer the questions.

Your body needs energy to grow and heal itself. Your body also needs energy to move and think. That energy comes from the food you eat. It also comes from what you drink. How can you tell how much energy you get when you eat and drink? You can look at the calories. Most foods and drinks have labels that tell you how many calories they have. That number tells you how much energy you could get from eating or drinking something. You need the right number of calories every day. That way, your body can stay healthy. But what is the right number? Everyone is different. Most kids need between 1,600 and 2,500 calories every day. Your doctor can help you decide how many calories you should get.

1. Which title summarizes this text?

- (A) All About Calories
- (B) Cooking a Great Dinner!
- (C) The Earth's Energy
- (D) New Food For You to Try

2. Where does your body get energy?

- (A) from growing
- (B) from healing itself
- (C) from food and drinks
- (D) from labels

3. When the author claims that people need the *right* number of calories, what can you infer about the meaning of that phrase?

- (A) It means that everyone should eat the exact same number of calories.
- (B) It means finding the healthy amount for each individual's body.
- (C) It means not exceeding 2,500 calories.
- (D) It means only consuming certain types of calories.

4. What is a grammatical feature of this sentence: *Your body needs energy to grow and heal itself.*

- (A) It has only one noun.
- (B) It has a compound predicate.
- (C) It has five predicates.
- (D) It has four verbs.

5. Which is the tone of this text?

- (A) informative
- (B) humorous
- (C) fearful
- (D) sorrowful

SCORE

1. Ⓨ Ⓝ
2. Ⓨ Ⓝ
3. Ⓨ Ⓝ
4. Ⓨ Ⓝ
5. Ⓨ Ⓝ

___ / 5 **Total**

NAME: ____________________ **DATE:** ____________

DIRECTIONS Read the text and then answer the questions.

SCORE

1. Ⓨ Ⓝ
2. Ⓨ Ⓝ
3. Ⓨ Ⓝ
4. Ⓨ Ⓝ
5. Ⓨ Ⓝ

___ / 5 Total

What does your body do with the calories you eat and drink? Your body uses that energy to help you move and think. Your body also uses calories to help you grow. If you do not get enough calories, you do not have much energy. You cannot think as well. You do not grow properly and it is hard for your body to heal properly. Your hair, skin, and nails are not at their healthiest. Your body needs calories for growing, for healing, and for energy. So it is very important to get enough calories. What happens if you get more calories than you need? Your body stores that energy. You use that energy when you are active. If you do not use that energy, you can gain weight. Being overweight is not healthy. So it is important to be active. It is also important not to get more calories than you need.

1. Which is **not** a way that your body uses calories?

Ⓐ thinking
Ⓑ growing
Ⓒ healing
Ⓓ getting rid of energy

2. Which sentence reflects a fact from this text?

Ⓐ Calories are not important.
Ⓑ It is a good idea to eat as much as you can.
Ⓒ It is important to get the right number of calories.
Ⓓ You should not get any calories.

3. Which prefix could be added to *properly* to make its antonym?

Ⓐ *pre–*
Ⓑ *im–*
Ⓒ *ab–*
Ⓓ *pro–*

4. Which of these words is an adverb?

Ⓐ properly
Ⓑ grow
Ⓒ heal
Ⓓ you

5. Which word is a synonym for *gain*?

Ⓐ lose
Ⓑ increase
Ⓒ notice
Ⓓ calculate

NAME: ____________________ **DATE:** ____________

DIRECTIONS Read the text and then answer the questions.

Some foods are higher in calories than other foods. Foods that are high in fat often have more calories than foods that are low in fat. For example, a small serving of french fries has 14.5 grams of fat and 271 calories, but two ounces of turkey has just over 1.5 grams of fat and only 85 calories. Healthy foods such as lean meat, whole grains, fruits, and vegetables are usually low in fat. They are also very good for you. That doesn't mean you can never have french fries or potato chips, but it is a good idea to make sure that most of the calories you eat are healthy calories. Eat plenty of fruits and vegetables and protein, and get most of your calories from these foods. Save high-fat foods, such as candy, potato chips, and fried food, for treats.

1. Which of these is **not** a high-calorie food?

Ⓐ lean meat
Ⓑ cookies
Ⓒ french fries
Ⓓ fried chicken

2. How would a reader use a title such as "Choosing Healthy Foods" to understand more about this text?

Ⓐ The title would hint at the main idea of the text.
Ⓑ The title would be a joke from the author to the reader.
Ⓒ The title would reveal the words that are most common in the text.
Ⓓ The title would describe a picture.

3. What is the definition of *usually*?

Ⓐ never
Ⓑ most of the time
Ⓒ once in a while
Ⓓ every week

4. If the author recommends that readers eat plenty of fruits, vegetables, and protein, what does the word *plenty* tell you?

Ⓐ Eat no vegetables.
Ⓑ Eat a few pieces of fruit.
Ⓒ Eat no fruits, vegetables, or protein.
Ⓓ Eat lots of fruits, vegetables, and protein.

5. What does the phrase *most of* mean?

Ⓐ none of
Ⓑ a few of
Ⓒ the majority of
Ⓓ some of

SCORE

1. Ⓨ Ⓝ
2. Ⓨ Ⓝ
3. Ⓨ Ⓝ
4. Ⓨ Ⓝ
5. Ⓨ Ⓝ

___ / 5
Total

NAME: ______________________________ **DATE:** ________________

SUPERSIZED

Have you eaten at a fast-food restaurant lately? Many restaurants serve much bigger portions of food than they used to serve. A *portion* is the amount of food that you get when you order. For example, in the 1950s, a portion of french fries was about 2.4 ounces. Today's portion can be as high as 7 ounces or more. In the 1950s, a regular soda was 8 ounces. Today, that size soda is more likely to be 24 ounces.

Why does it matter if portion sizes are bigger now? Isn't that a good thing for customers? Not if you want to eat a healthy diet. Bigger portions have more food in them, and the more food you eat, the more calories your body gets. If you eat a lot of fast food, you are probably getting many more calories than you need, and those calories may not be healthy calories. Here is just one example: A meal with a large burger, fries, and a soda at one major fast-food restaurant has 1,200 calories. That is one-half to three-quarters of the number of calories most kids should eat in one day. That meal has a lot of fat and salt without a lot of the vitamins and minerals that your body needs. So, that meal gives you a lot of calories but not much nutrition.

You can enjoy fast food sometimes without overeating. Most restaurant menus tell you the number of calories in each item. Look for a food choice with a lower number of calories. Chances are you will find something you like. When you do order fried foods or other high-fat foods, order a small portion. You will still enjoy the taste! Don't eat too quickly—it takes your brain up to twenty minutes to realize that your stomach is full. So eat your food more slowly to give your brain time to catch up. Then, you will feel satisfied with less food. And remember that fast food is best if you have it as a treat once in a while—not every day.

NAME: ______________________ **DATE:** ______________

DIRECTIONS Read "Supersized" and then answer the questions.

1. Which fact is true about restaurants in the 1950s?

Ⓐ They served bigger portions.
Ⓑ They did not serve soda.
Ⓒ They did not serve french fries.
Ⓓ They served smaller portions.

2. Which is a likely purpose for reading this text?

Ⓐ I want to know how to supersize my own meals at home.
Ⓑ I want to understand why restaurants are getting bigger.
Ⓒ I want to read about the history of farms that grow our food.
Ⓓ I want to learn about healthy portion sizes.

3. What is the author hoping readers will do?

Ⓐ eat a lot of fast food
Ⓑ eat fast food wisely
Ⓒ never eat fast food again
Ⓓ eat as quickly as you can

4. Why are bigger portions a problem?

Ⓐ They have too many calories.
Ⓑ They are too expensive.
Ⓒ They do not taste good.
Ⓓ They do not fit on plates.

5. Since it takes the brain up to twenty minutes to know the stomach is full, which conclusion makes sense?

Ⓐ Meals should not be longer than twenty minutes.
Ⓑ Meals should take only twenty minutes.
Ⓒ Eating slowly prevents you from getting too full.
Ⓓ Brains work slowly.

6. Which is likely the author's opinion?

Ⓐ A healthy diet is important.
Ⓑ Fast food is very good for you.
Ⓒ A healthy diet doesn't matter.
Ⓓ Kids should eat more fast food.

7. It takes Celia thirty minutes to eat lunch, but it takes Lisa fifteen minutes. What can you infer?

Ⓐ Celia will not feel satisfied.
Ⓑ Lisa and Celia are not friends.
Ⓒ Celia will feel satisfied with less food than Lisa will.
Ⓓ Lisa will be very hungry.

8. Which conclusion about people in the 1950s is the most realistic?

Ⓐ They ate more fast food than we do.
Ⓑ They ate less fast food than we do.
Ⓒ They ate the same amount of fast food as we do.
Ⓓ They ate no fast food at all.

SCORE

1. Ⓨ Ⓝ
2. Ⓨ Ⓝ
3. Ⓨ Ⓝ
4. Ⓨ Ⓝ
5. Ⓨ Ⓝ
6. Ⓨ Ⓝ
7. Ⓨ Ⓝ
8. Ⓨ Ⓝ

___ / 8 Total

NAME: ______________________ **DATE:** ______________

DIRECTIONS Reread "Supersized." Then, read the prompt and respond on the lines below.

SCORE

___ / 4

How can you make smart food choices at your favorite fast-food restaurant? Write about what you could do to make smart food choices.

NAME: ____________________ **DATE:** ____________

DIRECTIONS Read the text and then answer the questions.

Brooke had been in her school's library for half an hour, looking unsuccessfully for some information for a project. She was nearly ready to give up in frustration when she spotted the school's librarian. "Mrs. Jordan," Brooke pleaded, "can I please have some help finding some things?"

"I'll certainly do my best, Brooke. What is it that you need?" Mrs. Jordan asked.

"I need good resources for my project on ancient Assyria, but there's not much here."

"I'm sorry you're not finding what you need," Mrs. Jordan said with some embarrassment. "I wish we had more material on ancient Assyria, but we just don't have the funding we need for all the books we would like to have."

Mrs. Jordan helped Brooke as best she could, but Brooke couldn't help thinking the school ought to hold a fund-raiser for more library materials.

1. What is Brooke's problem?

- (A) Mrs. Jordan is angry with her.
- (B) She does not like being in the library.
- (C) She can't find the material she needs.
- (D) She has lost a library book.

2. How does the text explain why the library does **not** have the material it needs?

- (A) The material is hard to find.
- (B) There is not enough funding.
- (C) Mrs. Jordan does not like the material.
- (D) The library is too small.

3. Which two words are synonyms?

- (A) *resources* and *project*
- (B) *material* and *ancient*
- (C) *project* and *library*
- (D) *funding* and *money*

4. What does the prefix *un–* in the word *unsuccessfully* tell the reader about Brooke's search?

- (A) She finds everything she needs.
- (B) She is successful.
- (C) She is not successful.
- (D) She is afraid to ask for help.

5. Which word is used to describe what a group holds in order to raise money?

- (A) fund-raiser
- (B) library
- (C) material
- (D) project

SCORE

1. Ⓨ Ⓝ
2. Ⓨ Ⓝ
3. Ⓨ Ⓝ
4. Ⓨ Ⓝ
5. Ⓨ Ⓝ

___ / 5 Total

NAME: ______________________ **DATE:** ______________

DIRECTIONS Read the text and then answer the questions.

SCORE

1. Ⓨ Ⓝ

2. Ⓨ Ⓝ

3. Ⓨ Ⓝ

4. Ⓨ Ⓝ

5. Ⓨ Ⓝ

___ / 5
Total

Brooke was working on a project about ancient Assyria. She had looked in her school's library for material, but there wasn't very much. So she had to go to the public library. Brooke got what she needed at the public library, but she kept thinking that the school's library should have more resources. Mrs. Jordan, the librarian, told Brooke that the library didn't have the funding it needed. That was why there wasn't enough material. So Brooke decided to ask if there could be a fund-raiser to get more library books and materials. She talked to Mrs. Archer, who was head of the school's booster club. Mrs. Archer thought a library fund-raiser was a terrific idea. She and Brooke talked about what to do for a fund-raiser and finally they hit on the perfect idea—a block party where everyone would bring food and a small donation.

1. Who is Mrs. Jordan?

Ⓐ Brooke's teacher
Ⓑ the librarian
Ⓒ the head of the booster club
Ⓓ none of the above

2. How do Brooke and Mrs. Archer plan to solve the library's funding problem?

Ⓐ a block party fund-raiser
Ⓑ a bigger library
Ⓒ a trip to the public library
Ⓓ a new booster club

3. Which word is a synonym for *donation*?

Ⓐ discussion
Ⓑ library
Ⓒ party
Ⓓ contribution

4. What is an example of a proper noun?

Ⓐ Assyria
Ⓑ Mrs. Jordan
Ⓒ Brooke
Ⓓ all of the above

5. Which word is an antonym of *public*?

Ⓐ library
Ⓑ large
Ⓒ private
Ⓓ terrific

NAME: ____________________ **DATE:** ______________

DIRECTIONS Read the text and then answer the questions.

SCORE

1. Ⓨ Ⓝ
2. Ⓨ Ⓝ
3. Ⓨ Ⓝ
4. Ⓨ Ⓝ
5. Ⓨ Ⓝ

___ / 5 Total

Don't Miss the Fabulous Blowout Block Party Potluck!

Do you enjoy eating delicious homemade food? Do you like to play games, watch movies, and spend time with your friends? Then, you want to be there for the amazing Blowout Block Party Potluck! The Block Party Potluck will be held at Mason Street School on Saturday, September 17, from 1:00 p.m. until 5:00 p.m. Bring a potluck dish to share, and sample some of the finest cooking in town! There will be music, movies, games, and prizes, too! Don't miss out on this spectacular event!

Get your tickets now: Adult tickets are $5.00, and student tickets are $4.00.

All proceeds from ticket sales will benefit the Mason Street School library, so get ready to have a great time and help the library, too!

1. Which information is **not** provided in this flyer?

Ⓐ the date of the block party
Ⓑ the time and place of the block party
Ⓒ the price of the tickets
Ⓓ titles of the movies that will be shown

2. Why is a flyer helpful for a reader?

Ⓐ It is small.
Ⓑ It is colorful.
Ⓒ It includes the most important facts.
Ⓓ It only includes pictures.

3. Which word is a synonym for *sample*?

Ⓐ taste
Ⓑ cook
Ⓒ attend
Ⓓ ticket

4. What does the adjective *delicious* tell you about the food?

Ⓐ It is hard to find.
Ⓑ It is expensive.
Ⓒ It tastes very good.
Ⓓ It is easy to make.

5. Which word is **not** a compound word?

Ⓐ blowout
Ⓑ potluck
Ⓒ homemade
Ⓓ spectacular

NAME: ______________________ **DATE:** ______________

THE BLOWOUT BLOCK PARTY

Brooke was concerned because the library at her school needed more books and other materials. But Mrs. Jordan, the librarian, told Brooke that there wasn't enough funding for new materials. So Brooke decided to ask if the school could have a fund-raiser for the library. She talked to Mrs. Archer, the head of the booster club, and they settled on a block party potluck. Each person would be asked to buy a ticket and bring a dish to share as the price of admission. The money from the ticket sales would be given to the library to buy new materials.

Brooke worked with her friends and Mrs. Archer, and together they created flyers and got tickets printed. Mrs. Archer arranged for the party to be held at the school and got permission to use some of the rooms. One room would be used to show movies. There was even going to be popcorn. There would be games outside, with prizes for the winners. There would also be long tables set up outside for the food and drinks. Mrs. Archer knew someone who played in a local band, so there would be music at the party, too.

Once everything was planned, the next step was to publicize the party and let everyone know about it. Brooke and her friends passed out the flyers, posted a notice about the party on the school's website, and called everyone they knew. They posted notices in the local newspaper, too, and called some of the radio stations to ask them to help spread the word.

Brooke was really hoping that the party would be a success. It certainly seemed that it would be. It was a beautiful day. The party was to begin at one o'clock, but when Brooke got to the school at twelve-thirty, there were already people waiting! She knew then that her idea had worked.

The fund-raising party raised hundreds of dollars for the library. Before long, the school was able to buy many new books and computer programs. Now, Brooke and the other students would have more resources, and it was all because of a party!

NAME: ______________________ **DATE:** ______________

DIRECTIONS Read "The Blowout Block Party" and then answer the questions.

1. Which is a good word to describe Brooke?

Ⓐ fearful
Ⓑ organized
Ⓒ selfish
Ⓓ athletic

2. Which word in this text would help a reader understand the relevant definition of *band*?

Ⓐ programs
Ⓑ music
Ⓒ tables
Ⓓ books

3. What do you think might happen if it rained during the party?

Ⓐ Brooke would not play in the band.
Ⓑ The money would not be given to the library.
Ⓒ The party would be held outside.
Ⓓ People would go inside and have the party there.

4. Which statement reflects a purpose for reading this text?

Ⓐ I want to learn how to cook for my friends.
Ⓑ I want to find out why someone would throw a blowout block party.
Ⓒ I want to see a map of a block party.
Ⓓ I want to know where my own block party is in my neighborhood.

5. How does Brooke likely feel, given that her idea worked so well?

Ⓐ proud
Ⓑ jealous
Ⓒ fearful
Ⓓ curious

6. What do you think Mrs. Jordan's opinion is about the fund-raiser?

Ⓐ She probably thinks the fund-raiser is not a good idea.
Ⓑ She is probably happy that money was raised for the library.
Ⓒ She is probably angry about the fund-raiser.
Ⓓ She is probably afraid to get new materials for the library.

7. What indicates that the party will be a success?

Ⓐ It rains on the day of the party.
Ⓑ People stay up all night the night before the party.
Ⓒ A few students go to the party.
Ⓓ When Brooke gets to the school, there are already people there.

8. Which is a theme in this text?

Ⓐ determination
Ⓑ dishonesty
Ⓒ discrimination
Ⓓ conceitedness

SCORE

1. Ⓨ Ⓝ
2. Ⓨ Ⓝ
3. Ⓨ Ⓝ
4. Ⓨ Ⓝ
5. Ⓨ Ⓝ
6. Ⓨ Ⓝ
7. Ⓨ Ⓝ
8. Ⓨ Ⓝ

___ / 8
Total

NAME: ______________________________ **DATE:** ________________

DIRECTIONS Reread "The Blowout Block Party." Then, read the prompt and respond on the lines below.

SCORE

___ / 4

What kind of fund-raiser would you plan for your school? Write about what you would do for your fund-raiser, and where the money would go.

NAME: ______________________ **DATE:** ______________

DIRECTIONS Read the text and then answer the questions.

If you watch television, you have probably seen advertisements. In fact, the average kid sees 20,000 televised ads every year! And that doesn't include the ads that you see on the Internet and in magazines. Why are they there, and how do they get there? The basic purpose of ads is to get you to buy products or services. Companies know that people watch television, and they want people to watch their ads. They also know that it can be very expensive to make TV shows. So they find out which TV shows are the most popular shows. Then, companies pay the people who make those TV shows to show their ads. The people who make TV shows then use that money to pay for making the shows.

1. What is the main purpose of advertisements?

Ⓐ to be on television

Ⓑ to get you to buy products or services

Ⓒ to be on the Internet

Ⓓ to pay for TV shows

2. Which statement is **not** true?

Ⓐ Companies want people to watch their ads.

Ⓑ The people who make TV shows use the money from ads to make their shows.

Ⓒ Most kids do not see many ads.

Ⓓ Companies know that it can be expensive to make TV shows.

3. Which is the definition of *average* in this text?

Ⓐ typical

Ⓑ largest

Ⓒ smallest

Ⓓ unusual

4. Which word has the same root word as the noun *products*?

Ⓐ prefabricate

Ⓑ pore

Ⓒ prompt

Ⓓ produce

5. Which word has the same meaning as *purpose*?

Ⓐ work

Ⓑ history

Ⓒ picture

Ⓓ reason

SCORE

1. Ⓨ Ⓝ

2. Ⓨ Ⓝ

3. Ⓨ Ⓝ

4. Ⓨ Ⓝ

5. Ⓨ Ⓝ

___ / 5

Total

NAME:______________________ DATE:______________

DIRECTIONS Read the text and then answer the questions.

SCORE

1. Ⓨ Ⓝ

2. Ⓨ Ⓝ

3. Ⓨ Ⓝ

4. Ⓨ Ⓝ

5. Ⓨ Ⓝ

___ / 5
Total

Companies want their ads to bring them lots of customers. So they pay the people who make TV shows to put their ads on the shows. But creating ads and paying the people who make TV shows is expensive. So companies want to be certain they choose shows that are popular with their target market. A *target market* is the group of people a company thinks will be most likely to buy its product or service. For instance, suppose a company makes snacks for kids. Kids like you are that company's target market. Now, suppose that company creates a new snack and makes an ad for the new product. The company wants to be sure that its target market sees the ad, so it carefully selects TV shows that kids like you watch. Those are the shows the company uses for its ads.

1. What is this text about?

- Ⓐ how to make a good ad
- Ⓑ how to make a TV show
- Ⓒ how companies choose where to put their ads
- Ⓓ snacks for kids

2. Which title would help a reader understand the main idea?

- Ⓐ Watching TV
- Ⓑ Ads for Dollars
- Ⓒ Money Talks
- Ⓓ Targeted Advertisements

3. Which two words are synonyms?

- Ⓐ *new* and *snack*
- Ⓑ *certain* and *carefully*
- Ⓒ *make* and *create*
- Ⓓ *product* and *service*

4. Which sentence below uses the word *target* as an adjective?

- Ⓐ The teacher wanted to *target* counting as an important skill.
- Ⓑ I see the *target* across the field.
- Ⓒ The soldier hit his *target*.
- Ⓓ Our *target* date for moving is September 1st.

5. When the author claims that a company is *certain* of something, what does that mean?

- Ⓐ The company is sure.
- Ⓑ The company is confused.
- Ⓒ The company is careful.
- Ⓓ The company is busy.

NAME: ____________________ **DATE:** ____________

DIRECTIONS Read the text and then answer the questions.

Companies want to be sure that their target markets see their ads. So they carefully select shows that are popular with their target markets. But how do they know which shows to choose? Companies often use information they get from Nielsen Media Research. That is a company that collects information on what people watch on TV. Some people keep Nielsen TV diaries where they write down what they watch. Some people use Nielsen People Meters. People Meters are placed on all televisions in a participant's home to keep track of all the shows watched in the household. Nielsen Media Research gathers information on how many people watch each TV show. It also gathers information on the kinds of people who watch each show. That information helps companies decide where to place their ads.

1. How do companies know which shows are popular with their target markets?

- (A) They often use information from Nielsen Media Research.
- (B) They try to guess which shows are popular.
- (C) They talk to people to ask which shows they watch.
- (D) They do not know which shows are popular.

2. What is Nielsen Media Research?

- (A) a company that creates TV shows
- (B) a company that makes and sells TV sets
- (C) a company that gathers information on what people watch on TV
- (D) a company that sells products and services on TV

3. Which word is a synonym for *gathers*?

- (A) discards
- (B) collects
- (C) shows
- (D) asks

4. What does the verb *place* mean in the following sentence: *That information helps companies decide where to place their ads.*

- (A) finish
- (B) locate
- (C) invest
- (D) put

5. Which word has a meaning similar to *select*?

- (A) carefully
- (B) choose
- (C) place
- (D) keep

SCORE

1. Ⓨ Ⓝ

2. Ⓨ Ⓝ

3. Ⓨ Ⓝ

4. Ⓨ Ⓝ

5. Ⓨ Ⓝ

___ / 5 Total

NAME: ____________________ **DATE:** ______________

COMMERCIAL BREAK

Advertisements are everywhere. Every time you watch a TV show, use the Internet, or read a magazine, you see them. Some ads are funny, some are beautiful, and some are action-packed. But all of them have one important purpose: to get you to buy a product or service. Ads can be useful. For instance, that is how stores let you know when they are having sales. Ads also let you know about new products or services. Without ads, you might not know about those things. Ads are important for companies, too—that's how they reach customers.

When you see an ad, it is important to remember why it is there. The company that made the ad wants you to buy that product or service. The ad is made so that when you see it, you will want to buy. For example, ads for restaurants are designed to make you feel hungry for the food in the ad. Ads for clothes are designed so that you will want to buy those clothes. Ads for cell phones and music players are designed so that you will believe you are missing out if you don't have those things. It is important to think carefully and make up your own mind before you buy. Don't buy something just because an ad says that you should.

How do companies create ads that get people to buy things? They start with a product or service they want to sell. Then, they figure out what special thing that product or service has that will make people want to buy it. It might be a low price, a particular taste, or something else. Then, companies design ads that tell people about that special thing. The ads use color, sound, and other things to get people's attention. When the ads are finished, some companies show them to a group of people and get their opinions. If people like what they see, those companies use the ads they created. If people don't like what they see, the ads are changed.

NAME: ______________________________ **DATE:** ________________

DIRECTIONS Read "Commercial Break" and then answer the questions.

1. What do the title and photograph indicate about this text?

- (A) It describes how to set up a TV.
- (B) It describes TV ads.
- (C) It is about moving to a new place.
- (D) It explains things to do outdoors.

2. Which is **not** a way in which ads can be useful?

- (A) Companies use ads to find out what people want to buy.
- (B) Companies use ads to reach their customers.
- (C) Ads publicize sales.
- (D) Ads introduce new products and services.

3. What is likely the author's opinion?

- (A) Companies use ads poorly.
- (B) Ads are important, and you should believe what they say.
- (C) There should be no ads.
- (D) Ads are important tools, but it is important to make up your own mind.

4. What can you infer when you see an ad for a new style of jeans?

- (A) Everyone should wear jeans.
- (B) Those jeans are the best jeans.
- (C) You really need new jeans.
- (D) The company wants you to buy their jeans.

5. Before they create an ad, companies

- (A) show it to people to get their opinions.
- (B) tell people about a product or service.
- (C) create a product or service to sell.
- (D) change the ad if people don't like it.

6. Which sentence reflects an opinion?

- (A) The company that made the ad wants you to buy that product or service.
- (B) Without ads, you might not know about those things.
- (C) Some ads are funny, some are beautiful, and some are action-packed.
- (D) The ads use color, sound, and other things to get people's attention.

7. Which of these summarizes the second paragraph?

- (A) Ads can make you hungry.
- (B) Companies design ads that make you want to buy things.
- (C) Ads are designed to make you want to buy a new pair of jeans.
- (D) Ads keep you from missing out.

8. What might a restaurant's ad share?

- (A) how good the food tastes
- (B) where you can find shoes
- (C) how many people they employ
- (D) how to make the restaurant's food

SCORE

1. Ⓨ Ⓝ
2. Ⓨ Ⓝ
3. Ⓨ Ⓝ
4. Ⓨ Ⓝ
5. Ⓨ Ⓝ
6. Ⓨ Ⓝ
7. Ⓨ Ⓝ
8. Ⓨ Ⓝ

___ / 8
Total

NAME: ______________________ DATE: ______________

SCORE

___ / 4

DIRECTIONS Reread "Commercial Break." Then, read the prompt and respond on the lines below.

What kinds of ads get your attention? Why? Describe the kinds of ads you notice most.

NAME: ______________________ **DATE:** ______________

DIRECTIONS Read the text and then answer the questions.

Jared was planning to play basketball with some of his friends. His mom said he could, but she insisted that he take his little brother, Max, with him. Max was only five years old, and Jared was afraid that he would slow everyone down. He was embarrassed to even think about that. But Jared's mom repeated that Max would have to go along with Jared; she had some errands she needed to do, and Max couldn't remain at home alone. "Besides," Mom added, "Max doesn't want to be left out. He admires you, you know."

Jared was aware of that, but it wasn't very comforting. He reluctantly told Max that he was going to play basketball and that Max could join him. Max was so excited to go that Jared couldn't stay upset for long.

1. Initially, how does Jared feel about taking Max with him?

- Ⓐ embarrassed
- Ⓑ excited
- Ⓒ curious
- Ⓓ jealous

2. Which word best describes Jared?

- Ⓐ annoyed
- Ⓑ angry
- Ⓒ cooperative
- Ⓓ irresponsible

3. Which word or phrase means *admire*?

- Ⓐ ride
- Ⓑ dislike
- Ⓒ look up to
- Ⓓ follow

4. What does the adverb *reluctantly* tell the reader?

- Ⓐ Jared is happy about talking to Max.
- Ⓑ Jared does not want to tell Max where he is going.
- Ⓒ Jared cannot hear Max.
- Ⓓ Jared does not know where Max is.

5. Which word is a synonym for *remain*?

- Ⓐ work
- Ⓑ leave
- Ⓒ stay
- Ⓓ travel

SCORE

1. Ⓨ Ⓝ
2. Ⓨ Ⓝ
3. Ⓨ Ⓝ
4. Ⓨ Ⓝ
5. Ⓨ Ⓝ

___ / 5 Total

NAME: ______________________ **DATE:** ______________

DIRECTIONS Read the text and then answer the questions.

SCORE

1. Ⓨ Ⓝ
2. Ⓨ Ⓝ
3. Ⓨ Ⓝ
4. Ⓨ Ⓝ
5. Ⓨ Ⓝ

___ / 5
Total

Jared often met his friends after school and on the weekends to play basketball. They would play until it was time to go home for dinner. But today, Jared wasn't looking forward to playing basketball. His mom had insisted that he take his little brother, Max, with him, and Jared wasn't happy about it. When he first told Max that he could go along, Max was so excited that Jared couldn't stay unhappy about it. But now, on the way to the basketball court, it was all coming back. What was he going to do with Max while he played basketball? Jared was so preoccupied that he didn't even notice when they got to the basketball court. Then he looked up and couldn't believe what he saw—there were three other little kids Max's age! Jared wasn't the only kid who had brought his younger sibling along. Now, he wouldn't have to worry about what Max would do while he played.

1. Why does Jared bring Max to the basketball court?

Ⓐ His mom insisted that he bring Max.
Ⓑ Max begged to go along.
Ⓒ Jared's friends want to meet Max.
Ⓓ Jared's teacher says he should bring Max.

2. How is Jared's problem solved?

Ⓐ It starts to rain, so nobody can play basketball.
Ⓑ Jared decides not to play basketball.
Ⓒ Max decides to go home.
Ⓓ There are other kids Max's age at the basketball court.

3. Which word is a synonym for *preoccupied*?

Ⓐ sad
Ⓑ joyful
Ⓒ worried
Ⓓ furious

4. What does the verb *insisted* tell you in the sentence: *His mom had insisted that he take his little brother, Max, with him, and Jared wasn't happy about it*?

Ⓐ She didn't know where Jared was.
Ⓑ She didn't notice Max.
Ⓒ She asked Jared if he wanted to take Max.
Ⓓ She said Jared had to take Max.

5. What is the meaning of the phrase *it was all coming back*?

Ⓐ Jared and Max are going back home.
Ⓑ The basketball court is going somewhere.
Ⓒ Jared remembers why he was unhappy.
Ⓓ Jared forgets where he and Max are going.

NAME: ______________________ **DATE:** ______________

DIRECTIONS Read the text and then answer the questions.

Jared and his friends played basketball as often as they could. The basketball court they used had a fence all around it and a solid gate. During the day, the gate was unlocked so that players could come in and play basketball. At night, the gate was locked for safety. Today, Jared was bringing his little brother, Max, to the basketball court for the first time. Some of Jared's friends had brought their little brothers and sisters, too. When Jared and Max got to the basketball court, Jared was surprised to see all of his friends outside the gate. "The gate's locked," one of Jared's friends said. "We can't get in to play." Everyone looked at one another in dismay. It looked as though there would be no basketball that day.

1. What is the setting of the text?

- (A) Jared's home
- (B) the cafeteria
- (C) the basketball court
- (D) the swimming pool

2. Which repeated word in the text indicates the setting?

- (A) brothers
- (B) gate
- (C) court
- (D) play

3. What does the word *dismay* tell readers about the characters?

- (A) They are unhappy.
- (B) They are excited.
- (C) They are jealous.
- (D) They are joyful.

4. What does the adjective *solid* indicate about the gate?

- (A) It is strong.
- (B) It is locked.
- (C) It is easy to open.
- (D) It is tall.

5. Which of these is another way to say *looked as though*?

- (A) worked at
- (B) promised
- (C) looked at
- (D) seemed that

SCORE

1. Ⓨ Ⓝ
2. Ⓨ Ⓝ
3. Ⓨ Ⓝ
4. Ⓨ Ⓝ
5. Ⓨ Ⓝ

___ / 5 Total

NAME:______________________ DATE:______________

LITTLE BROTHER, BIG HELP!

Jared's mom had insisted that he bring his little brother, Max, to the basketball court where Jared planned to meet his friends. Jared was reluctant to bring Max, but he didn't have a choice, so he trudged to the basketball court with Max happily skipping at his side. To Jared's relief, a few of his friends had brought their little brothers and sisters, too, so at least Max would have some kids his own age to occupy him during the game. Then, Jared noticed what the others had already seen: The gate into the basketball court was locked.

For a few minutes, everyone waited helplessly, trying to figure out what to do. Then, from around the corner strode Mr. Giles, the maintenance manager at the community center where the basketball court was located. Mr. Giles hastily approached the boys and said apologetically, "Sorry I'm behind schedule today, guys. I had a flat tire." He unhooked a bunch of keys from his belt and reached over to unlock the gate. But instead, Mr. Giles accidentally dropped the keys on the other side of the fence!

There was a long silence. Then Max piped up, "I can get them." Everyone ignored him until he repeated himself, this time more loudly.

When he finally heard Max, Jared snapped, "How can you possibly help?"

Max simply answered, "Watch what I can do." He dropped to the ground and squirmed underneath the gate. Within a minute, he had emerged on the opposite side. He grabbed the keys and passed them through to Jared, who returned them to Mr. Giles. In seconds, Mr. Giles had the gate unlocked. The boys trooped onto the basketball court, calling out their thanks to Mr. Giles as they surged toward the net.

Mr. Giles responded, "Don't thank me. Max is the one who saved the day. He was the only one small enough to squeeze under that gate." After that, Jared resolved to never again think of his brother as an inconvenience.

NAME: ______________________ **DATE:** ______________

DIRECTIONS Read "Little Brother, Big Help!" and then answer the questions.

1. Why does Max repeat himself?

- (A) Nobody is there at first.
- (B) He does not know how to talk.
- (C) Everyone ignores him at first.
- (D) Jared tells him to be quiet.

2. What do context clues indicate the meaning of the word *flat* in the text?

- (A) smooth
- (B) level
- (C) lacking excitement
- (D) not full of air

3. Which will likely happen the next time Jared and his friends play basketball?

- (A) Jared will not tell Max he is going to play basketball.
- (B) Jared will bring Max with him.
- (C) Jared will not play basketball.
- (D) Jared will be very angry with Max.

4. Which reflects a purpose for reading this text, based on the title?

- (A) I want to learn about helping my own brother.
- (B) I am curious about how the little brother becomes a big help.
- (C) I want to read about a real brother who helps someone.
- (D) I want to find out why brothers do not get along and help each other.

5. How does Mr. Giles likely feel about dropping the keys?

- (A) excited
- (B) curious
- (C) proud
- (D) embarrassed

6. What can the reader infer about the weather?

- (A) It is too windy to go outside.
- (B) It is snowy and freezing.
- (C) It is cold and rainy.
- (D) It is warm and sunny.

7. Which is a theme in this text?

- (A) uncertainty
- (B) helpfulness
- (C) sorrow
- (D) jealousy

8. Which summarizes the problem in the text?

- (A) The gate is locked.
- (B) The basketball is missing.
- (C) Jared has a broken leg.
- (D) The boys are not allowed to play basketball.

SCORE

1. Ⓨ Ⓝ
2. Ⓨ Ⓝ
3. Ⓨ Ⓝ
4. Ⓨ Ⓝ
5. Ⓨ Ⓝ
6. Ⓨ Ⓝ
7. Ⓨ Ⓝ
8. Ⓨ Ⓝ

___ / 8 Total

NAME: ______________________________ **DATE:** ____________________

DIRECTIONS

Reread "Little Brother, Big Help!" Then, read the prompt and respond on the lines below.

SCORE

___ / 4

Do you have brothers or sisters? Has someone younger than you ever helped you? Write about a time your brother, sister, or a friend helped you.

NAME: ______________________ **DATE:** ______________

DIRECTIONS Read the text and then answer the questions.

The United States government has three branches: the legislative branch, the judicial branch, and the executive branch. The legislative branch makes and passes laws. It also coins money and has other powers. The judicial branch can stop a law if it is not fair or if it goes against the Constitution. It also makes decisions in some court cases. The executive branch runs the country and *executes*, or carries out, laws. The executive branch is headed by the president, who has special powers. For instance, Congress makes and passes laws. But those laws do not go into effect until the president signs them. The president also has veto power. That means the president can stop a law if it is not a good law. All three branches must work together. They do that so that no branch becomes too powerful. This is called the *system of checks and balances.*

1. What is something the president can do?

- (A) make decisions in some court cases
- (B) make and pass laws
- (C) veto laws
- (D) coin money

2. Who is the head of the executive branch?

- (A) Congress
- (B) the president
- (C) the judicial branch
- (D) checks and balances

3. Which definition of *execute* is used in this text?

- (A) carry out
- (B) kill
- (C) write
- (D) get rid of

4. Which of these sentences has a compound predicate?

- (A) This is called the *system of checks and balances*.
- (B) The president also has veto power.
- (C) The executive branch runs the country and *executes*, or carries out, laws.
- (D) It also makes decisions in some court cases.

5. Which word means *the power to stop a law*?

- (A) the Constitution
- (B) the president
- (C) Congress
- (D) veto

SCORE

1. Ⓨ Ⓝ
2. Ⓨ Ⓝ
3. Ⓨ Ⓝ
4. Ⓨ Ⓝ
5. Ⓨ Ⓝ

___ / 5

Total

NAME: ____________________ **DATE:** ______________

DIRECTIONS Read the text and then answer the questions.

SCORE

1. Ⓨ Ⓝ
2. Ⓨ Ⓝ
3. Ⓨ Ⓝ
4. Ⓨ Ⓝ
5. Ⓨ Ⓝ

___ / 5 Total

The president has many powers. For example, laws do not go into effect until the president signs them. And the president can veto laws if they are not good laws. The president is also the commander in chief of the troops. This means that the president is in charge of the military. The president also chooses ambassadors. An *ambassador* represents the United States in other countries. The president also names justices to the Supreme Court. Congress must *confirm*, or agree with, those choices. The president can veto a law. But Congress can override that veto. That means Congress can vote for a law even if the president vetoes it. There are limits to what the president can do.

1. What is this text mostly about?

Ⓐ what the president can do
Ⓑ what the Supreme Court does
Ⓒ what ambassadors do
Ⓓ how a veto works

2. Which statement is true?

Ⓐ The president can override a veto.
Ⓑ The president chooses justices.
Ⓒ The president's power has no limits.
Ⓓ The president is not in charge of the military.

3. Who represents the United States in other countries?

Ⓐ a veto
Ⓑ the commander in chief
Ⓒ a justice
Ⓓ an ambassador

4. Which word from the text is **not** a verb?

Ⓐ choose
Ⓑ confirm
Ⓒ ambassador
Ⓓ override

5. Which has the same meaning as *agree with*?

Ⓐ choose
Ⓑ veto
Ⓒ confirm
Ⓓ vote

NAME: ____________________ **DATE:** ____________

DIRECTIONS Read the text and then answer the questions.

To be elected president, a person must be at least thirty-five years old. The president must also have been born in the United States. Finally, the president must have lived in the United States for at least fourteen years. These rules are in the Constitution. The president serves for four years. That is called one *term*. Presidents can be in office for only two terms. The president lives and works in the White House in Washington, DC. Part of the White House is living quarters for the president and the president's family. Many people beside the president work in the White House, so many rooms in the White House are used for meetings and offices. If you visit Washington, DC, you can take a tour of the White House.

1. Where can you find the rules about who can be president?

Ⓐ in the White House
Ⓑ in the Constitution
Ⓒ in the term
Ⓓ in the office

2. Which word or phrase reflects the main idea?

Ⓐ Constitution
Ⓑ Washington, DC
Ⓒ president
Ⓓ White House

3. What is a four-year presidential job called?

Ⓐ Constitution
Ⓑ White House
Ⓒ a term
Ⓓ quarters

4. Which verb means *elected*?

Ⓐ served
Ⓑ called
Ⓒ born
Ⓓ chosen

5. What does the word *quarters* mean in the text?

Ⓐ rooms where people reside
Ⓑ coins
Ⓒ periods of time in a sporting event
Ⓓ one-fourth

SCORE

1. Ⓨ Ⓝ
2. Ⓨ Ⓝ
3. Ⓨ Ⓝ
4. Ⓨ Ⓝ
5. Ⓨ Ⓝ

___ / 5 Total

NAME: ______________________ **DATE:** ______________

THE EXECUTIVE BRANCH

The president is the head of the executive branch of the U.S. government. But the president is only one part of it. There are many other people in that branch. For example, the vice president is a member of that branch. The vice president works with the president and also with Congress. The president also has a team of experts. Those people are called the president's *cabinet*. Each person in the cabinet is an expert in one area. For instance, there is an expert on education. There is also an expert on other countries. There are other experts in the cabinet, too. The experts in the cabinet meet with the president. They give the president advice and special information. The president makes a lot of very difficult decisions, so that information is important.

The president also gets a lot of help and advice from the people who work at the White House. For example, the president has a press secretary who talks to television and newspaper reporters. The press secretary's job is to tell those reporters what the president is doing. Then, the reporters tell people who read and watch the news. The president also works with people who help make policies. A *policy* is a set of rules and ways of doing things. Other advisors also work with the president and provide information. That way, the president can make smart decisions.

The president is a very busy person. So, there are people at the White House who help plan what the president does. There are also people who help the president prepare speeches. Other people do other jobs at the White House, such as answering letters and telephone calls. When you think of the executive branch of our government, you may think of the president. And the president leads that branch. But as you can see, the president can't run the government alone. The president depends on many people to get the job done.

The White House

NAME: ______________________ DATE: ______________

DIRECTIONS Read "The Executive Branch" and then answer the questions.

1. What do the title and picture help readers to predict?

(A) This text is about the executive branch of government.
(B) This text is about a leader of a business.
(C) This text is about a large house.
(D) This text is about the workplace.

2. What is a *policy*?

(A) a room in the White House
(B) politics
(C) a set of rules and ways of doing things
(D) the president's agenda

3. What is the author's purpose?

(A) to tell about all of our presidents
(B) to get you to visit the White House
(C) to tell about the executive branch
(D) to tell a personal story

4. Which statement is a reasonable conclusion about the vice president?

(A) He or she visits Congress often.
(B) He or she doesn't work hard.
(C) He or she lives far from Washington.
(D) He or she doesn't know the president.

5. Why does the president need a group of experts?

(A) The experts work very hard.
(B) The experts make the decisions.
(C) The president needs to talk to TV reporters.
(D) The president needs their information to make decisions.

6. Which of the following is an opinion?

(A) The president is friendly with his advisors.
(B) The president depends on many people.
(C) The cabinet helps the president make decisions.
(D) The president is the head of the executive branch.

7. What might happen if the president did **not** have a cabinet?

(A) The executive branch would be big.
(B) It would be harder for the president to make smart decisions.
(C) There would be no press secretary.
(D) There would be no executive branch.

8. Which is true about the White House?

(A) The president works there.
(B) The president lives there.
(C) There are many offices there.
(D) all of the above

SCORE

1. Ⓨ Ⓝ
2. Ⓨ Ⓝ
3. Ⓨ Ⓝ
4. Ⓨ Ⓝ
5. Ⓨ Ⓝ
6. Ⓨ Ⓝ
7. Ⓨ Ⓝ
8. Ⓨ Ⓝ

___ / 8
Total

NAME: ______________________ **DATE:** ______________

SCORE

___ / 4

DIRECTIONS

Reread "The Executive Branch." Then, read the prompt and respond on the lines below.

What are some things that you would do if you were the president? Write about what you would do.

NAME: ______________________________ **DATE:** ________________

DIRECTIONS Read the text and then answer the questions.

Ashley loved music and talking about music. So when her friend Tara mentioned an online music chat group, Ashley wanted to join it. Ashley talked to her parents about the group, too. At first, they didn't want her to join. They explained that online chat groups can be very dangerous for kids. But Ashley kept begging, and finally, her mom and dad consented. They told her that she could join, but she could only enter the chat room when one of them was home. Ashley didn't like that rule at all. Her mom and dad explained that it was important for Ashley to be safe. So she agreed to follow their rule and only enter the chat room when an adult was home. At least she would get the chance to talk to other kids who loved music as much as she did.

1. How does Ashley find out about the chat room?

- (A) Her mom tells her about it.
- (B) Her friend Tara mentions it.
- (C) Her dad tells her about it.
- (D) She finds it online.

2. Which title would hint at the text's main idea?

- (A) Online Safety
- (B) Chatting in Rooms
- (C) A Tough Choice
- (D) Following School Rules

3. What is the definition of the word *consented*?

- (A) asked questions
- (B) yelled
- (C) refused
- (D) gave permission

4. What does the verb *begging* tell the reader?

- (A) Ashley really wants to join the chat room.
- (B) Ashley doesn't care about the chat room.
- (C) Ashley is angry with her mom and dad.
- (D) Ashley has never met Tara.

5. What does *mention* mean?

- (A) talk about
- (B) ignore
- (C) read about
- (D) listen to

SCORE

1. Ⓨ Ⓝ
2. Ⓨ Ⓝ
3. Ⓨ Ⓝ
4. Ⓨ Ⓝ
5. Ⓨ Ⓝ

___ / 5 Total

NAME: ______________________________ DATE: ____________________

DIRECTIONS Read the text and then answer the questions.

SCORE

1. Ⓨ Ⓝ

2. Ⓨ Ⓝ

3. Ⓨ Ⓝ

4. Ⓨ Ⓝ

5. Ⓨ Ⓝ

___ / 5
Total

Ashley's parents had allowed her to join an online music chat group. At first, they had been reluctant to let her join. Chat rooms can be dangerous for kids because it is very hard to tell who someone really is when you are online. But Ashley promised to be careful, and she was. She only entered the chat room when her mom or dad was home. She did not give anyone her telephone number or address, and she didn't post pictures of herself, either. She was also careful about what she said in the chat room. And she loved having the chance to talk about music. She found a lot of kids in the chat room who loved music just as much as she did. They talked about bands, concerts, and music lessons, and they suggested songs to one another.

1. What does Ashley do to be careful online?

Ⓐ She talks about bands and concerts.
Ⓑ She joins a chat room.
Ⓒ She does not join the chat room.
Ⓓ She does not give anyone her telephone number.

2. What do Ashley and the people in her chat group love to talk about?

Ⓐ sports
Ⓑ music
Ⓒ math
Ⓓ books

3. What does *post* mean in this text?

Ⓐ to mail
Ⓑ a piece of wood
Ⓒ a job
Ⓓ to display online

4. Which word is a synonym for *allowed*?

Ⓐ permitted
Ⓑ denied
Ⓒ asked
Ⓓ required

5. What do the phrases *post pictures* and *suggested songs* exemplify?

Ⓐ similes
Ⓑ metaphors
Ⓒ alliteration
Ⓓ personification

NAME: ______________________ **DATE:** ______________

DIRECTIONS Read the text and then answer the questions.

Ashley was a member of an online music chat group. She got a lot of music news from the other members of the group, and she shared music news, too. She and her group also talked about bands, singers, and concerts. One day, everyone in the group was talking about some very big news. A band called Seven Wonders was going to release a new CD. Lots of kids in the group, including Ashley, were fans of Seven Wonders and couldn't wait to get their new music. Ashley saved up her allowance for three weeks. She wanted to have enough money to buy the new CD when it was released. The other kids in her online chat group were just as excited. Everyone talked about how amazing their music was.

1. How will Ashley pay for the CD she wants to buy?

- (A) Ashley's mom and dad will buy it for her.
- (B) She is saving up her allowance.
- (C) Her online chat group will buy it for her.
- (D) She will not buy the CD.

2. Which title would best fit this text?

- (A) Seven Wonders Release
- (B) Ashley's Friends
- (C) Online Talk
- (D) Concert Chat

3. Which definition of *release* is used in this text?

- (A) dismiss
- (B) rent or lease again
- (C) free or let out
- (D) make available for sale

4. Which part of speech is the word *her* in the sentence: *Ashley saved up her allowance for three weeks.*

- (A) an adjective
- (B) a possessive pronoun
- (C) an auxiliary verb
- (D) a predicate

5. What is the meaning of the phrase *just as*?

- (A) not
- (B) less
- (C) equally
- (D) fair

SCORE

1. Ⓨ Ⓝ
2. Ⓨ Ⓝ
3. Ⓨ Ⓝ
4. Ⓨ Ⓝ
5. Ⓨ Ⓝ

___ / 5 Total

NAME: ______________________________ **DATE:** ____________________

WHO'S IN THE ROOM?

Ashley was very excited. Seven Wonders, one of her favorite bands, had just released a new CD. She had saved up her money, and she was ready to buy the CD when it was released this weekend. She talked about the music with her online music chat group. A lot of the other kids in the group were going to buy the CD, too. In fact, that was the main thing everyone in the chat room was talking about one afternoon.

All of a sudden, Ashley got a chat message from Stephanie, one of the kids in the chat room. The message said that Stephanie wanted to meet Ashley at the mall. Then they could buy the new CD together. Ashley told her mom about the message, and her mom asked, "Do you know Stephanie from school?"

"No," Ashley admitted. "We've only chatted online. I don't think she goes to my school."

"Listen," Ashley's mom said, "I want you to have friends, but sometimes, people online aren't who they say they are. And when you're online, you can't always tell. So I don't think it's a good idea for you to meet this person."

"But, Mom," Ashley pleaded, "what if it *is* just a kid named Stephanie who wants to buy a CD with me?"

Ashley's mom considered that for a moment. Then she said, "Let's do this. Dad and I will go with you to the mall to buy the CD with Stephanie. If Stephanie really is just a kid who wants to meet you in person, that's great. If not, you'll be safe."

Ashley didn't like that idea. It made her feel like a baby. But she knew her mom was right about safety, and besides, she wouldn't be allowed to get the CD if she didn't agree, so she finally nodded. Then she answered Stephanie's message. She told Stephanie that she and her parents would be at the mall the next afternoon.

The next day, Ashley went to the mall with her mom and dad so that she could get her CD. When Stephanie never showed up and then disappeared from the chat room, Ashley knew her parents had been right to be concerned. She was glad they were there to take care of her.

NAME: ____________________ **DATE:** ____________

DIRECTIONS Read "Who's in the Room?" and then answer the questions.

1. Which answers the title's question, *who's in the room*?

- (A) There is music playing in the room.
- (B) Ashley and Stephanie are alone in the room.
- (C) The room is empty.
- (D) The room is a virtual room online with unknown visitors.

2. What does it mean that two people *chatted online*?

- (A) They talked on the phone.
- (B) They talked in person.
- (C) They communicated on the computer.
- (D) They talked by text messages.

3. What do you think will happen the next time someone wants to meet Ashley in person?

- (A) Ashley will not tell her parents about it.
- (B) Ashley will meet that person.
- (C) Ashley will tell her parents about it.
- (D) Ashley will not be concerned about it.

4. How does Ashley's mom feel when Ashley tells her about Stephanie?

- (A) suspicious
- (B) bored
- (C) jealous
- (D) very glad

5. What is the point of view of this text?

- (A) first person
- (B) second person
- (C) third person
- (D) There is no point of view.

6. At the end of the text, how does Ashley feel about her parents going with her to the mall?

- (A) She is afraid.
- (B) She is upset.
- (C) She is grateful.
- (D) She is jealous.

7. How would this text be different if Ashley and Stephanie were in the same class?

- (A) Stephanie and Ashley would not know each other.
- (B) Stephanie might tell Ashley not to buy the new CD.
- (C) Ashley might not want the new CD.
- (D) Ashley's mom might let her go alone to meet Stephanie at the mall.

8. Which is a lesson from the text?

- (A) Parents don't care about their children's safety.
- (B) It is very important to use caution on the Internet.
- (C) Chat rooms are fun and informative.
- (D) Kids should never go to the mall without their parents.

SCORE

1. Ⓨ Ⓝ
2. Ⓨ Ⓝ
3. Ⓨ Ⓝ
4. Ⓨ Ⓝ
5. Ⓨ Ⓝ
6. Ⓨ Ⓝ
7. Ⓨ Ⓝ
8. Ⓨ Ⓝ

___ / 8 Total

NAME: ______________________ DATE: ______________

SCORE

___ / 4

DIRECTIONS Reread "Who's in the Room?" Then, read the prompt and respond on the lines below.

Do you go online? If you do, what do you do to stay safe? Write about how to stay safe online.

NAME: ______________________ **DATE:** ______________

DIRECTIONS Read the text and then answer the questions.

What would it be like if library books weren't put into any kind of order? You probably wouldn't be able to find the book you wanted. That is why library books are organized. Most public libraries separate books for children and teens from books for adults. That way, children, teens, and adults can find the books they want more easily. Most libraries also separate fiction books from nonfiction books. Fiction books are alphabetized by the author's last name. So if you are looking for a children's fiction book, begin by going to the children's section. Next, look for the fiction books in that section. Finally, search alphabetically for the last name of the author, and you will likely find the book.

1. What is this text mostly about?

- (A) how books are made
- (B) why libraries were invented
- (C) how to find a library near you
- (D) how library books are organized

2. How are fiction books organized?

- (A) by number of pages
- (B) by title, in alphabetical order
- (C) by author's last name, in alphabetical order
- (D) by the number of chapters

3. Which prefix could be added to the word *organized* to make its antonym?

- (A) *dis–*
- (B) *bi–*
- (C) *pro–*
- (D) *con–*

4. Which of these sentences is an imperative sentence?

- (A) Then, look for the fiction books in that section.
- (B) Fiction books are in alphabetical order by the author's last name.
- (C) Most public libraries separate books for children and teens from books for adults.
- (D) What would it be like if library books weren't put into any kind of order?

5. Which word is a synonym for *separate*?

- (A) unite
- (B) divide
- (C) search
- (D) begin

SCORE

1. (Y)(N)
2. (Y)(N)
3. (Y)(N)
4. (Y)(N)
5. (Y)(N)

___ / 5
Total

NAME: ______________________ DATE: ________________

DIRECTIONS Read the text and then answer the questions.

SCORE

1. Ⓨ Ⓝ

2. Ⓨ Ⓝ

3. Ⓨ Ⓝ

4. Ⓨ Ⓝ

5. Ⓨ Ⓝ

___ / 5

Total

One of the best ways to find what you are looking for in a library is to use the library's catalogue (KAT-uh-log). Libraries used to have card catalogues, which are groups of drawers that hold sets of cards. Each card has the title and author of a book. It also tells you the book's topic and where it is located. You can search for a book by the title, by the author's name, or by the topic. Most libraries now have their catalogues on computers. The process of looking for a book on the computer is a lot like using a card catalogue. You can search for a book by author, by title, or by subject. Then, you can go to the section of the library that has that book and get what you need.

1. Which of these is **not** a way to search for a book?

Ⓐ by author

Ⓑ by title

Ⓒ by date

Ⓓ by subject

2. What does this text tell readers?

Ⓐ how to get to a local library

Ⓑ how to use a library's catalogue

Ⓒ what the best books are

Ⓓ how many libraries there are

3. Which word is a synonym for *process*?

Ⓐ catalogue

Ⓑ book

Ⓒ method

Ⓓ library

4. Which noun is the location where people can find a library's list of books?

Ⓐ catalogue

Ⓑ subject

Ⓒ author

Ⓓ section

5. What is the phrase *looking for a book on the computer is a lot like using a card catalogue* an example of?

Ⓐ alliteration

Ⓑ a metaphor

Ⓒ personification

Ⓓ a comparison

NAME: ______________________ **DATE:** ______________

DIRECTIONS Read the text and then answer the questions.

Once you find a book in the catalogue, how do you find it in the library? Many libraries use the Dewey Decimal System, or DDS. The DDS divides books into ten topics. Each topic has its own number. You can find each book's number when you look that book up in the catalogue. For example, *art* has the Dewey number of 700, so if you search for a book about art, you will find that art books have numbers that start with 7. Each topic has topics within it. Suppose you are interested in drawing. Drawing is a kind of art, and the Dewey number for books about art is 700, so start at the section of your library labeled "700." Books about drawing have the Dewey number of 730. Go to that section of the art books. You will probably find what you want.

1. What is this text mostly about?

- (A) the Dewey Decimal System
- (B) art books
- (C) the history of libraries
- (D) how to write a book

2. Which statement is **not** true about the DDS?

- (A) It is a way of organizing books.
- (B) It separates books into ten topics.
- (C) Each topic has its own number.
- (D) The DDS has fifteen topics.

3. Which means *look up*?

- (A) admire
- (B) talk about
- (C) draw
- (D) search for

4. What does the pronoun *it* refer to in the sentence: *Once you find a book in the catalogue, how do you find it in the library?*

- (A) the library
- (B) the catalogue
- (C) a book
- (D) you

5. Which of these is an interrogative sentence?

- (A) Many libraries use the Dewey Decimal System, or DDS.
- (B) Once you find a book in the catalogue, how do you find it in the library?
- (C) You will probably find what you want.
- (D) Go to that section of the art books.

SCORE

1. Ⓨ Ⓝ
2. Ⓨ Ⓝ
3. Ⓨ Ⓝ
4. Ⓨ Ⓝ
5. Ⓨ Ⓝ

___ / 5 **Total**

NAME: ______________________ **DATE:** ______________

MELVIL DEWEY

Today, it is easy to find what you want when you go to the library. For that, you can thank Melvil Dewey. Melvil was born in Adams Center, New York, in 1851. His parents, Joel and Eliza, owned a general store. He was always interested in books and words. That interest continued when he went to Amherst College. In 1872, he began working at the college library.

Melvil thought that it was important for people to be educated. He also thought that libraries could play a big role in teaching people, so he wanted them to be easy to use. At the time, it was hard for people to use libraries. Books were not organized. So, books on the same subject might be in several parts of a library. It was hard to find books on one subject because there was no good way to know which books in a library were about which topics. So Melvil invented a new system of organizing books. That system is called the *Dewey Decimal System* (DDS). It was so successful that many libraries still use it today. It is an easy way to keep track of books and an easy way to find books.

Melvil did more than invent the DDS. He wanted libraries and librarians to work together, so he helped to found the American Library Association in 1876. He also founded the *Library Journal*. Melvil did a lot for librarians. At the time, there was no place for a person to learn to be a librarian. So librarians had to learn on the job as best they could. Melvil opened the world's first school for librarians in 1887. He also set up the first traveling library. Today's bookmobiles are based on that library. Melvil Dewey died in 1931, but his work still helps people use libraries today.

Melvil Dewey

NAME: ____________________ **DATE:** ____________

DIRECTIONS Read "Melvil Dewey" and then answer the questions.

1. Knowing about which topic will help readers better understand this text?

Ⓐ libraries
Ⓑ colleges
Ⓒ stores
Ⓓ boats

2. What did Melvil do before he invented the DDS?

Ⓐ He started the first school for librarians.
Ⓑ He founded the *Library Journal*.
Ⓒ He founded the American Library Association.
Ⓓ He went to Amherst College.

3. How did Melvil help solve the problem of training people to be librarians?

Ⓐ He went to Amherst College.
Ⓑ He organized library books.
Ⓒ He became a librarian.
Ⓓ He started the first school for librarians.

4. Which did Melvil **not** use to organize libraries?

Ⓐ numbers
Ⓑ computers
Ⓒ labels
Ⓓ titles

5. Which purpose for reading makes the most sense for this topic?

Ⓐ to learn about the DDS
Ⓑ to learn about the accomplishments of Melvil Dewey
Ⓒ to learn about bookmobiles
Ⓓ all of the above

6. Which of these is a good word to describe Melvil?

Ⓐ organized
Ⓑ athletic
Ⓒ sloppy
Ⓓ lazy

7. Which statement is **not** an important idea from the text?

Ⓐ Organizing books in a library helps us use the library more effectively.
Ⓑ Education was not important to Melvil Dewey.
Ⓒ Librarians have benefitted from Melvil Dewey's work.
Ⓓ Successful ideas can help people.

8. Which of these is a problem that Melvil solved?

Ⓐ There were no libraries.
Ⓑ Libraries had no books.
Ⓒ Library books were not organized.
Ⓓ Many people could not read.

SCORE

1. Ⓨ Ⓝ
2. Ⓨ Ⓝ
3. Ⓨ Ⓝ
4. Ⓨ Ⓝ
5. Ⓨ Ⓝ
6. Ⓨ Ⓝ
7. Ⓨ Ⓝ
8. Ⓨ Ⓝ

___ / 8
Total

NAME: ______________________ **DATE:** ______________

DIRECTIONS

Reread "Melvil Dewey." Then, read the prompt and respond on the lines below.

SCORE

___ / 4

How do you find a library book when you are looking for one? Give an example. Write about how to find a book in a library.

NAME: ____________________ **DATE:** ______________

DIRECTIONS Read the text and then answer the questions.

Carlos opened the back door of his house to let his puppy, Lucky, back inside. He and his family had only had Lucky for a few weeks, but Lucky was already learning a lot of things. As Carlos glanced out at the sky, he saw dark clouds that threatened rain. It was going to be a very soggy afternoon. The thought of taking Lucky out in the pouring rain made Carlos think that it would be nice if Lucky had a doghouse. Then, the puppy could have a place to go to stay dry in the rain and cool in the heat. Carlos looked at doghouses online, but he couldn't find one that was exactly right for Lucky. So he decided that he would build a doghouse himself.

1. How will Carlos solve the problem of not finding a doghouse to buy?

- (A) He will ask a friend for help.
- (B) He will go to pet stores.
- (C) He will not get Lucky a doghouse.
- (D) He will build a doghouse himself.

2. Which chapter title is most appropriate for this text?

- (A) Wet Lucky
- (B) Carlos Gets an Idea
- (C) A Rainy Day
- (D) A Boy and His Puppy

3. Which word is a synonym for *soggy*?

- (A) parched
- (B) damp
- (C) very wet
- (D) cloudy

4. What does the verb *glanced* tell you about how Carlos looked at the sky?

- (A) He stared at the sky for a long time.
- (B) He looked at the sky very quickly.
- (C) He did not look outside.
- (D) He wanted another puppy.

5. Which is the meaning of *threatened* in this text?

- (A) bullied
- (B) warned
- (C) removed
- (D) protected

SCORE

1. (Y)(N)
2. (Y)(N)
3. (Y)(N)
4. (Y)(N)
5. (Y)(N)

___ / 5 Total

NAME: ____________________ **DATE:** ____________

DIRECTIONS Read the text and then answer the questions.

SCORE

1. Ⓨ Ⓝ
2. Ⓨ Ⓝ
3. Ⓨ Ⓝ
4. Ⓨ Ⓝ
5. Ⓨ Ⓝ

___ / 5 Total

Carlos wanted his puppy, Lucky, to have a doghouse, but he hadn't been able to find exactly what he wanted online. So he decided that the best idea would be to build a doghouse himself. Carlos had not done a project like that before, and he knew he would need help. So he asked his dad about building a doghouse. Carlos's dad suggested that they look at some websites for building a doghouse. He also thought it would be a good idea to go to a building-supply store and ask some questions. People there would probably have helpful advice. Carlos agreed. Together, they visited some do-it-yourself websites. They also visited a few local home-improvement stores. Soon, they knew what supplies they would need to build a doghouse.

1. Which action does Carlos take to get help with his doghouse?

- Ⓐ He asks the vet about doghouses.
- Ⓑ He talks to his friends.
- Ⓒ He asks his dad about building a doghouse.
- Ⓓ He takes a class on building doghouses.

2. How do the characters discover what supplies they will need for a doghouse?

- Ⓐ They visit a few local home-improvement stores.
- Ⓑ They ask a friend.
- Ⓒ They ask Carlos's teacher.
- Ⓓ They visit a local animal shelter.

3. What does the word *local* mean?

- Ⓐ enormous
- Ⓑ new
- Ⓒ expensive
- Ⓓ nearby

4. Which word is a conjunction in the sentence: *Carlos hadn't done a project like that before, and he knew he would need some help.*

- Ⓐ project
- Ⓑ and
- Ⓒ hadn't
- Ⓓ some

5. What does *exactly* mean?

- Ⓐ precisely
- Ⓑ nearly
- Ⓒ the opposite of
- Ⓓ happily

NAME: ______________________ **DATE:** ______________

DIRECTIONS Read the text and then answer the questions.

Carlos and his father went to The Fix-It Place, a local home-improvement store, to get supplies for making a doghouse. They made a list of what they would need so they wouldn't forget anything. The first thing they would need was wood. They would need solid lumber for the frame of the doghouse, and plywood, a kind of thin wooden board, for the walls. They were also going to need nails, paint, and some other supplies. As they went through the store, they checked their list and put what they needed into their shopping cart. Finally, they had all their supplies. Carlos was really beginning to get excited about this project. He knew it would be a challenge, but he was looking forward to getting started.

1. Where does this text take place?

Ⓐ at a park
Ⓑ at school
Ⓒ in Carlos's backyard
Ⓓ at The Fix-It Place

2. Which will Carlos **not** need to build the doghouse?

Ⓐ nails
Ⓑ paint
Ⓒ tile
Ⓓ lumber

3. What is a kind of thin wooden board?

Ⓐ a list
Ⓑ a frame
Ⓒ plywood
Ⓓ paint

4. Which word is a synonym for *supplies*?

Ⓐ materials
Ⓑ boards
Ⓒ lists
Ⓓ improvements

5. Which word signals that the action of the text is ending?

Ⓐ started
Ⓑ finally
Ⓒ forget
Ⓓ supplies

SCORE

1. Ⓨ Ⓝ
2. Ⓨ Ⓝ
3. Ⓨ Ⓝ
4. Ⓨ Ⓝ
5. Ⓨ Ⓝ

___ / 5
Total

NAME: ______________________ **DATE:** ______________

THE DOGHOUSE

Carlos and his father were about to build a doghouse for their puppy, Lucky. Carlos wanted Lucky to have a place to stay dry when it rained and stay cool when it was hot. Carlos and his dad had gone to The Fix-It Place to get their supplies, and now they were ready to begin the project. Carlos's dad explained that the first thing they would need to do would be to measure Lucky. The doghouse would have to be big enough so Lucky could turn around and lie down, and big enough to hold food and water.

After they measured Lucky, it was time to build the frame. Carlos and his dad used strong boards for the frame so the doghouse would be sturdy. Then, they measured and cut plywood for the walls and floor. They also made sure to cut an opening that was big enough for Lucky to go in and out. Once they attached it to the frame, it was time to start working on the roof.

Carlos and his dad started with strong boards for the roof frame, and then they used other boards for the rafters. They used plywood to complete the shape of the roof. The roof would need to protect Lucky from rain and too much sun, so they also put shingles on the roof. Carlos thought the doghouse roof looked a lot like the roof of his own house—it even had the same shape. His dad explained that the pitched roof would help the rain fall off the roof instead of collecting on top of it.

Finally, the doghouse was ready to be decorated. Carlos painted it bright red, and painted Lucky's name above the door. As a finishing touch, Carlos put a piece of carpet and a blanket in the doghouse. Lucky was going to be a comfortable puppy! Carlos couldn't believe how good the doghouse looked. He was glad he had thought of this idea.

NAME: ______________________ **DATE:** ______________

DIRECTIONS Read "The Doghouse" and then answer the questions.

1. How does Carlos's dad likely feel when the doghouse is done?

- (A) angry
- (B) proud
- (C) suspicious
- (D) unsure

2. Why do Carlos and his dad have to start by measuring Lucky?

- (A) Lucky has gotten very big.
- (B) Lucky is afraid of the doghouse.
- (C) They want the doghouse to be the right size.
- (D) They want to make the doghouse very small.

3. What do you think might have happened if they had built the roof first?

- (A) The roof might be made of paper.
- (B) It might not rain.
- (C) Carlos and his dad might not have built the rest of the doghouse.
- (D) The roof might not be the right size.

4. What can you infer about Carlos based on the text?

- (A) He likes dogs.
- (B) He likes baseball.
- (C) He does not like to make things.
- (D) He does not live in a house.

5. What is the point of view of this text?

- (A) first person
- (B) second person
- (C) third person
- (D) There is no point of view.

6. According to the author's tone, how will Lucky likely feel about the doghouse?

- (A) He will not fit.
- (B) He will refuse to go inside.
- (C) He will like it.
- (D) He will not see it.

7. What problem do Carlos and his dad solve?

- (A) Lucky is too big for his doghouse.
- (B) Lucky does not have a place to stay out of the rain and the heat.
- (C) Lucky does not know how to go downstairs.
- (D) Carlos is afraid of dogs.

8. What theme is communicated in this text?

- (A) Hard work can be rewarding.
- (B) Dogs do not make good pets.
- (C) It is better to work alone than with help.
- (D) There is not much planning involved with building projects.

SCORE

1. Ⓨ Ⓝ
2. Ⓨ Ⓝ
3. Ⓨ Ⓝ
4. Ⓨ Ⓝ
5. Ⓨ Ⓝ
6. Ⓨ Ⓝ
7. Ⓨ Ⓝ
8. Ⓨ Ⓝ

___ / 8
Total

NAME: ______________________ **DATE:** ______________

DIRECTIONS Reread "The Doghouse." Then, read the prompt and respond on the lines below.

SCORE

___ / 4

If you were going to build something, what would you build? Write about the supplies you would use and how you would build the object.

NAME: ____________________ **DATE:** ____________

DIRECTIONS Read the text and then answer the questions.

Your body does a lot of things amazingly well. But as incredible as your body is, it can still be attacked by germs. Germs can invade your body, and until your body gets rid of them, you feel sick. There are many different kinds of germs, and all of them are too small for you to see without a microscope. One kind of germ is *bacteria* (bak-TEER-ee-uh). Bacteria are one-celled forms of life. They can grow outside the body, but they can also grow inside the body. Ear infections and strep throat are caused by bacteria. Food poisoning is also caused by bacteria. Some bacteria are actually good for your body. They help you digest what you eat and drink. But many kinds of bacteria can make you very sick.

1. What is the text mostly about?

- Ⓐ bacteria
- Ⓑ how your body grows
- Ⓒ microscopes
- Ⓓ cells

2. How does this text feature help a reader: *(bak-TEER-ee-uh)*?

- Ⓐ It tells readers a word's part of speech.
- Ⓑ It tells readers how to spell a word.
- Ⓒ It tells readers how to pronounce a word.
- Ⓓ It tells readers how to write a word.

3. What does the prefix *micro–* tell you about a *microscope*?

- Ⓐ It lets you see very large things.
- Ⓑ It lets you see very small things.
- Ⓒ It lets you see orange things.
- Ⓓ It lets you see square things.

4. Which sentence is a passive sentence?

- Ⓐ But many kinds of bacteria can make you very sick.
- Ⓑ Food poisoning is also caused by bacteria.
- Ⓒ Your body does a lot of things amazingly well.
- Ⓓ Bacteria are one-celled forms of life.

5. Which word describes one-celled forms of life?

- Ⓐ microscopes
- Ⓑ bodies
- Ⓒ bacteria
- Ⓓ ear infections

SCORE

1. Ⓨ Ⓝ
2. Ⓨ Ⓝ
3. Ⓨ Ⓝ
4. Ⓨ Ⓝ
5. Ⓨ Ⓝ

___ / 5
Total

NAME: ____________________ DATE: ______________

DIRECTIONS Read the text and then answer the questions.

SCORE

1. Ⓨ Ⓝ
2. Ⓨ Ⓝ
3. Ⓨ Ⓝ
4. Ⓨ Ⓝ
5. Ⓨ Ⓝ

___ / 5
Total

There are a few types of germs that can invade your body and make you sick. Some of those germs are viruses. Viruses are a little different from bacteria. While bacteria are one-celled forms of life, viruses are not. In fact, many scientists don't consider viruses to be alive until they are in a cell. That is because viruses need to be inside a cell to grow. When a virus gets inside a cell, it uses that cell as a host and lives on the nutrients in the cell. Then, it reproduces itself and makes more viruses. Those viruses invade more cells and use them as hosts. Viruses are smaller than bacteria, but they can still make you very sick. Most colds are caused by viruses. Viruses cause the flu, chicken pox, and measles, too.

1. Which index entry would include this text?

Ⓐ doctors
Ⓑ kinds of germs
Ⓒ nutrition
Ⓓ hosting a party

2. Which word in the text is important to know and could be shown in bold or italicized print?

Ⓐ sick
Ⓑ bacteria
Ⓒ chicken pox
Ⓓ viruses

3. Which word is a synonym for *reproduce*?

Ⓐ remove
Ⓑ copy
Ⓒ erase
Ⓓ move

4. What is the phrase *inside a cell* an example of?

Ⓐ conjunction
Ⓑ predicate
Ⓒ subject
Ⓓ prepositional phrase

5. Which word has the same meaning as *invade*?

Ⓐ attack
Ⓑ grow
Ⓒ feed
Ⓓ study

NAME: ______________________ **DATE:** ______________

DIRECTIONS Read the text and then answer the questions.

Viruses and bacteria can make you very sick. But there are several things you can do to prevent a lot of them from invading your body. One important thing to do is wash your hands. Many viruses can live on doorknobs. They can also live on telephones, remote controls, and computer keyboards. If you touch those things, you can get germs on your hands. So wash your hands, especially before you eat and after you use the bathroom. Germs are contagious. If your friends are sick, wait until they are well again before you visit. And if you are sick, wait until you are well before spending time with your friends.

1. Which title best fits the text?

Ⓐ What to Do if You Are Sick
Ⓑ How to Cook Your Food Properly
Ⓒ Where Viruses Live
Ⓓ How to Keep from Spreading Germs

2. Which is a true statement about this topic?

Ⓐ Germs cannot spread from one person to another.
Ⓑ You can do several things to prevent germs from making you sick.
Ⓒ Washing your hands isn't very important.
Ⓓ Bacteria cannot grow on food.

3. Which word is an antonym of *prevent*?

Ⓐ stop
Ⓑ open
Ⓒ permit
Ⓓ operate

4. Which prefix could be added to the word *visit* to make a word that means *visit again*?

Ⓐ *pre–*
Ⓑ *re–*
Ⓒ *non–*
Ⓓ *un–*

5. What does the word *contagious* mean?

Ⓐ unhealthy
Ⓑ disgusting
Ⓒ can be passed around
Ⓓ moves quickly

SCORE

1. Ⓨ Ⓝ
2. Ⓨ Ⓝ
3. Ⓨ Ⓝ
4. Ⓨ Ⓝ
5. Ⓨ Ⓝ

___ / 5
Total

NAME: ______________________ **DATE:** ______________

STOP THE INVADERS

Even if you take good care of your body, you can still get sick sometimes. Germs can invade even a healthy body! Getting sick can make you feel miserable, but there are some things that you can do to help yourself get better quickly and be more comfortable.

The first thing to do when you are not feeling well is to let your parents know. Sometimes it is hard to tell whether you have a cold, the flu, or something more serious. So your parents may take you to the doctor. Your doctor can do tests that will let you know what is making you sick.

You may be sick because of bacteria. Strep throat is an example of an illness caused by bacteria. If bacteria has made you sick, your doctor will give you antibiotics. *Antibiotics* are medicines that are designed to help your body get rid of the bacteria that is making you sick. It is important to take all of the medicine the doctor gives you because your body needs all of the medicine in order to kill the germs. It is also important to get plenty of rest because your body needs rest to heal. Drinking plenty of liquids such as water and juice also helps.

Your doctor may tell you that you have a virus, like the flu. If you do, the best thing to do is get plenty of rest. Even if you are not asleep, rest as much as you can. It is also important to drink lots of fluids. Water, juice, and soup are especially good for you. Your parents can give you medicine for your fever and aches. Tell your parents if you start to feel a lot worse or if you have trouble breathing. They will take you back to the doctor.

If you have a cold, there are things you can do to be more comfortable. Warm liquids like chicken soup soothe your throat and help clear your nose. Liquids such as juice and water are very helpful, too. You can also help soothe your throat and clear your sinuses with a hot bath or a shower. And don't forget to blow your nose frequently—that will help your body get rid of mucus, too. Germs can invade anyone's body, but you can help your body fight back.

NAME: ______________________ **DATE:** ______________

DIRECTIONS Read "Stop the Invaders" and then answer the questions.

1. What is an example of bacteria making you sick?

Ⓐ cold
Ⓑ the wrong medicine
Ⓒ strep throat
Ⓓ a broken leg

2. What does it mean for germs to *invade* your body?

Ⓐ Germs make you hot.
Ⓑ Germs get inside your body.
Ⓒ Germs are only in animal bodies.
Ⓓ Germs only go into your body through your nose.

3. What does the author likely want the reader to do?

Ⓐ avoid medicine
Ⓑ drink very little water
Ⓒ get the flu
Ⓓ feel better more quickly when he or she is sick

4. Why might a doctor need to do tests to find out what is making you sick?

Ⓐ You may have the flu, but feel fine.
Ⓑ Sometimes it is hard to tell what is causing your symptoms.
Ⓒ You may have strep throat, but not feel sick.
Ⓓ Tests cannot tell whether you have a cold or the flu.

5. Which is a purpose for reading this text?

Ⓐ to learn how to find a good doctor
Ⓑ to learn how to become a doctor
Ⓒ to learn how to make your own juice
Ⓓ to learn how to take care of yourself when you are sick

6. What might happen if you do not finish all of an antibiotic?

Ⓐ You might get better more quickly.
Ⓑ You might not kill all the bacteria and you could get sick again.
Ⓒ You might sleep better at night.
Ⓓ You might get very hungry.

7. What should you do when you feel sick?

Ⓐ Tell your parents and then try to get a lot of rest.
Ⓑ Get extra exercise.
Ⓒ Get up early and go to school.
Ⓓ Tell the doctor that you feel fine.

8. Why is it important to get a lot of rest when you are sick?

Ⓐ Your body does not need much rest when you are sick.
Ⓑ Rest helps you to feel less bored.
Ⓒ Your body needs a lot of rest in order to heal.
Ⓓ Rest is not important when you are feeling well.

SCORE

1. Ⓨ Ⓝ
2. Ⓨ Ⓝ
3. Ⓨ Ⓝ
4. Ⓨ Ⓝ
5. Ⓨ Ⓝ
6. Ⓨ Ⓝ
7. Ⓨ Ⓝ
8. Ⓨ Ⓝ

___ / 8
Total

NAME: ______________________ **DATE:** ______________

SCORE

___ / 4

DIRECTIONS Reread "Stop the Invaders." Then, read the prompt and respond on the lines below.

When was the last time you were sick? What was it like? Write about what happened and what you did to feel better.

NAME: ______________________ **DATE:** ______________

DIRECTIONS Read the text and then answer the questions.

Vanessa usually got to class before the bell sounded, but today she was running late and barely made it. She and her friends had been talking about a rumor they had heard, and she hadn't paid attention to the time. A few people had seen a new girl walking around, and everyone wondered whose class she would be in. A lot of stories about the new student had been passed around already, so Vanessa was curious about her. Just then, Mr. Sharpe came into the classroom followed by a girl Vanessa had never seen before. This must be the new student, and she was going to be in Vanessa's class. "Okay, everyone," Mr. Sharpe announced, "I want you all to meet Niki. She's just moved here, and moving isn't easy, so let's all make her welcome."

1. What is the setting of this text?

- (A) the school library
- (B) the cafeteria
- (C) a classroom
- (D) the gym

2. What kind of picture might help a reader understand this text?

- (A) a picture of a new student
- (B) a picture of a test
- (C) a picture of a baseball game
- (D) a picture of a teacher

3. What does the word *barely* tell readers about Vanessa?

- (A) She was not feeling well.
- (B) She was very curious.
- (C) She had a lot of time.
- (D) She was almost late.

4. Which noun means the same as *rumor*?

- (A) question
- (B) gossip
- (C) interest
- (D) friend

5. Which means that someone may not be on time?

- (A) curious
- (B) running late
- (C) passed around
- (D) paid attention

SCORE

1. Ⓨ Ⓝ
2. Ⓨ Ⓝ
3. Ⓨ Ⓝ
4. Ⓨ Ⓝ
5. Ⓨ Ⓝ

___ / 5
Total

NAME: ______________________ **DATE:** ______________

DIRECTIONS Read the text and then answer the questions.

SCORE

1. Ⓨ Ⓝ

2. Ⓨ Ⓝ

3. Ⓨ Ⓝ

4. Ⓨ Ⓝ

5. Ⓨ Ⓝ

___ / 5 Total

Niki was a new student in Vanessa's class. She had only been there for a few days, but rumors about her were already spreading around. Some of Vanessa's friends said that Niki was really rich and she was a stuck-up snob. Other people spread the rumor that Niki got good grades but only because she cheated on all of her tests. Vanessa heard other stories, too, and she didn't know which ones to believe. She didn't know what to say to Niki, either. Niki never talked very much unless the teacher called on her. Vanessa had tried to talk to her a few times. But every time she did, Niki ended the conversation as soon as possible. Vanessa didn't want to be rude or mean, but if Niki didn't want to talk to her, maybe she was a snob just as Vanessa had heard she was.

1. Why does Vanessa think that Niki might be a snob?

Ⓐ Niki doesn't talk very much.

Ⓑ Niki tells her she is a snob.

Ⓒ Vanessa's teacher tells her Niki is a snob.

Ⓓ Vanessa's mother tells her Niki is a snob.

2. Which title best describes this text's main idea?

Ⓐ Making a Friend

Ⓑ The First Day of School

Ⓒ Rumor Has It

Ⓓ Starting Over

3. Which has the same meaning as the word *mean* in the last sentence?

Ⓐ unkind

Ⓑ cheap

Ⓒ average

Ⓓ friendly

4. What kind of sentence is: *Niki was a new student in Vanessa's class.*

Ⓐ compound

Ⓑ simple

Ⓒ complex

Ⓓ interrogatory

5. What are the phrases *really rich* and *stuck-up snob* examples of?

Ⓐ similes

Ⓑ metaphors

Ⓒ personification

Ⓓ alliteration

NAME: ______________________ **DATE:** ______________

DIRECTIONS Read the text and then answer the questions.

Vanessa had tried to talk to Niki, the new student, but Niki never said much. Vanessa was beginning to think that Niki was a snob—that's what the rumor was about her, anyway. Well, if Niki wanted to be a snob, that was just fine with Vanessa. So for several days, Vanessa didn't speak to Niki at all. Then one day, Vanessa noticed that Niki had forgotten her notebook in class. Vanessa decided to try one last time to talk to Niki. Holding the notebook, she followed Niki out of the classroom.

When she caught up with Niki, she said, "Here, I think you forgot this."

Niki thanked her and abruptly turned away. Then, she suddenly turned back, smiled, and said, "Thanks for being nice to me."

Vanessa couldn't believe Niki had actually spoken to her. Maybe she wasn't such a snob.

1. What is the turning point in the text's plot?

- (A) Vanessa hears a new rumor about Niki.
- (B) Niki smiles and talks to Vanessa.
- (C) Vanessa's mother asks her to be nice to Niki.
- (D) Niki is nice to one of Vanessa's friends.

2. How is the main event of this text—Vanessa is trying to get to know Niki—described to readers?

- (A) through the actions of the characters
- (B) only through dialogue
- (C) with foreshadowing
- (D) with a picture

3. What does the word *abruptly* tell readers about Niki's action?

- (A) She moves loudly.
- (B) She moves slowly.
- (C) She moves quickly.
- (D) She moves happily.

4. Which word from the text is an adverb?

- (A) spoken
- (B) snob
- (C) suddenly
- (D) said

5. Which word is a synonym for *actually*?

- (A) never
- (B) possibly
- (C) really
- (D) quietly

SCORE

1. Ⓨ Ⓝ
2. Ⓨ Ⓝ
3. Ⓨ Ⓝ
4. Ⓨ Ⓝ
5. Ⓨ Ⓝ

___ / 5
Total

NAME: ______________________ **DATE:** ______________

DON'T BELIEVE THE RUMORS

Vanessa and Niki had just begun a friendship. Niki was new at school, and Vanessa had thought she was a snob. That was mostly because Niki barely said anything, and besides, that was the rumor about her. But then, Niki had forgotten her notebook in the classroom by accident, and Vanessa had returned it to her. Then the two girls started to talk, and they got to know each other. Now Vanessa knew that Niki wasn't a snob, but she still didn't understand why Niki wouldn't talk to anyone.

One day, Niki explained herself. "I don't really know anyone here except you, and I'm kind of shy. I know everybody thinks I'm a snob, but I'm not. I just don't know what to say to people."

Vanessa understood that, and it made her feel guilty for thinking Niki was a snob. She shouldn't have believed the rumors about Niki.

Vanessa had an idea for helping Niki. "If my other friends get to know you," she told Niki, "they'll like you, too, just like I do. So why don't you sit with my friends and me at lunch tomorrow? Then everybody will see what you're like." Niki was very doubtful, but she was tired of everyone thinking she was a snob. So she reluctantly agreed to have lunch with Vanessa and her friends.

The next day, Vanessa and Niki waited in the cafeteria for Vanessa's other friends. Niki was nervous, but Vanessa said, "Don't worry. Just be yourself. You'll be fine." Finally, everyone else arrived.

One of Vanessa's friends took one look at Niki and asked, "Why are you sitting with the snob, Vanessa? Come on and eat with us." Niki's eyes filled with tears.

Vanessa took a breath and then said, "I'm sitting with Niki because she's my friend and she's nice. How about finding out for yourself instead of believing every rumor you hear?" For a moment, everyone stared at each other. Then, very slowly, the other girls sat down at the table. At first, nobody said much, but soon, they started talking. By the time lunch was over, Niki realized that Vanessa was right—all she had to do was be herself. And all everyone else needed to do was stop believing rumors.

NAME: ______________________ **DATE:** ______________

DIRECTIONS Read “Don't Believe the Rumors” and then answer the questions.

1. Whom is the conflict between?

- (A) Vanessa and her math teacher
- (B) Vanessa and her mom
- (C) Vanessa and Niki
- (D) Vanessa and her friends

2. Why doesn't Niki say very much?

- (A) She doesn't speak the same language.
- (B) She is a snob.
- (C) She is shy and doesn't know what to say.
- (D) She doesn't like Vanessa.

3. What might happen the following day?

- (A) Vanessa will eat lunch alone.
- (B) Vanessa will be very angry with Niki.
- (C) Niki will stop speaking to Vanessa.
- (D) Niki will have lunch with Vanessa and her friends again.

4. How do Vanessa's friends likely feel when they first see that she is sitting with Niki?

- (A) excited
- (B) surprised
- (C) frightened
- (D) joyful

5. Which statement reflects a purpose for reading this text?

- (A) I want to learn how to make friends.
- (B) I want to read about how some kids checked out the truth behind rumors.
- (C) I want to know how to spread rumors.
- (D) I want to know about the family backgrounds of the characters.

6. Which conclusion makes the most sense?

- (A) Vanessa has several friends.
- (B) Niki has more friends than Vanessa does.
- (C) Vanessa is not a good student.
- (D) Niki wants to be a swimmer.

7. What lesson does Vanessa learn?

- (A) She learns that Niki is a snob.
- (B) She learns not to believe rumors.
- (C) She learns that her other friends are snobs.
- (D) She learns not to sit with her friends at lunch.

8. How does Vanessa feel about no longer believing the rumors?

- (A) She feels angry.
- (B) She feels guilty.
- (C) She feels proud.
- (D) She feels afraid.

SCORE

1. (Y) (N)
2. (Y) (N)
3. (Y) (N)
4. (Y) (N)
5. (Y) (N)
6. (Y) (N)
7. (Y) (N)
8. (Y) (N)

___ / 8 Total

NAME: ______________________ DATE: ______________

DIRECTIONS

Reread "Don't Believe the Rumors." Then, read the prompt and respond on the lines below.

SCORE

___ / 4

Have you ever heard rumors about people? What did you do? Write about what you have done about a rumor or how you would handle gossip.

NAME: ______________________ **DATE:** ______________

DIRECTIONS Read the text and then answer the questions.

Companies want to sell products or services that people will buy. But in order to do that, they need to understand their *market*—the people who will buy from them. So, many companies use market research to find out about their customers. For example, imagine a company is planning to make a new kind of video game. The company wants to make a game people want. So the company decides to find out the *mean*, or average, age of video-game players. To do that, the company finds out the ages of a group of players. Then, the company adds up all of the ages and divides that total by the number of players. That is the mean age. Then, the company can interview people in that age group and find out what they want in a game.

1. What is this text mostly about?

Ⓐ video games
Ⓑ how companies make their products
Ⓒ how companies find out about their customers
Ⓓ adding

2. Which chapter title reflects the main idea?

Ⓐ Going to the Market
Ⓑ Means and Averages
Ⓒ Market Research
Ⓓ A Mean Age

3. Which word is a synonym for *mean*?

Ⓐ division
Ⓑ group
Ⓒ total
Ⓓ average

4. Which word below is both a noun and a verb?

Ⓐ people
Ⓑ products
Ⓒ decides
Ⓓ group

5. What is a tool for finding out about customers?

Ⓐ a video game
Ⓑ market research
Ⓒ a company
Ⓓ totaling

SCORE

1. Ⓨ Ⓝ
2. Ⓨ Ⓝ
3. Ⓨ Ⓝ
4. Ⓨ Ⓝ
5. Ⓨ Ⓝ

___ / 5 Total

NAME: ______________________ **DATE:** ______________

DIRECTIONS Read the text and then answer the questions.

SCORE

1. Ⓨ Ⓝ
2. Ⓨ Ⓝ
3. Ⓨ Ⓝ
4. Ⓨ Ⓝ
5. Ⓨ Ⓝ

___ / 5
Total

Imagine a company has decided to make a new kind of video game. The company knows that if the game costs too much, people will not buy it. If the game does not cost enough, the company will not earn much money. So the company wants to find out how much money people are willing to spend on video games. The company knows that a few people will spend a lot of money on video games and a few people will only spend a little. The company wants to sell its game to the most people. So the company wants to find out how much most people are willing to spend on video games. To do that, the company uses the median price that people will pay. To find the median, the company lists all of the prices people will pay, from lowest to highest price. The number in the middle of that list is the median price.

1. What is the first step in finding a median price?

Ⓐ Look for the price in the middle.
Ⓑ List all of the prices from lowest to highest.
Ⓒ Put a price on a video game.
Ⓓ Add up the prices.

2. What kind of text feature would help explain this information?

Ⓐ a graph of the most popular video games
Ⓑ a photograph of a television
Ⓒ a chart showing the range of prices for a game
Ⓓ a picture of a video game

3. What does the root *medi–* in *median* mean?

Ⓐ middle
Ⓑ price
Ⓒ company
Ⓓ money

4. Which prefix could be added to make an antonym of *willing*?

Ⓐ *bi–*
Ⓑ *un–*
Ⓒ *epi–*
Ⓓ *sub–*

5. Which word means *find out*?

Ⓐ report
Ⓑ earn
Ⓒ learn
Ⓓ ask

NAME: ______________________ **DATE:** ______________

DIRECTIONS Read the text and then answer the questions.

Imagine that a video game company makes several different games. The company wants to make a lot of copies of the most popular games. That way, there will be enough copies of those games for everyone who wants one. The company doesn't want to make a lot of copies of games that are not popular. If it does, there will be a lot of unsold copies of those games. The company won't earn money that way. So the company finds out how many copies it sells of each game. It makes a list of games and the number of copies sold. The game that appears the most often on that list is the *mode*—it is the most frequently bought game. The company will make more copies of that game than it will make of other games since it will probably sell more of that game.

1. Why does a company want to make a lot of copies of popular video games?

Ⓐ so there will be enough copies for everyone who wants one

Ⓑ so those games will not be popular

Ⓒ so there will only be a few copies of those games

Ⓓ so the company will make new games

2. According to this text, what does the mode explain?

Ⓐ which games companies make

Ⓑ which item appears the least often on a list

Ⓒ how much a video game costs

Ⓓ which item appears the most often on a list

3. In any group of numbers, what is the *mode*?

Ⓐ the smallest number

Ⓑ the largest number

Ⓒ the number that appears most often

Ⓓ always the middle number

4. Which part of speech is the word *frequently*?

Ⓐ verb

Ⓑ noun

Ⓒ adverb

Ⓓ adjective

5. Which word is a synonym for *enough*?

Ⓐ never

Ⓑ some

Ⓒ sufficient

Ⓓ sparse

SCORE

1. Ⓨ Ⓝ

2. Ⓨ Ⓝ

3. Ⓨ Ⓝ

4. Ⓨ Ⓝ

5. Ⓨ Ⓝ

___ / 5 Total

NAME: ____________________ **DATE:** ____________

GAME ON

Imagine that BestGames wants to make a new video game called *Dragon Days*. BestGames wants to make a game that people want to buy, so the company will do some market research. One thing that BestGames wants to know is the mean age of video-game buyers. So BestGames finds out the ages of a group of video-game buyers. Then, it adds up those ages and divides that total by the number of buyers. Here is what BestGames learns about video-game buyers:

Video-Game Buyers

Total video-game buyers	100
Sum of buyers' ages	2,200
Mean age of video-game buyers	22

BestGames also wants to know how much people will pay for *Dragon Days*. So BestGames asks a number of people how much they will pay for a game. BestGames wants to know how much most people will pay, so it will list all of the prices people are willing to pay, from lowest to highest. The number in the middle is the median. That number will give BestGames a good idea of what most people will pay. Here is what BestGames learns about the median price people will pay:

Prices Video-Game Buyers Will Pay

Lowest price	$1.00
Highest price	$75.00
Median price	$25.00

Once the game is in stores, BestGames needs to monitor its sales. So each month, the company lists the game that sells the most copies. The game that is on that list most often is the mode. That is the most popular game. If *Dragon Days* is the mode, BestGames will make a lot of copies of that game. That is because it will probably sell most of them. Here is what BestGames learns about its sales.

Most Popular Games

Month	Highest Sales
January	*New World*
February	*Dragon Days*
March	*Dragon Days*
April	*Dragon Days*
May	*Your City*
June	*Your City*

NAME: ____________________ **DATE:** ____________

DIRECTIONS Read "Game On" and then answer the questions.

1. What is the average age of video-game buyers?

(A) 22
(B) 100
(C) 2,200
(D) 12

2. Based on the text, what can you tell about the definition of the word *mean*?

(A) not nice
(B) have good intentions
(C) intend to do something
(D) average

3. Which game will BestGames likely make the most copies of for sale?

(A) Your City
(B) Dragon Days
(C) New World
(D) April

4. What would BestGames do if the mean age of game buyers were 8?

(A) find out the mean age of game sellers
(B) not make any more games
(C) make more games for adults
(D) make more games for kids

5. Which was the least popular game between January and June?

(A) New World
(B) Dragon Days
(C) Your City
(D) BestGames

6. What would BestGames likely do if *Your City* became the mode?

(A) stop making video games
(B) make a lot of copies of *Dragon Days*
(C) stop selling it
(D) make more copies of it

7. Who might be most interested in this type of data?

(A) a journalist who works for a video-game magazine
(B) a kindergarten math teacher
(C) a supermarket owner
(D) a movie theater worker

8. What does this text tell you about market research?

(A) It is only helpful to video-game companies.
(B) It is mostly about making guesses.
(C) Companies rely on it to make many decisions.
(D) Most businesses do not think it is very important.

SCORE

1. (Y)(N)
2. (Y)(N)
3. (Y)(N)
4. (Y)(N)
5. (Y)(N)
6. (Y)(N)
7. (Y)(N)
8. (Y)(N)

___ / 8
Total

NAME: ______________________ **DATE:** ______________

DIRECTIONS

Reread "Game On." Then, read the prompt and respond on the lines below.

SCORE

___ / 4

How do you find the mean of a set of numbers? How do you find the median of a set of numbers? Explain how to find the mean and the median of a set of numbers.

NAME: ______________________ **DATE:** ______________

DIRECTIONS Read the text and then answer the questions.

Josh got tired of losing his things, especially important things like money. He admitted that it was mostly his own fault. He didn't keep his room very organized and he didn't clean it often. Whenever he lost something, his mom or dad offered to help him look for it, but Josh didn't want them going through his things. One day, he lost a game that belonged to his friend Ian, and although he looked for a long time, he couldn't find it. That was when he knew he needed to do something about his room. That night at dinner, he asked his parents, "Can I have some crates or boxes or something for my stuff? I don't want to keep losing everything." His mom and dad thought that would be a very good idea for Josh's room, so they agreed to take him shopping.

1. Who is the main character?

- (A) Ian
- (B) Ian's mom
- (C) Josh
- (D) Ian's dad

2. What is Josh's problem?

- (A) His room is too large.
- (B) He keeps losing things.
- (C) He is angry with his parents.
- (D) He is angry with his friend Ian.

3. Which word is an antonym of *admitted*?

- (A) sang
- (B) confessed
- (C) realized
- (D) denied

4. Which is the meaning of the noun *stuff* in this text?

- (A) things
- (B) fill
- (C) eat too much
- (D) push

5. What does the phrase *tired of* mean?

- (A) annoyed with
- (B) sleepy
- (C) excited about
- (D) new to

SCORE

1. Ⓨ Ⓝ
2. Ⓨ Ⓝ
3. Ⓨ Ⓝ
4. Ⓨ Ⓝ
5. Ⓨ Ⓝ

___ / 5 Total

NAME: ______________________ **DATE:** ______________

DIRECTIONS Read the text and then answer the questions.

SCORE

1. Ⓨ Ⓝ
2. Ⓨ Ⓝ
3. Ⓨ Ⓝ
4. Ⓨ Ⓝ
5. Ⓨ Ⓝ

___ / 5
Total

Josh and his parents went to the home-supply store to get some things to help him organize his room. Josh had a bad habit of losing things, and he was tired of it. He wanted some way to keep track of everything, and he didn't want to ask for help every time he lost something. When they got to the store, Josh's dad asked him what kinds of things he wanted. At first, Josh wasn't sure—he had never made an effort to organize his things before. But soon, he chose a storage cart with four drawers in it and a storage bin that fit under his bed. Josh's mom suggested a laundry hamper so Josh would have a separate place for his dirty clothes. Josh had the feeling it wasn't going to be easy to organize his things, but now he had the tools he needed to do it.

1. Why do Josh and his parents go to the home-supply store?

Ⓐ Josh needs to buy a new bed.
Ⓑ Josh's parents need to buy some sheets and towels.
Ⓒ Josh wants a way to keep track of his things.
Ⓓ His parents want to see what the store is like.

2. How are events ordered in this text?

Ⓐ in order of importance
Ⓑ in the order they occur
Ⓒ in alphabetical order
Ⓓ in numerical order

3. Which word is a synonym for *lose*?

Ⓐ mistake
Ⓑ discover
Ⓒ misplace
Ⓓ discuss

4. Which verb means to *keep track of*?

Ⓐ clean
Ⓑ lose
Ⓒ monitor
Ⓓ throw

5. What does the phrase *make an effort* mean?

Ⓐ talk
Ⓑ shop
Ⓒ clean
Ⓓ try

NAME: ______________________________ **DATE:** ________________

DIRECTIONS Read the text and then answer the questions.

Josh knew that he would have a lot of work to do. His parents had just gotten him some new storage bins and a laundry hamper so he could organize his room. But his room was such a mess that he didn't quite know where to begin. The easiest thing to do was separate clothes from everything else. So the first thing Josh did was to toss all of his dirty clothes into his new laundry hamper. Once that was done, he looked around to see what else he could separate from everything. There were a lot of movies and video games lying around, so Josh gathered them all up and put them into one of his storage bins. Then, he picked up books and papers and put them into another storage bin. It wasn't long before everything was put away.

1. What is the setting of this text?

- (A) the home-supply store
- (B) school
- (C) the living room
- (D) Josh's room

2. Why is Josh's first action to put his dirty clothes in the hamper?

- (A) Josh doesn't have any clean clothes.
- (B) His mom tells Josh to start with clothes.
- (C) It is easiest to separate clothes from everything else.
- (D) Josh puts all of his clothes away.

3. What does the word *gotten* mean in this text?

- (A) taken
- (B) bought
- (C) talked about
- (D) washed

4. Which is the root word in *lying*?

- (A) lie
- (B) lay
- (C) loaf
- (D) light

5. What does the phrase *know where to begin* mean?

- (A) get ready to go
- (B) begin at the starting line
- (C) how to get started
- (D) start walking

SCORE

1. Ⓨ Ⓝ
2. Ⓨ Ⓝ
3. Ⓨ Ⓝ
4. Ⓨ Ⓝ
5. Ⓨ Ⓝ

___ / 5 Total

NAME:______________________ DATE:______________

JOSH COMES CLEAN

Josh was tired of always losing things, so his parents bought him storage bins and other things to organize his room. Now he was finding it easier than ever to keep track of his belongings. He even found some overdue library books and returned them. He found a game that belonged to his friend Ian, too, and gave it back. Josh noticed how much time he saved just by using storage bins and a laundry hamper. He was beginning to understand now why his parents always nagged him about cleaning his room.

One day, Josh decided to get his skateboard out of the garage and ride it for a while. When he got to the garage, though, he couldn't find his skateboard. The garage was just as disorganized as his room had been. Josh thought about it for a while and then decided he might as well clean the garage. At least that way he would be able to find his skateboard, bike, and helmet. He asked his parents if they could get more storage bins, and they were happy to agree to that! His dad even said there were some bins in the basement, and that Josh could use them.

So one Saturday morning, his mom moved the car out of the garage, and Josh got to work. First, he made separate piles for everything. There was a pile for gardening supplies, a pile for tools, and a pile for bike and skateboard equipment. There was also a pile for painting and cleaning supplies. By the time Josh was done, there were seven different piles of things. After everything was sorted out, Josh started putting everything into different bins. It took a long time because the garage was a big mess. But when Josh was finished, it looked a lot neater. When everything was stored, Josh swept the garage. His family said the garage looked great, and Josh knew that the next time he wanted his skateboard, he would be able to find it.

NAME: ______________________ **DATE:** ______________

DIRECTIONS Read "Josh Comes Clean" and then answer the questions.

1. What is the last thing that Josh does?

- (A) He sweeps the garage.
- (B) He makes separate piles for everything.
- (C) He puts things into different bins.
- (D) He looks for his skateboard.

2. What does it mean that Josh was *tired of* something?

- (A) He needed sleep.
- (B) He was ready for a change.
- (C) He needed to change a tire.
- (D) He had too much energy.

3. What will likely happen the next time Josh wants his skateboard?

- (A) He will lose it.
- (B) He will find it quickly.
- (C) He will not ride it.
- (D) His dad will take it.

4. Which purpose for reading is most appropriate for this text?

- (A) to know how someone stays organized
- (B) to know how to keep my dog clean
- (C) to read about a character who apologizes for a lie
- (D) to read about how to better clean my house

5. From which point of view is this text told?

- (A) third person
- (B) first person
- (C) second person
- (D) There is no point of view.

6. Why might Josh wait until the very end to sweep the garage?

- (A) There is no room for him to sweep until he stores everything.
- (B) His parents tell him that it's not safe to sweep.
- (C) The broom is broken and Josh has to get a new one.
- (D) Josh is too tired to sweep at first.

7. How do Josh's parents likely feel about the way the garage looks at the end of the text?

- (A) angry
- (B) confused
- (C) afraid
- (D) happy

8. Which of these sayings is a good summary of the theme of this text?

- (A) Too many cooks spoil the broth.
- (B) The early bird catches the worm.
- (C) A place for everything, and everything in its place.
- (D) Do unto others as you would have them do unto you.

SCORE

1. Ⓨ Ⓝ
2. Ⓨ Ⓝ
3. Ⓨ Ⓝ
4. Ⓨ Ⓝ
5. Ⓨ Ⓝ
6. Ⓨ Ⓝ
7. Ⓨ Ⓝ
8. Ⓨ Ⓝ

___ / 8
Total

NAME: ______________________ **DATE:** ______________

DIRECTIONS Reread "Josh Comes Clean." Then, read the prompt and respond on the lines below.

SCORE
___ / 4

How organized are you? Write about how you keep track of your things.

NAME: ______________________ **DATE:** ______________

DIRECTIONS Read the text and then answer the questions.

Have you ever passed a construction site? Putting up a house or another building takes a lot of time and knowledge. If the building isn't constructed well, it could be very dangerous. If a building is constructed on land that can't support a building, that could be dangerous, too. So the people who design and make buildings have to be good at their jobs. There are several steps to designing and constructing buildings. First, an architect (AHRK-i-tekt) draws up the plans for the building. The architect makes a small model of the building so everyone will know what the building will look like. Then, a construction company uses those plans to make the house, store, or other building. When the building is finished, a building inspector goes through it to make sure that everything is safe. Finally, the building is ready for people to use it.

1. What does a building inspector do?

- (A) A building inspector draws up plans for a building.
- (B) A building inspector makes buildings.
- (C) A building inspector goes through a building to be sure it is safe.
- (D) A building inspector makes a model of a building.

2. What is the first step in constructing a building?

- (A) A building inspector goes through the building.
- (B) An architect draws up the plans.
- (C) A construction company makes the building.
- (D) People can use the building.

3. Which word is a synonym for *construct*?

- (A) build
- (B) destruct
- (C) pour
- (D) model

4. Which word from the text can be both a noun and a verb?

- (A) architect
- (B) plan
- (C) safe
- (D) several

5. Which of these is **not** a word that tells you the order of things?

- (A) then
- (B) finally
- (C) first
- (D) have

SCORE

1. Ⓨ Ⓝ

2. Ⓨ Ⓝ

3. Ⓨ Ⓝ

4. Ⓨ Ⓝ

5. Ⓨ Ⓝ

___ / 5 Total

NAME: ______________________ **DATE:** ______________

DIRECTIONS Read the text and then answer the questions.

SCORE

1. Ⓨ Ⓝ
2. Ⓨ Ⓝ
3. Ⓨ Ⓝ
4. Ⓨ Ⓝ
5. Ⓨ Ⓝ

___ / 5
Total

In most cities, people cannot put up buildings wherever they want because different kinds of buildings are used for different things. For example, factories are used to make things. Sometimes, the people who work there use dangerous equipment. Factories can also be extremely loud. So it wouldn't be wise to have a factory next to a school. But factories can be near each other. And schools and houses can be near each other—in fact, a lot of schools and houses are very near each other. So how do people know what kinds of buildings they can put up in an area? Most cities and towns have laws called *zoning laws*. Those laws tell which parts, or zones, of a city are for houses and schools, for factories, and for stores and other businesses.

1. Which title best describes what this text is about?

Ⓐ An Architect's Dream
Ⓑ Building Up
Ⓒ City Zones
Ⓓ Living Together

2. Which type of book would likely include this information in a chapter?

Ⓐ a book of maps
Ⓑ a book about city government
Ⓒ a history book about a small town
Ⓓ a newspaper article about homes for sale

3. What is another term for an *area* of a city or town?

Ⓐ zone
Ⓑ building
Ⓒ factory
Ⓓ law

4. Which noun describes rules for the parts of a city that are for different kinds of buildings?

Ⓐ area laws
Ⓑ business laws
Ⓒ factory laws
Ⓓ zoning laws

5. What does the phrase *put up* mean in this text?

Ⓐ tolerate
Ⓑ pay for
Ⓒ build
Ⓓ crash

NAME: ______________________ **DATE:** ______________

DIRECTIONS Read the text and then answer the questions.

It is important that buildings are safe for people. So most cities and states have laws that tell how buildings must be constructed. Those laws are called *building codes*. For example, codes tell how floors and walls must be made. They also tell what materials can be used for basements, attics, and roofs. There are other codes, too, that builders must follow when they construct houses, factories, and other buildings. In fact, before a building can be used, a building inspector goes through the building. The building inspector checks to make sure that the building has been constructed properly. If the builders have followed the codes, then walls and floors are sturdy and roofs are safe and strong. Electrical wiring has been done properly. And stairs are wide enough and strong enough to be safe. Once the building inspector is sure that the building follows the codes, then people can use the building.

1. What is this text mostly about?

- (A) what building codes are and what they do
- (B) electrical wiring
- (C) factories and houses
- (D) a day in the life of a building inspector

2. Why do cities and states have building codes?

- (A) All buildings must have stairs.
- (B) Many buildings have basements and attics.
- (C) Buildings have walls and roofs.
- (D) It is important that buildings are safe for people to use.

3. Which prefix could be added to make an antonym of *properly*?

- (A) *hyper–*
- (B) *sub–*
- (C) *per–*
- (D) *im–*

4. If a building is described using the adjective *sturdy*, what does that mean?

- (A) It is expensive.
- (B) It is tall.
- (C) It is strong.
- (D) It is nearby.

5. Which word or phrase shows that the author thinks building codes are important?

- (A) safe and strong
- (B) constructed properly
- (C) sturdy
- (D) all of the above

SCORE

1. Ⓨ Ⓝ
2. Ⓨ Ⓝ
3. Ⓨ Ⓝ
4. Ⓨ Ⓝ
5. Ⓨ Ⓝ

___ / 5
Total

NAME:______________________ DATE:______________

CIVIL ENGINEERS

How are houses, stores, and other buildings designed? What about roads, bridges, and tunnels? Many of these are designed by civil engineers. They manage all kinds of construction projects. They design tunnels, bridges, and office buildings. They design houses and apartment buildings, too. Some work for cities and states. Others work for construction companies. One of their jobs is to see that construction projects are safe. Another is to be sure that they do not harm the environment. They also must be sure their projects are completed on time.

Sometimes, civil engineers are hired by towns or cities. For example, if a city is planning to build a new mall or office building, it will need civil engineers. If a company wants to build a new apartment complex, it may hire a civil engineer. If a state wants to build a new system of roads or improve the roads it has, it will hire civil engineers.

How do civil engineers learn their jobs? Most people who want to be civil engineers go to college. They study math, physics, and other kinds of science. After college, they often work with an experienced engineer. They do their job for four years, and then they take a special exam. If they pass that exam, they get a license. With that license, they can work directly with people or they can be hired by companies.

Civil engineers often work near construction sites. Many work near larger towns and cities where buildings are being planned. Civil engineers are responsible for a lot of things. They must be sure that their projects follow building codes and are completed by the deadline. They also have to be sure that their projects do not harm the environment or cost more than the budget allows.

NAME: ______________________ **DATE:** ______________

DIRECTIONS Read "Civil Engineers" and then answer the questions.

1. Which question is **not** answered in the text?

- (A) What do civil engineers do?
- (B) How much money do civil engineers earn?
- (C) How do civil engineers learn their jobs?
- (D) Who hires civil engineers?

2. Which words in the text help the reader understand the meaning of the word *engineer*?

- (A) *building* and *designed*
- (B) *civil* and *responsible*
- (C) *towns* and *cities*
- (D) *budget* and *cost*

3. What might be a purpose for reading this text?

- (A) to learn what civil engineers do
- (B) to learn how to build a house
- (C) to find the nearest big city
- (D) to learn to take care of the environment

4. What does a civil engineer have to know?

- (A) the best commuting routes
- (B) a city's building codes
- (C) how to operate a train
- (D) how to mix paints

5. Which of these projects would a civil engineer manage?

- (A) building a new kind of computer
- (B) designing a new style of jeans
- (C) designing a new kind of car
- (D) building a new shopping center

6. Which is likely the author's opinion about civil engineers?

- (A) They do not work hard.
- (B) They are professional athletes.
- (C) They are not interesting.
- (D) They do important work.

7. Who would most likely work with a civil engineer?

- (A) a company that wants to make a new snack
- (B) a person who wants to buy a car
- (C) a city that wants to build a mall
- (D) a teacher who wants new supplies

8. Why are civil engineers important?

- (A) They know all about bridges and tunnels.
- (B) They work near construction sites.
- (C) There are not many places for civil engineers to work.
- (D) They ensure that construction projects are safe and do not harm the environment.

SCORE

1. Ⓨ Ⓝ
2. Ⓨ Ⓝ
3. Ⓨ Ⓝ
4. Ⓨ Ⓝ
5. Ⓨ Ⓝ
6. Ⓨ Ⓝ
7. Ⓨ Ⓝ
8. Ⓨ Ⓝ

___ / 8
Total

NAME: ______________________ **DATE:** ______________

DIRECTIONS Reread "Civil Engineers." Then, read the prompt and respond on the lines below.

SCORE

___ / 4

What do you think it might be like to be a civil engineer? Write about what would be the best and the hardest parts of the job.

NAME: ____________________ **DATE:** ____________

DIRECTIONS Read the text and then answer the questions.

This morning, the weather was cloudy and the forecast was for very rainy weather, so Melanie wore a hooded jacket to school. At school, Mrs. Jackson explained that a low-pressure weather system was going to pass through the area. That meant that the air would be warmer, so it would rise, and that would bring wind, clouds, and a lot of rain. Mrs. Jackson told the class that low-pressure systems sometimes lead to major storms, such as hurricanes. When she heard that, Melanie wondered if this particular low-pressure system would bring a hurricane. Mrs. Jackson said, "Well, there is a hurricane forming out over the ocean, but we don't know if it will hit land yet. And fortunately, we're not very near the ocean, so it probably won't be a serious storm here."

1. What is Melanie worried about in this text?

- (A) the weather
- (B) her grades
- (C) her family
- (D) one of her friends

2. What does the important vocabulary in this text teach readers?

- (A) how hurricanes are formed from low-pressure weather systems
- (B) what to do if a hurricane hits
- (C) why Mrs. Jackson was a nice teacher
- (D) where Melanie lived

3. What is a *hurricane*?

- (A) a kind of jacket
- (B) a kind of storm
- (C) a kind of ocean
- (D) a kind of cloud

4. Which verb has a similar meaning as the word *forming*?

- (A) flying
- (B) disappearing
- (C) developing
- (D) swimming

5. What is the meaning of *hit* in this text?

- (A) to bat
- (B) to score
- (C) to win
- (D) to strike

SCORE

1. (Y)(N)
2. (Y)(N)
3. (Y)(N)
4. (Y)(N)
5. (Y)(N)

___ / 5 Total

NAME: ______________________ DATE: ______________

DIRECTIONS Read the text and then answer the questions.

SCORE

1. Ⓨ Ⓝ
2. Ⓨ Ⓝ
3. Ⓨ Ⓝ
4. Ⓨ Ⓝ
5. Ⓨ Ⓝ

___ / 5 Total

Melanie had heard in class and in weather reports that there was going to be a major storm. A hurricane was forming over the ocean, and it was possible that it might hit land. One morning, the weather report mentioned that the barometric pressure was starting to fall. That meant that a low-pressure system was starting to move through the area. Melanie asked her parents what they would do if a hurricane did strike land. They told Melanie that they lived inland—not very near the ocean. So the storm probably wouldn't be severe. "Besides," her mom told Melanie, "even if it is a serious storm, we're ready. We've got flashlights and lanterns in case we lose power. And there's plenty of food and bottled water."

1. What does Melanie's mom say about the weather?

- Ⓐ She doesn't know about the weather.
- Ⓑ There will probably not be any rain.
- Ⓒ The family is ready in case there is a storm.
- Ⓓ The weather is sunny and warm.

2. What makes Melanie think there might be a storm?

- Ⓐ Melanie's friends have told her there will be a storm.
- Ⓑ A hurricane is forming over the ocean.
- Ⓒ Her mom and dad are very worried about the weather.
- Ⓓ Melanie is afraid of hurricanes.

3. Which word is a synonym for *severe*?

- Ⓐ serious
- Ⓑ cloudy
- Ⓒ distant
- Ⓓ brilliant

4. Which verb has a similar meaning to the word *mentioned*?

- Ⓐ shouted
- Ⓑ asked
- Ⓒ stated
- Ⓓ surveyed

5. Which word or phrase means *the pressure of a mass of air*?

- Ⓐ ocean pressure
- Ⓑ land
- Ⓒ hurricane
- Ⓓ barometric pressure

NAME:______________________ DATE:______________

DIRECTIONS Read the text and then answer the questions.

A major storm was predicted to strike within the next few days. Melanie and her parents weren't worried about it because they had the supplies they would need. But they still wanted to be sure that they were prepared. So they checked to make sure that everything was ready in case the storm was severe. Melanie checked each flashlight and lantern to be sure that all of them were working. Her dad checked that the windows and doors were sealed properly. Her mom checked to be sure that the basement was sealed off so water wouldn't leak in. The family also went over their emergency plan. Then they made sure they had plenty of canned food and water. When they were done, they knew that they were ready if bad weather came.

1. Which action is **not** part of this text's plot?

Ⓐ The family checks that the basement is sealed.
Ⓑ The family checks that the smoke alarms are working.
Ⓒ The family checks that the flashlights are all working.
Ⓓ The family checks that the doors and windows are sealed.

2. How do the characters feel about the storm?

Ⓐ They are not worried.
Ⓑ They are happy.
Ⓒ They are excited.
Ⓓ They have no feelings.

3. Which two words are synonyms?

Ⓐ *canned* and *food*
Ⓑ *sealed* and *properly*
Ⓒ *storm* and *strike*
Ⓓ *ready* and *prepared*

4. What does the adjective *plenty* tell the reader about the family's supply of canned food and water?

Ⓐ They have more than enough.
Ⓑ They have no supplies.
Ⓒ They have only a little.
Ⓓ The supplies are spoiled.

5. What does the phrase *went over* mean in this text?

Ⓐ telephoned
Ⓑ traveled
Ⓒ reviewed
Ⓓ wrote

SCORE

1. Ⓨ Ⓝ
2. Ⓨ Ⓝ
3. Ⓨ Ⓝ
4. Ⓨ Ⓝ
5. Ⓨ Ⓝ

___ / 5
Total

NAME:________________________________ DATE:____________________

STORM FRONT

A major storm had been predicted for a few days. Finally one afternoon, it struck. Melanie had just gotten home from school when the sky began to get unusually dark and the wind began to blow harder. She hurried around the house shutting the windows so that rain wouldn't pour in. For a while, not much happened, although it did start to sprinkle. Fortunately, Melanie's mom and dad got home from work before the weather got terribly bad.

Then, all of a sudden, the skies opened up. The rain poured down as though someone had overturned a bucket of water. It lashed against the roofs and churned down the streets. It beat a loud drumbeat on the windowpanes and ran like a river down driveways. It was raining so hard that Melanie could barely see through the windows, but she could certainly hear the wind. It whipped the tree limbs around and rattled against the windows and doors.

Before long, the wind had raised its voice from a moan to a loud scream as the storm blew through. Then, everything went dark. For a moment, everybody sat silently, but then Melanie felt her way to the kitchen for some flashlights. Melanie's dad went to get lanterns and her mom pulled some blankets out of the closet. Everyone got comfortable in the living room as they waited for the storm to pass.

After a while, Melanie got hungry. Her mom and dad said they were ready to eat, too. So they took flashlights back to the kitchen and found the peanut butter, the jelly, and some bread. Melanie's dad grabbed a bag of potato chips, and Melanie found some cookies. It wasn't a normal kind of dinner, but then, this wasn't a normal kind of evening. They ate their sandwiches in the living room and told ghost stories. Finally, everyone drifted off to sleep.

By the next morning, the storm had blown away. There were tree limbs on the ground, and everything was soaked from the heavy rain. But everyone was safe, and there had been no real damage. Melanie and her family felt lucky about that. It had actually been kind of fun—it certainly had been an adventure!

NAME: ____________________ **DATE:** ______________

DIRECTIONS Read "Storm Front" and then answer the questions.

1. What do the title and picture tell readers about the topic of the text?

- Ⓐ It is about a swimming pool party.
- Ⓑ It is about moving to a new town.
- Ⓒ It is about buying a new house.
- Ⓓ It is about a major storm.

2. Why does everything go dark?

- Ⓐ The lightbulb burns out.
- Ⓑ The storm makes the house lose power.
- Ⓒ Melanie cannot remember anything.
- Ⓓ The family falls asleep.

3. Why might the author use words such as *churned* and *lashed*?

- Ⓐ to get readers to use candles and flashlights
- Ⓑ to get readers to go out in the rain
- Ⓒ to show how afraid Melanie is
- Ⓓ to show how powerful the storm is

4. How do Melanie and her parents solve the problem of getting food without electricity?

- Ⓐ They decide not to eat dinner.
- Ⓑ They make peanut butter and jelly sandwiches.
- Ⓒ They go out to a restaurant.
- Ⓓ They go to a neighbor's house.

5. From which point of view is this text told?

- Ⓐ third person
- Ⓑ first person
- Ⓒ second person
- Ⓓ There is no point of view.

6. Which inference makes the most sense, based on the text?

- Ⓐ The wind blew the tree limbs down.
- Ⓑ Melanie is very, very afraid of storms.
- Ⓒ The family has no flashlights.
- Ⓓ The storm will go on for many days.

7. What can a reader learn from this text?

- Ⓐ Family is important.
- Ⓑ Eating sandwiches for dinner is fun.
- Ⓒ Preparation is critical for getting through a disaster.
- Ⓓ Storms are scary.

8. Why is the family able to get through the storm so easily?

- Ⓐ They are very well prepared, with food and extra sources of light.
- Ⓑ Peanut butter and jelly is their favorite meal.
- Ⓒ The power is out and they cannot use any electricity.
- Ⓓ They enjoy listening to the wind and rain.

SCORE

1. Ⓨ Ⓝ
2. Ⓨ Ⓝ
3. Ⓨ Ⓝ
4. Ⓨ Ⓝ
5. Ⓨ Ⓝ
6. Ⓨ Ⓝ
7. Ⓨ Ⓝ
8. Ⓨ Ⓝ

___ / 8
Total

NAME: ______________________ DATE: ______________

DIRECTIONS

Reread "Storm Front." Then, read the prompt and respond on the lines below.

SCORE

___ / 4

Tell about the worst storm you can remember. What was it like? Write about the storm.

NAME: ____________________ **DATE:** ____________

DIRECTIONS Read the text and then answer the questions.

How do you learn about what's going on in the world? Many people get their news by reading a daily newspaper. Newspapers generally have several sections. Each section focuses on one kind of story. The front section is for major national stories. World news is in the front section, too. There is often another section that gives local and regional news. Many newspapers have a section for sports news, too. Some have a section for business news. Newspapers also often have a section that lists movies and TV shows. Opinions are often given in a newspaper's editorial section. That's where the newspaper prints letters to the editor. And finally, newspapers usually have a classified section. That section lists ads for jobs, personal ads, and items to be bought or sold.

1. What is this text mostly about?

- (A) what is in newspapers
- (B) how to write a news story
- (C) where to buy a newspaper
- (D) the history of newspapers

2. Which will you probably **not** find in a newspaper?

- (A) major national stories
- (B) letters to the editor
- (C) directions to the nearest park
- (D) sports and business news

3. Which word is a synonym for *region*?

- (A) major
- (B) city
- (C) area
- (D) newspaper

4. Which section of a newspaper lists ads for jobs?

- (A) front
- (B) editorial
- (C) sports
- (D) classified

5. What is the tone of the text?

- (A) informative
- (B) silly
- (C) persuasive
- (D) serious

SCORE

1. (Y)(N)
2. (Y)(N)
3. (Y)(N)
4. (Y)(N)
5. (Y)(N)

___ / 5 Total

NAME: ______________________ **DATE:** ______________

DIRECTIONS Read the text and then answer the questions.

SCORE

1. Ⓨ Ⓝ
2. Ⓨ Ⓝ
3. Ⓨ Ⓝ
4. Ⓨ Ⓝ
5. Ⓨ Ⓝ

___ / 5 Total

Many people get their news by listening to the radio. There are some advantages to listening to the radio to get news. For one thing, news can be reported on the radio as it is happening. People don't have to wait until the newspaper is delivered to find out what is going on. For another, radio news is convenient. People can find out the news while they are *commuting*, or traveling to work. In fact, radio news is so popular that there are many all-news radio stations. Radio stations often report the news every hour. Some report it every half-hour. At rush hour, they also have traffic reports. Radio news stories often do not have a lot of detail. That is because radio stations tend to have short news breaks.

1. Which statement is **not** true about radio news?

Ⓐ Radio news stories often do not have a lot of detail.

Ⓑ Radio news is reported only in the morning.

Ⓒ At rush hour, many radio stations have traffic reports.

Ⓓ Many radio stations report news every hour or half-hour.

2. Which of these is **not** an advantage of getting news on the radio?

Ⓐ News can be reported as it is happening.

Ⓑ Radio news is convenient.

Ⓒ People can find out the news while they are commuting.

Ⓓ Radio news stories are long and detailed.

3. Which prefix could be added to *advantages* to make its antonym?

Ⓐ *acro–*

Ⓑ *multi–*

Ⓒ *bi–*

Ⓓ *dis–*

4. What part of speech is the word *news* in the first sentence?

Ⓐ noun

Ⓑ verb

Ⓒ adjective

Ⓓ conjunction

5. What does the phrase *traveling to work* also mean?

Ⓐ commuting

Ⓑ reporting

Ⓒ traveling

Ⓓ rush hour

NAME: ______________________________ **DATE:** ________________

DIRECTIONS Read the text and then answer the questions.

Since 1926, news has been reported on television. Until the late 1940s, though, most people did not have TVs, so most people listened to the radio for their news. As more people have gotten TVs, television news has become more and more important. Today, most people have TVs, and most TV stations have news programs. There are a few kinds of news programs. One of them is local news. Local news focuses on stories from the area served by the TV station. Reporters go to places where news is happening and report their stories. Local news programs have three sections: news, sports, and weather. Other kinds of news programs report world and national news. Those programs do not usually have sports and weather sections. Some news programs are called *news magazines.* Those programs report stories in greater depth. There are a few news-only stations that have both shorter news programs and news magazines.

1. How does the text compare local TV news and national TV news?

(A) National TV news is not on TV.

(B) National TV news does not usually have sports and weather.

(C) National TV news always covers stories in great depth.

(D) National TV news focuses on stories from the area served by the TV station.

2. Which vocabulary word is essential to the text and could be shown in boldface?

(A) sections

(B) stations

(C) important

(D) news

3. Which word is a synonym for *sections*?

(A) parts

(B) days

(C) pictures

(D) stories

4. Which part of speech is the word *news* in the phrase *news magazines*?

(A) an adjective

(B) a verb

(C) a pronoun

(D) a conjunction

5. Which phrase has the same meaning as *happening*?

(A) taking place

(B) reporting on

(C) listening to

(D) taking a break

SCORE

1. (Y)(N)

2. (Y)(N)

3. (Y)(N)

4. (Y)(N)

5. (Y)(N)

___ / 5

Total

NAME:______________________________ **DATE:**________________

EXTRA! EXTRA!

Today there are many ways in which people can follow news stories. Many people listen to the news on the radio while they are going to and from work. Other people read the newspaper to get their news. But more than ever before, people get their news from the Internet. In a survey of 2,259 adults, 61 percent said they get their news from the Internet.

There are a lot of different ways to get news on the Internet. Some people go to news websites where they read articles about different news events. Other people go to blogs and other websites where people write about news events and discuss them. Some people go to video websites where they watch videos of news stories. All of those ways can help you learn about what is happening in the news, but there are important things to keep in mind. First, it is important to be sure you are going to safe sites. Second, it is important to remember that some blogs and social media sites give their own points of view about events. Just because you read a story on a blog or on a social site doesn't mean the story is true. It's a good idea to check any story at a news site to be sure it is true. It's also a good idea to check out some news sites so you know what is happening.

Many, many people also get their news from TV. In fact, 78 percent of people in the survey said they get their news from TV. Both TV news programs and TV news magazines can tell you what is going on, too. Again, it's a good idea to find out what different TV programs say about a story so you know the whole story. You can even use the Internet and TV to follow a story. That is what 92 percent of people in the survey said they do. Today more than ever, there are a lot of ways to follow a news story.

NAME: ______________________ **DATE:** ______________

DIRECTIONS Read "Extra! Extra!" and then answer the questions.

1. Why should readers check stories on a news site?

- (A) There are not many news sites.
- (B) There are many news sites.
- (C) News sites have a lot of videos.
- (D) News sites help readers be sure a story is true.

2. If a reader forgets how many people get their news from the Internet, what could he or she do?

- (A) Look it up in a dictionary.
- (B) Read the last sentence.
- (C) Read the title.
- (D) Reread the first paragraph.

3. What is the author's purpose?

- (A) to instruct
- (B) to persuade
- (C) to inform
- (D) to entertain

4. How do people who drive a long distance to work likely get their news?

- (A) only from the Internet
- (B) on the radio while they are in their cars
- (C) only from newspapers
- (D) on billboards

5. What is a fact about blogs and social media sites?

- (A) They are not current.
- (B) They give their own points of view.
- (C) They only share lies.
- (D) They are hard to access.

6. Which is likely to be true about the author?

- (A) The author is bored by news.
- (B) The author reads news stories.
- (C) The author does not enjoy the Internet.
- (D) The author does not enjoy watching TV.

7. What does the text say about how to follow the news?

- (A) There are many ways to follow the news.
- (B) TV is the best way.
- (C) The Internet is not an effective way.
- (D) Radio is outdated.

8. Which summarizes how most people get their news?

- (A) from newspapers and TV
- (B) from the Internet and TV
- (C) from TV and the radio
- (D) from the radio and newspapers

SCORE

1. Ⓨ Ⓝ
2. Ⓨ Ⓝ
3. Ⓨ Ⓝ
4. Ⓨ Ⓝ
5. Ⓨ Ⓝ
6. Ⓨ Ⓝ
7. Ⓨ Ⓝ
8. Ⓨ Ⓝ

___ / 8
Total

NAME: ______________________________ **DATE:** __________________

DIRECTIONS Reread "Extra! Extra!" Then, read the prompt and respond on the lines below.

SCORE

___ / 4

What kind of news stories do you think are interesting? Write about how and where you get news.

NAME: ______________________ **DATE:** ______________

DIRECTIONS Read the text and then answer the questions.

Shawn had an uneasy feeling right from the beginning that this was going to be an annoying day. For one thing, he almost missed the school bus and had to race to get to the bus stop on time. Then, when Shawn arrived at school, things quickly went downhill. In English class, Mr. Matthews announced that everyone would be writing persuasive essays. Shawn hated writing any kind of essay—he could never figure out what to write, and he always ended up waiting until the last minute. Mr. Matthews announced that the class would have a week to do the assignment and that he would be available to answer questions after school. Shawn decided he was going to have to do something—maybe talk to Mr. Matthews—because he had no idea how to get started on his essay.

1. How does Shawn plan to solve his problem?

- (A) He will ask Mr. Matthews for help.
- (B) He will not write the essay.
- (C) He will ask a friend for help.
- (D) He will ask his parents for help.

2. How does Shawn feel about writing an essay?

- (A) excited
- (B) very unhappy
- (C) curious
- (D) proud

3. Which prefix would be added to make an antonym of *available*?

- (A) *uni–*
- (B) *sub–*
- (C) *un–*
- (D) *pre–*

4. What does the adjective *persuasive* tell a reader about an essay?

- (A) The essay tells how to do something.
- (B) The essay tells a personal story.
- (C) The essay gets people to do something or believe something.
- (D) The essay gives a list of facts as information.

5. What is the meaning of the phrase *things went downhill*?

- (A) got a lot better
- (B) slid down a hill
- (C) got worse
- (D) were easy to do

SCORE

1. Ⓨ Ⓝ
2. Ⓨ Ⓝ
3. Ⓨ Ⓝ
4. Ⓨ Ⓝ
5. Ⓨ Ⓝ

___ / 5
Total

NAME: ______________________________ **DATE:** ____________________

DIRECTIONS Read the text and then answer the questions.

SCORE

1. Ⓨ Ⓝ
2. Ⓨ Ⓝ
3. Ⓨ Ⓝ
4. Ⓨ Ⓝ
5. Ⓨ Ⓝ

___ / 5 Total

Mr. Matthews had assigned the class a persuasive essay, and Shawn had no idea how to begin. He really disliked writing essays, but he also didn't want to do poorly on the assignment. So one day, he remained after school to try to get some advice from Mr. Matthews. When he had caught Mr. Matthews's attention, Shawn explained his situation. "I never know how to get started with essays," he began. "I get nervous about it, so I just stare at the blank page until the assignment's due, and then I scribble whatever comes to my mind. I know that's a terrible way to write, but I don't know any other way."

Mr. Matthews replied, "You're not the only one in that situation, Shawn. Let me offer you a few pointers for getting started, and hopefully, they will help you organize your ideas."

1. What is the setting of this text?

Ⓐ a classroom
Ⓑ a cafeteria
Ⓒ a gymnasium
Ⓓ a principal's office

2. How does the author share a solution to Shawn's problem?

Ⓐ Shawn realizes his own solutions in a dream.
Ⓑ Mr. Matthews suggests solutions.
Ⓒ The author describes the solution for the reader.
Ⓓ The author does not include a solution.

3. Which word is an antonym of *remain*?

Ⓐ stay
Ⓑ leave
Ⓒ study
Ⓓ explain

4. What does the verb *scribble* indicate about Shawn?

Ⓐ He writes slowly and carefully.
Ⓑ He takes a lot of time to write.
Ⓒ He plans his work weeks in advance.
Ⓓ He writes quickly and without a plan.

5. What does the phrase *a few pointers* mean?

Ⓐ advice or tips
Ⓑ arrows
Ⓒ papers
Ⓓ words

NAME: ______________________ **DATE:** ______________

DIRECTIONS Read the text and then answer the questions.

Mr. Matthews was helping Shawn plan a persuasive essay he was assigned to write. "The first step," Mr. Matthews explained, "is to develop an opinion on something that's important to you." Shawn wanted very much to be on the school's football team. He had tried out for the team, but he hadn't been selected, so he decided to write a persuasive essay explaining why he should be allowed to be a part of the team even if he didn't play in every game. Mr. Matthews agreed that Shawn had a workable idea for a persuasive essay, and he asked Shawn to write it down. Then, Mr. Matthews asked Shawn to list all of the strongest reasons he could think of—reasons that would convince someone that Shawn was right for the team. When Shawn was finished, he had the ingredients for his essay.

1. What is Mr. Matthews helping Shawn to do?

- (A) study for a big test
- (B) manage his time better
- (C) write a persuasive essay
- (D) practice baseball

2. How does the author organize the plot of this text?

- (A) It is told in the order that Shawn should take to write his essay.
- (B) It is told in the order of what happened over a week.
- (C) It compares Shawn's experience with another student.
- (D) It is told as a persuasive tale.

3. Which word is a synonym for *persuade*?

- (A) explain
- (B) agree
- (C) essay
- (D) convince

4. Which verb has the same meaning as *allowed*?

- (A) called
- (B) permitted
- (C) told
- (D) forbidden

5. What is the tone of the text?

- (A) informative
- (B) silly
- (C) mysterious
- (D) encouraging

SCORE

1. Ⓨ Ⓝ
2. Ⓨ Ⓝ
3. Ⓨ Ⓝ
4. Ⓨ Ⓝ
5. Ⓨ Ⓝ

___ / 5 **Total**

NAME: ______________________ **DATE:** ______________

SHAWN DOES THE WRITE THING

Shawn and his class were working on a new assignment. They were writing persuasive essays. When Shawn first learned about the assignment, he was unhappy. Shawn disliked writing essays, and he wasn't sure how to go about planning and writing a powerful essay that would persuade someone to do something. So he asked Mr. Matthews for extra help planning his essay.

Mr. Matthews suggested that Shawn begin by selecting a topic that was important to him. Shawn wanted to be on the football team, so he decided to write a paper explaining why he should be on the team. Next, Mr. Matthews suggested that Shawn list the strongest and best reasons he could think of that would persuade people. When Shawn had listed his reasons, he was ready to start writing.

First, Shawn wrote a draft of the paper. He began with his main point—that he should be allowed to be on the football team. Then, he explained why he should be on the team, using the reasons he had listed. Then, he wrote the conclusion—the end of the paper. After Shawn had his draft finished, he was ready to revise what he had written.

Shawn read the paper aloud to himself and to his parents. His mom and dad suggested ways that he could revise the paper to make it more convincing. Then, Shawn read the paper again. This time, he thought of a few persuasive details himself. After the revisions were finished, it was time to edit.

To edit his paper, Shawn read it carefully to be certain that he had spelled everything the way it should be spelled. He also checked his paper for grammatical mistakes. Mr. Matthews had explained to the class that a paper is more persuasive if it is written carefully. By the time Shawn was finished editing his paper, it was written well enough that Mr. Matthews gave him a very good grade. The football coach read Shawn's paper, too, and was so convinced by Shawn's reasons that he permitted Shawn to work with the team!

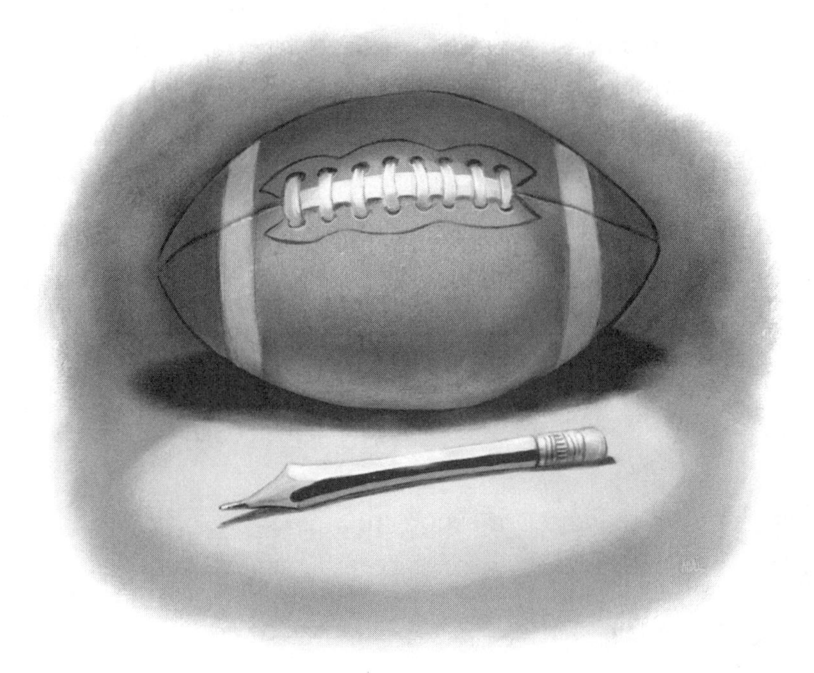

NAME: ____________________ DATE: ____________

DIRECTIONS Read "Shawn Does the Write Thing" and then answer the questions.

1. What is notable about the title?

Ⓐ It indicates that the story is about Shawn.

Ⓑ It uses a homophone to hint that the story is about writing.

Ⓒ It hints that the text is about being right.

Ⓓ The story teaches the difference between right and wrong.

2. Why does Shawn look for errors in his essay?

Ⓐ Essays are more persuasive if they are written well.

Ⓑ Shawn is very good at spelling and never makes mistakes.

Ⓒ Shawn's mom and dad do not like what Shawn has written.

Ⓓ Correct spelling and grammar are not important in essays.

3. Shawn asked Mr. Matthews to

Ⓐ help him get on the football team.

Ⓑ persuade his parents to let him play football.

Ⓒ do the right thing.

Ⓓ help him write a powerful essay.

4. What is the first thing Mr. Matthews suggests that Shawn do?

Ⓐ edit his essay

Ⓑ revise his essay

Ⓒ choose a topic that he likes

Ⓓ read his essay aloud

5. From which point of view is this text told?

Ⓐ third person

Ⓑ first person

Ⓒ second person

Ⓓ There is no point of view.

6. Which inference makes the most sense?

Ⓐ Mr. Matthews does not know who Shawn is.

Ⓑ Shawn likes football.

Ⓒ The football coach does not like Shawn's essay.

Ⓓ Shawn's parents will not help him.

7. What will likely happen the next time Shawn has to write an essay?

Ⓐ He will not write another essay.

Ⓑ It will be harder for him.

Ⓒ It will be easier for him.

Ⓓ He will not know what to do.

8. What lesson does this text share about writing essays?

Ⓐ You must always ask for a teacher's help.

Ⓑ You should never have your parents write an essay for you.

Ⓒ It is not rewarding.

Ⓓ It is a process that takes planning and hard work, but is also satisfying.

SCORE

1. Ⓨ Ⓝ
2. Ⓨ Ⓝ
3. Ⓨ Ⓝ
4. Ⓨ Ⓝ
5. Ⓨ Ⓝ
6. Ⓨ Ⓝ
7. Ⓨ Ⓝ
8. Ⓨ Ⓝ

___ / 8
Total

NAME: ______________________________ **DATE:** __________________

DIRECTIONS Reread "Shawn Does the Write Thing." Then, read the prompt and respond on the lines below.

SCORE

___ / 4

Do you think Shawn should be allowed to work with the football team even though he was not chosen? Why? Explain your answer.

NAME: ____________________ DATE: ____________

DIRECTIONS Read the text and then answer the questions.

Do you live near a river? People have made their homes and built towns and cities near rivers for thousands of years. A nearby river helps people in many ways. One way is that rivers offer a steady supply of water. Water is essential for life. People have used river water to cook, clean, drink, raise animals, and grow crops for a very long time. Another thing that makes rivers very appealing is that they provide a good source of food. Fish and other water animals have been a part of people's diets for thousands of years. Finally, rivers provide good transportation. They allow people to travel from one place to another, and they allow goods to be moved easily from one place to another. No wonder so many of the first cities were built near rivers.

1. Which statement is **not** a way that having a river nearby helps people?

- (A) It provides a steady supply of water.
- (B) It provides a supply of food.
- (C) It provides a means of transportation.
- (D) It provides a place for indoor activities.

2. Which title reflects the main idea of this text?

- (A) What Rivers Give Us
- (B) The History of Cities
- (C) The Biggest Rivers in the World
- (D) How to Sail on a River

3. Which word is a synonym for *essential*?

- (A) large
- (B) necessary
- (C) attractive
- (D) new

4. In this text, the word *drink* is which part of speech?

- (A) a verb
- (B) a noun
- (C) an adverb
- (D) an adjective

5. Which prefix could be added to make an antonym of *appealing*?

- (A) *maxi–*
- (B) *multi–*
- (C) *un–*
- (D) *sub–*

SCORE

1. (Y)(N)
2. (Y)(N)
3. (Y)(N)
4. (Y)(N)
5. (Y)(N)

___ / 5 **Total**

NAME: ______________________________ **DATE:** ____________________

DIRECTIONS Read the text and then answer the questions.

SCORE

1. Ⓨ Ⓝ

2. Ⓨ Ⓝ

3. Ⓨ Ⓝ

4. Ⓨ Ⓝ

5. Ⓨ Ⓝ

___ / 5 **Total**

What is the climate like where you live? Climate has a tremendous effect on the places where people live and on the kinds of homes and lives they have. A climate that is too cold makes it extremely hard to find and grow food. That means fewer people can live there, and those people who do live there don't get as much food. That's why most of the first cities weren't built in very cold climates. A climate that is too hot and dry doesn't allow people to grow food easily, either. That's one reason why the first cities weren't built in very hot climates. The first cities were built in places where the climate is warm and pleasant. That way, people could grow crops and have pastures for their animals.

1. Which statement is true about very cold climates?

- Ⓐ They do not have low temperatures.
- Ⓑ They make a good place for a city.
- Ⓒ They make it hard to find and grow food.
- Ⓓ They give people a place to grow crops.

2. Which vocabulary word is essential to this text?

- Ⓐ built
- Ⓑ climate
- Ⓒ cities
- Ⓓ pastures

3. Which word is a synonym for *tremendous*?

- Ⓐ enormous
- Ⓑ unimportant
- Ⓒ silly
- Ⓓ grateful

4. Which word is an antonym of *allow*?

- Ⓐ permit
- Ⓑ notice
- Ⓒ prevent
- Ⓓ labor

5. Which word or phrase has the same meaning as the word *pastures*?

- Ⓐ water
- Ⓑ barns
- Ⓒ cooking
- Ⓓ grazing land

NAME: ______________________ **DATE:** ______________

DIRECTIONS Read the text and then answer the questions.

Some places have many natural resources such as coal, iron, or trees. Other places do not. What happens to people who live in places without many natural resources? How can they get them? People who lived in early cities solved this problem. They developed a system of trade. People who lived in places with many natural resources traded those resources. They got goods such as clothes and tools. People who lived in places without natural resources made goods. They traded those goods for the things they needed. For example, they traded goods for iron and lumber. Trading allowed people to get what they needed. It also allowed different people to communicate. This meant that people could learn from one another. It also meant that people passed their language and culture along. This is called *cultural diffusion.*

1. Which action is **not** a result of trade?

- Ⓐ People did not settle into cities.
- Ⓑ People could learn from one another.
- Ⓒ People could get what they needed.
- Ⓓ People passed their language and culture along.

2. Which title best fits this text?

- Ⓐ Trading Resources
- Ⓑ Lumber and Iron
- Ⓒ Communication
- Ⓓ Cultural Roots

3. Which is **not** a natural resource?

- Ⓐ coal
- Ⓑ iron
- Ⓒ trees
- Ⓓ houses

4. What type of sentence is the following: *How can they get them?*

- Ⓐ an imperative sentence
- Ⓑ an exclamatory sentence
- Ⓒ an interrogatory sentence
- Ⓓ a declarative sentence

5. Which word or phrase means *the passing along of culture and language*?

- Ⓐ trading
- Ⓑ natural resources
- Ⓒ cultural diffusion
- Ⓓ a system

SCORE

1. Ⓨ Ⓝ
2. Ⓨ Ⓝ
3. Ⓨ Ⓝ
4. Ⓨ Ⓝ
5. Ⓨ Ⓝ

___ / 5 **Total**

NAME: ______________________________ **DATE:** ____________________

WHERE IT ALL BEGAN

Thousands of years ago, people did not live in cities. Instead, they moved around. They followed herds of animals and hunted. They gathered nuts, seeds, and other food as well. Then, people learned how to grow crops and herd animals. That meant that they could live in one place. The question was: Where would be a good place for people to settle? The first cities arose where they did for some very good reasons.

One reason that cities developed where they did is rivers. The city-state of Sumer (sue-MARE) was one early civilization. It developed in the Middle East. It was between the Tigris (TAHY-gris) and Euphrates (yoo-FREY-teez) rivers. The Indus (IN-duhs) Valley civilization was in India. It was located near the Indus River. The first Chinese civilizations developed near the Huang He, or Yellow River. The first cities in Egypt were built near the Nile River. Rivers were very important because they provided many things. They provided an easy source of water for drinking, cooking, and more. They also served as a good source of food. They also allowed people to travel more. Later, people used rivers for transportation.

The first cities were located in warm, pleasant climates. People needed warm climates so that they could grow crops and have pastures for their animals. All of the earliest cities were located in warm climates with plenty of rain.

Not all cities had everything people needed. So people developed a system of trade. They traded goods they made. They got natural resources from other places. They also learned from one another. They spread their own cultures and languages. That process is called *cultural diffusion*. Gradually, cities became larger, and more people lived in them. But it all started with a good source of water and a warm climate.

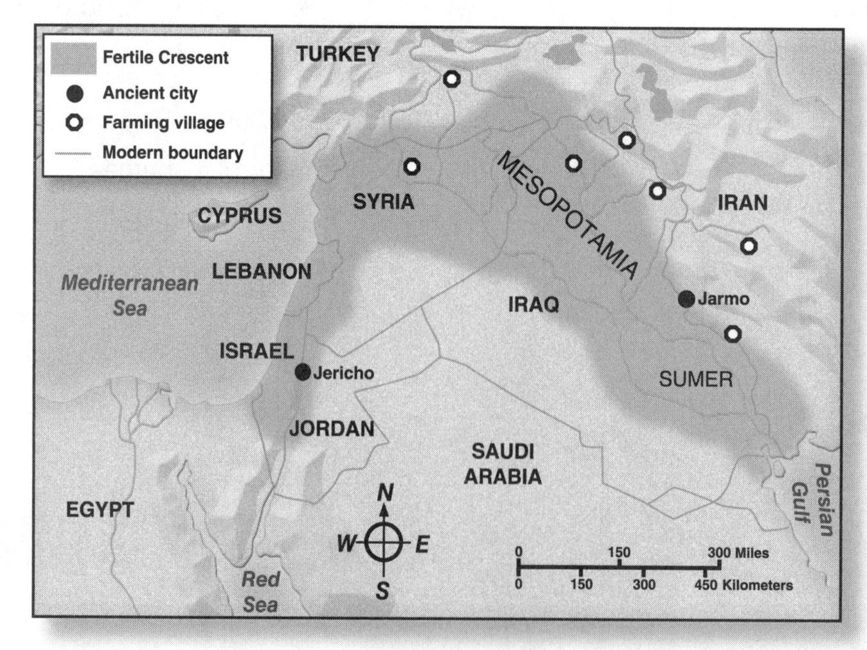

Ancient Sumer

NAME: ______________________ **DATE:** ______________

DIRECTIONS Read "Where It All Began" and then answer the questions.

1. What does the map tell you about Sumer?

Ⓐ It is in India.
Ⓑ It is in Egypt.
Ⓒ It is in Iraq.
Ⓓ It is in South America.

2. What could a reader do to understand how to pronounce the word *Euphrates*?

Ⓐ Check the pronunciation guide.
Ⓑ Read the title again.
Ⓒ Read the first sentence again.
Ⓓ Look at the map.

3. What happened after people settled in cities?

Ⓐ They gathered nuts, seeds, and other food.
Ⓑ They followed herds of animals.
Ⓒ They developed a system of trade.
Ⓓ They moved around a lot.

4. Which happened first?

Ⓐ People learned to grow crops.
Ⓑ People began to trade with people in other cities.
Ⓒ People built cities near rivers.
Ⓓ People followed herds of animals.

5. What is the author's purpose?

Ⓐ to persuade
Ⓑ to inform
Ⓒ to entertain
Ⓓ to instruct

6. Why do you think the earliest cities were **not** located in Alaska?

Ⓐ There are no rivers in Alaska.
Ⓑ There are too many rivers in Alaska.
Ⓒ The climate is too hot.
Ⓓ The climate is too cold.

7. Why did people long ago travel around?

Ⓐ They didn't know how to build cities.
Ⓑ They had to follow animals and gather food from different places to survive.
Ⓒ They had no materials to build homes with.
Ⓓ They did not want to live near other people.

8. What would happen if there was no trade?

Ⓐ There would not be cultural diffusion.
Ⓑ People would get the things they needed.
Ⓒ There would not be enough rivers.
Ⓓ People would travel much more.

SCORE

1. Ⓨ Ⓝ
2. Ⓨ Ⓝ
3. Ⓨ Ⓝ
4. Ⓨ Ⓝ
5. Ⓨ Ⓝ
6. Ⓨ Ⓝ
7. Ⓨ Ⓝ
8. Ⓨ Ⓝ

___ / 8
Total

NAME:______________________ DATE:______________

SCORE
___ / 4

DIRECTIONS

Reread "Where It All Began." Then, read the prompt and respond on the lines below.

Imagine you could start your own city. Where would you put it? Why? Explain your answer.

NAME: ______________________ **DATE:** ______________

DIRECTIONS Read the text and then answer the questions.

Stephanie's best friend, Lindsey, was having a birthday in a few weeks. The problem was that Stephanie had no idea what to get her. She didn't want to get Lindsey clothes or jewelry—everyone did that. Stephanie wanted her gift to be extra special. It didn't help matters that Stephanie didn't have a lot of money to spend. Whatever she got for Lindsey would have to be inexpensive. Stephanie thought about it for days but couldn't come up with any good ideas. Her mom usually had good ideas for presents. But even she couldn't think of an idea that Stephanie liked. As Lindsey's birthday got closer, Stephanie became more and more worried. What if she couldn't think of anything at all? She couldn't skip her best friend's birthday, but she didn't want to go to Lindsey's party without a good present.

1. What is the character's problem in this text?

Ⓐ Stephanie's birthday is coming soon, and she doesn't want presents.

Ⓑ Stephanie can't think of a good birthday present for her mom.

Ⓒ Stephanie can't think of a good birthday present for her best friend.

Ⓓ Stephanie's best friend Lindsey is angry with her.

2. Why doesn't Stephanie want to get Lindsey clothes or jewelry?

Ⓐ Lindsey doesn't like clothes or jewelry.

Ⓑ Her mom doesn't want Stephanie to buy those things.

Ⓒ Everyone says that clothes and jewelry are a bad idea.

Ⓓ Everyone does that, and Stephanie wants her gift to be extra special.

3. Which word is an antonym for *inexpensive*?

Ⓐ costly

Ⓑ cheap

Ⓒ comfortable

Ⓓ colorful

4. What is the correct meaning of the verb *skip* in this text?

Ⓐ hop

Ⓑ bounce

Ⓒ miss

Ⓓ discuss

5. What does the phrase *come up with* mean?

Ⓐ climb up

Ⓑ think of

Ⓒ stand

Ⓓ run around

SCORE

1. Ⓨ Ⓝ

2. Ⓨ Ⓝ

3. Ⓨ Ⓝ

4. Ⓨ Ⓝ

5. Ⓨ Ⓝ

___ / 5
Total

NAME: ______________________ **DATE:** ______________

DIRECTIONS Read the text and then answer the questions.

SCORE

1. Ⓨ Ⓝ
2. Ⓨ Ⓝ
3. Ⓨ Ⓝ
4. Ⓨ Ⓝ
5. Ⓨ Ⓝ

___ / 5
Total

Stephanie was worried because she couldn't think of a good birthday present for her best friend, Lindsey. And Lindsey's birthday was coming up soon. Stephanie would have to think of something fast. Finally, Stephanie decided that the best thing to do was just to ask Lindsey what she wanted. So one day, when Lindsey came over, Stephanie did just that. To Stephanie's shock, Lindsey said, "Forget about the whole birthday thing. Something terrible has happened! My parents just told me we're moving! I don't even want to think about my birthday! I don't even think I want presents." Both girls sat silently for a while. Stephanie couldn't believe this was happening! Her best friend was leaving her and there was nothing she could do about it. This was much worse than not having the perfect birthday present for Lindsey.

1. Why doesn't Lindsey want birthday presents?

Ⓐ She cannot think of anything to give Stephanie.
Ⓑ She already has everything she wants.
Ⓒ Her parents told her she cannot have presents.
Ⓓ Her family is moving, and she is upset about it.

2. How does Stephanie feel about Lindsey moving?

Ⓐ excited
Ⓑ unhappy
Ⓒ jealous
Ⓓ curious

3. What does the word *terrible* tell you about Lindsey?

Ⓐ She is very happy.
Ⓑ She is upset.
Ⓒ She is curious about something.
Ⓓ She is asleep.

4. What kind of sentence is the following: *My parents just told me we're moving!*

Ⓐ exclamatory
Ⓑ interrogative
Ⓒ imperative
Ⓓ declarative

5. What is the phrase *was worried* an example of?

Ⓐ a metaphor
Ⓑ a simile
Ⓒ alliteration
Ⓓ personification

NAME: ______________________ **DATE:** ______________

DIRECTIONS Read the text and then answer the questions.

Stephanie couldn't think of a good birthday gift for her best friend, Lindsey. She thought that was the worst of her troubles until Lindsey told her the bad news. Lindsey and her family were moving! Stephanie was terribly upset about it. Still, she wanted to give Lindsey a present. After a lot of thought, Stephanie finally hit on exactly the right present. She had a lot of good pictures of things she and Lindsey had done together. She also had plenty of pictures of places they'd been to and friends they shared. Stephanie decided she would make a photo album for Lindsey. First, she got Mom to take her to the store to buy just the right album. Then, she put all of the pictures together into the album. She labeled each picture and then added her own drawings. Finally, the photo album was done. Stephanie was really hoping Lindsey would like it.

1. Who is the main character in this text?

- (A) Lindsey
- (B) Mom
- (C) Stephanie
- (D) Dad

2. What will Stephanie give Lindsey for her birthday?

- (A) a photo album full of pictures
- (B) a label maker
- (C) new music
- (D) a drawing of a photo album

3. What does the phrase *hit on* mean?

- (A) smacked
- (B) played baseball
- (C) won
- (D) thought of

4. If the author didn't want to use the verb *labeled*, which verb has the same meaning?

- (A) drew
- (B) titled
- (C) colored
- (D) pasted

5. Which word indicates that you are about to read a set of steps in order?

- (A) pictures
- (B) album
- (C) first
- (D) drawings

SCORE

1. Ⓨ Ⓝ

2. Ⓨ Ⓝ

3. Ⓨ Ⓝ

4. Ⓨ Ⓝ

5. Ⓨ Ⓝ

___ / 5 Total

NAME:______________________________ **DATE:**__________________

THE BEST BIRTHDAY PRESENT EVER

Stephanie's best friend Lindsey was about to have a birthday. But neither girl felt like celebrating. Lindsey had just found out that she and her parents would be moving. The girls were heartbroken about it. But Stephanie still wanted to do something nice on Lindsey's birthday. So she'd made Lindsey a special photo album full of pictures. The pictures were of things the two girls had done together and friends they had made.

Lindsey's parents had said she could have a birthday party. But Lindsey didn't really want one. She just wanted Stephanie to come over for a while and keep her company. So on the day of Lindsey's birthday, Stephanie went over to her house with the photo album she'd made. When she got there, she gave Lindsey her present. Lindsey opened it reluctantly—she really wasn't in the mood for gifts. But then she saw the photo album and couldn't resist taking a peek inside. In no time at all, she and Stephanie were laughing at some of the pictures. They talked about the friends in other pictures and reminded each other of the good times they had had.

After a while, both girls began to feel just a little bit better. Then, Lindsey's father came into the living room where the girls were sitting. "I just talked to your parents," he told Stephanie. "I asked them if you could stay overnight, and they said that would be fine." Stephanie and Lindsey looked at each other and then both squealed. They hugged each other, and then they hugged Lindsey's father. Maybe Lindsey was going to be moving, but that didn't mean the girls couldn't enjoy the time they still had.

That night, Stephanie and Lindsey watched movies. They stuffed themselves with pizza and popcorn. They played video games, too. They stayed up very late and fell asleep in the living room with the TV still on. In the morning, Stephanie got ready to leave. Lindsey told her, "I'm so glad you came over, and I love this photo album! It's the best birthday present I have ever gotten!"

NAME: ______________________ **DATE:** ______________

DIRECTIONS Read "The Best Birthday Present Ever" and then answer the questions.

1. Why do you think Lindsey isn't in the mood for gifts?

- Ⓐ She's angry because nobody remembered her birthday.
- Ⓑ She already has too many gifts.
- Ⓒ It isn't her birthday.
- Ⓓ She is sad that her family is moving.

2. How do the two girls likely feel on the morning after the sleepover?

- Ⓐ rested
- Ⓑ angry
- Ⓒ exhausted
- Ⓓ startled

3. How does Lindsey likely feel about Stephanie coming to her house?

- Ⓐ grateful
- Ⓑ frightened
- Ⓒ jealous
- Ⓓ worried

4. Which prediction is most likely?

- Ⓐ Lindsey will not speak to Stephanie again.
- Ⓑ Stephanie will visit Lindsey in her new house.
- Ⓒ Stephanie will be upset with Lindsey.
- Ⓓ Lindsey will not keep the photo album.

5. What is one purpose for reading this text?

- Ⓐ to learn about how to give the perfect birthday present
- Ⓑ to enjoy a story of two good friends
- Ⓒ to find out about birthday parties
- Ⓓ to learn how to wrap a present

6. Which inference can be made based on the text?

- Ⓐ Lindsey does not like the photo album that Stephanie gives her.
- Ⓑ Lindsey's father does not want Stephanie to stay overnight.
- Ⓒ The two girls have never met before.
- Ⓓ The two girls are surprised when Lindsey's father invites Stephanie to stay overnight.

7. How do you think Stephanie feels about giving Lindsey a photo album?

- Ⓐ pleased
- Ⓑ ashamed
- Ⓒ jealous
- Ⓓ not sure

8. Why is the gift so special to Lindsey?

- Ⓐ She told Stephanie that was what she wanted for her birthday.
- Ⓑ It was expensive.
- Ⓒ It will remind her of her best friend, Stephanie, after she moves.
- Ⓓ Lindsey enjoys photography.

SCORE

1. Ⓨ Ⓝ
2. Ⓨ Ⓝ
3. Ⓨ Ⓝ
4. Ⓨ Ⓝ
5. Ⓨ Ⓝ
6. Ⓨ Ⓝ
7. Ⓨ Ⓝ
8. Ⓨ Ⓝ

___ / 8
Total

NAME: ______________________ DATE: ______________

SCORE

___ / 4

DIRECTIONS

Reread "The Best Birthday Present Ever." Then, read the prompt and respond on the lines below.

Have you ever had a good friend move away? Have you ever moved away from a good friend? Write about what happened and what it was like, or what it might be like to move.

NAME: ______________________ **DATE:** ______________

DIRECTIONS Read the text and then answer the questions.

What's the first thing you should do if there is an emergency? Your best choice is almost always to call 911. When you call 911, your call will be answered by a dispatcher, who will find out what your emergency is and send help. The dispatcher will ask you questions to help decide whether you need a police officer, an ambulance, a fire truck, or other help. The dispatcher may also give you some instructions. After that, the dispatcher will send help. What should you do when you call 911? Take a deep breath before you call. That way, you will be able to tell the dispatcher what the emergency is. Give the dispatcher as many details as you can. That way, the dispatcher will know what kind of help to send. Follow the dispatcher's instructions carefully. Then, wait for help to arrive.

1. What is this text mostly about?

- (A) how to become a police officer
- (B) what ambulances do
- (C) calling 911
- (D) dispatchers

2. Which action is **not** something that happens during a 911 call?

- (A) A dispatcher asks questions.
- (B) The dispatcher goes to the scene of the emergency.
- (C) The dispatcher gives instructions.
- (D) The dispatcher decides what kind of help to send.

3. Which word is a synonym for *instructions*?

- (A) directions
- (B) information
- (C) dispatchers
- (D) emergencies

4. Which is an interrogative sentence?

- (A) Follow the dispatcher's instructions carefully.
- (B) The dispatcher may also give you some instructions.
- (C) Then, wait for help to arrive.
- (D) What should you do when you call 911?

5. Who are the people who answer emergency calls and send help?

- (A) instructions
- (B) police officers
- (C) emergencies
- (D) dispatchers

SCORE

1. Ⓨ Ⓝ

2. Ⓨ Ⓝ

3. Ⓨ Ⓝ

4. Ⓨ Ⓝ

5. Ⓨ Ⓝ

___ / 5

Total

NAME: ______________________ **DATE:** ______________

DIRECTIONS Read the text and then answer the questions.

SCORE

1. Ⓨ Ⓝ
2. Ⓨ Ⓝ
3. Ⓨ Ⓝ
4. Ⓨ Ⓝ
5. Ⓨ Ⓝ

___ / 5 Total

Would you be prepared to help if your best friend were choking on something? You would if you've learned the Heimlich maneuver (HYM-lick muh-NOO-ver). The Heimlich maneuver is a special procedure that helps people who are choking to *expel*, or push out, the object that is caught in their throats. Follow these steps to perform the Heimlich maneuver:

1. Stand behind the choking person and wrap your arms around his or her waist.
2. Make a fist and place the thumb side of your fist against the person's upper abdomen, below the rib cage and above the navel (belly button).
3. Grasp your fist with your other hand and press into the person's upper abdomen with a quick upward thrust. Do not squeeze the person's rib cage; confine the force of the thrust to your hands.
4. Keep thrusting with your fist until the choking person expels the object.

1. What does this text explain?

Ⓐ how to perform the Heimlich maneuver
Ⓑ how to eat carefully so you won't choke
Ⓒ why people sometimes choke
Ⓓ the history of the Heimlich maneuver

2. How does the text feature below help a reader?
(*HYM-lick muh-NOO-ver*)

Ⓐ It tells readers a word's part of speech.
Ⓑ It tells readers how to spell a word.
Ⓒ It tells readers how to pronounce a word.
Ⓓ It tells readers how to write a word.

3. Which word means *to push something out*?

Ⓐ fist
Ⓑ expel
Ⓒ choke
Ⓓ wrap

4. What does the verb *thrust* refer to?

Ⓐ part of the body
Ⓑ type of food
Ⓒ kind of push
Ⓓ safety tip

5. Which term from the text means *a way of doing things*?

Ⓐ rib cage
Ⓑ procedure
Ⓒ expel
Ⓓ choke

NAME: ______________________ **DATE:** ______________

DIRECTIONS Read the text and then answer the questions.

How can you help if someone gets seriously cut? If it is a very serious cut, call 911 or call for other help immediately. While you're waiting, you can help stop the bleeding. Deep and serious cuts can lead to a lot of blood loss, and that's dangerous, so it's extremely important to stop the bleeding. Start by covering the wound with cloth. The best kind of cloth is *gauze*. Many large bandages are made of gauze. But if there's no gauze available, a towel is almost as effective. If you're outside or someplace without towels, even a shirt will work. After you've covered up the wound, put pressure directly on the covering. Pressure causes the blood to clot and the wound to close up so that it can heal. Don't take the cloth off the wound; otherwise, you'll open up the wound and the blood cannot clot as well. Keep pressure on the wound until medical help arrives.

1. What is the first step to stop bleeding?

- (A) Put pressure on the wound.
- (B) Cover the wound with cloth.
- (C) Do not take the cloth off the wound.
- (D) Keep pressure on the wound until help arrives.

2. Why is it important to follow steps to stop bleeding?

- (A) Put pressure on the wound.
- (B) Pressure causes the blood to clot and the wound to close.
- (C) Serious cuts can lead to blood loss, which is dangerous.
- (D) Don't take the cloth off the wound.

3. Which word is a synonym for *otherwise*?

- (A) or else
- (B) also
- (C) immediately
- (D) necessary

4. Which noun describes a special kind of cloth used in many large bandages?

- (A) clot
- (B) pressure
- (C) towel
- (D) gauze

5. What is the tone of the text?

- (A) informative
- (B) silly
- (C) persuasive
- (D) mysterious

SCORE

1. Ⓨ Ⓝ

2. Ⓨ Ⓝ

3. Ⓨ Ⓝ

4. Ⓨ Ⓝ

5. Ⓨ Ⓝ

___ / 5

Total

NAME: ______________________ **DATE:** ______________

EMERGENCY!

Nobody likes to think about being in an emergency, but they happen. If you know what to do when there is an emergency, you can save lives. In most emergencies, the best thing you can do is call 911. The 911 emergency system is set up to get people the help they need immediately. When you call 911, the dispatcher finds out what kind of help you need. Then the dispatcher gives you instructions for what to do while you wait for help. Next, the dispatcher sends help to you. It is very important to remember that 911 is only for emergencies. So don't call 911 unless you really need to; otherwise, people with emergencies might not be able to get through. If you do have a real emergency, the 911 system is there to help.

There are some other things you can learn to do that can save lives. One of them is the Heimlich maneuver. The Heimlich maneuver is used to help people who are choking expel the object that is making them choke. Learning how to do the Heimlich maneuver is not difficult, and it could save a life. So practice it and be able to use it in case you ever need to do so.

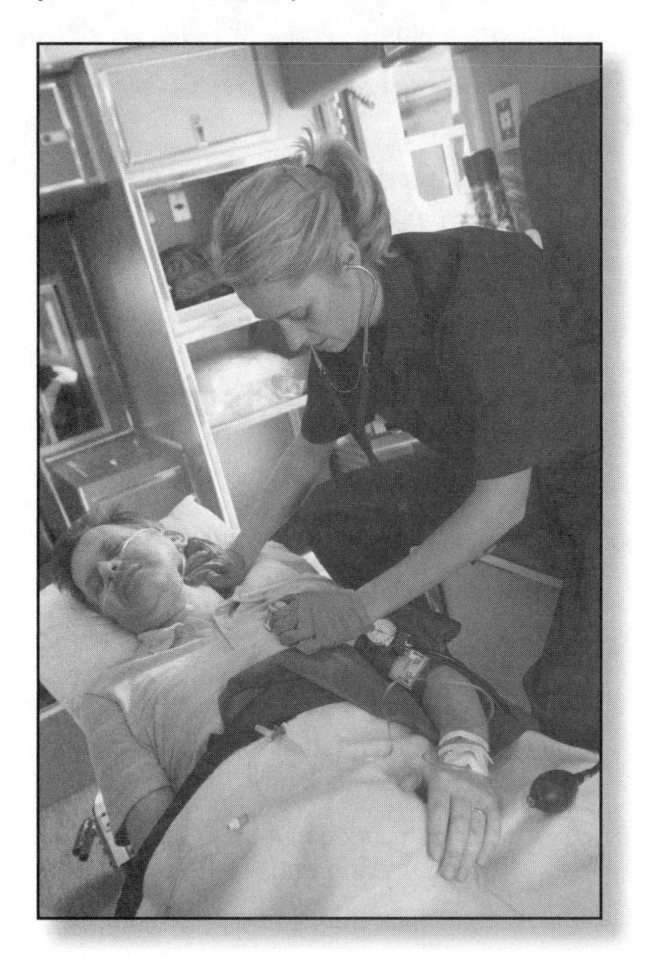

Another thing that you can learn to do in an emergency is to stop bleeding. Losing a lot of blood is very dangerous. So if someone is badly cut, the most important thing to do right away is to stop the bleeding. Applying direct pressure to a wound is the best way to do that. It's best to cover the wound first with gauze, but if you don't have gauze, a towel or even a shirt will work. Covering a wound and putting direct pressure on it will help stop bleeding and could save a life.

NAME: ______________________ **DATE:** ______________

DIRECTIONS Read "Emergency!" and then answer the questions.

1. Which sentence supports the idea that you can learn to stop bleeding?

(A) When you call 911, the dispatcher finds out what kind of help you need.
(B) One of them is the Heimlich Maneuver.
(C) Applying direct pressure to a wound is the best way to do that.
(D) If you do have a real emergency, the 911 system is there to help.

2. What could happen if too many people call 911 when there is **not** an emergency?

(A) There would be no emergencies.
(B) There would be fewer emergencies.
(C) People would call 911.
(D) People with real emergencies might not get help.

3. The author wants readers to

(A) have an emergency.
(B) know what to do in an emergency.
(C) call 911 when it is not necessary.
(D) lose a lot of blood.

4. A 911 dispatcher must be

(A) mean and judgmental.
(B) calm and helpful.
(C) able to drive an ambulance.
(D) a nurse.

5. Why might the author mention the Heimlich maneuver?

(A) It is very expensive and does not always work.
(B) It is not hard to learn and it can save lives.
(C) Only adults can learn it.
(D) It is too dangerous for people to use.

6. How might a person feel after helping someone in an emergency?

(A) hungry
(B) angry
(C) tired
(D) proud

7. Which question is answered in this text?

(A) What happens when you call 911?
(B) Why do emergencies happen?
(C) How many people choke every year?
(D) What happens when people go to the hospital?

8. Which summarizes what this text explains?

(A) where to buy gauze
(B) how to be a dispatcher
(C) what to do in an emergency
(D) the way to the nearest hospital

SCORE

1. Ⓨ Ⓝ
2. Ⓨ Ⓝ
3. Ⓨ Ⓝ
4. Ⓨ Ⓝ
5. Ⓨ Ⓝ
6. Ⓨ Ⓝ
7. Ⓨ Ⓝ
8. Ⓨ Ⓝ

___ / 8
Total

NAME: ______________________________ **DATE:** __________________

DIRECTIONS Reread "Emergency!" Then, read the prompt and respond on the lines below.

SCORE

___ / 4

Have you ever been in an emergency? If so, write about what happened and what you did. If not, write about how you would respond to an emergency.

NAME: ____________________ **DATE:** ______________

DIRECTIONS Read the text and then answer the questions.

Paul usually took the bus to and from school, but today, his mom picked him up. He had an appointment at the dentist, and they needed to be there on time. When they arrived at the dentist's office, Paul signed in, and he and his mom took seats in the waiting room. Soon, Paul's name was called, and he followed the dental hygienist (hahy-JEN-ist) back to an exam room. The dental hygienist cleaned Paul's teeth and took X-rays of them. A few minutes later, the dentist examined Paul's teeth, too, and looked at the X-rays. The dentist told Paul that he didn't have any cavities, and that was good news. But the dentist had other news: Paul was going to need braces.

1. What is the setting of the text?

- (A) the supermarket
- (B) Paul's home
- (C) school
- (D) the dentist's office

2. What news does the dentist give to Paul?

- (A) Paul has a cavity.
- (B) Paul will need braces.
- (C) Paul will not need braces.
- (D) Paul's teeth are not clean.

3. What is a *dental hygienist*?

- (A) a person who cleans teeth
- (B) a person who fixes cavities
- (C) a person who does not work with teeth
- (D) a person who does not take X-rays

4. Which word is an antonym of *arrived*?

- (A) visited
- (B) came
- (C) departed
- (D) noticed

5. What does the suffix *–ist* in *hygienist* mean?

- (A) clean
- (B) a person who does something
- (C) a dentist
- (D) greater than

SCORE

1. Ⓨ Ⓝ

2. Ⓨ Ⓝ

3. Ⓨ Ⓝ

4. Ⓨ Ⓝ

5. Ⓨ Ⓝ

___ / 5
Total

NAME: ______________________________ **DATE:** ____________________

DIRECTIONS Read the text and then answer the questions.

SCORE

1. Ⓨ Ⓝ

2. Ⓨ Ⓝ

3. Ⓨ Ⓝ

4. Ⓨ Ⓝ

5. Ⓨ Ⓝ

___ / 5 Total

Paul's dentist told him that he was going to need braces and recommended that Paul see an orthodontist. The orthodontist would work with Paul to straighten his teeth. Paul's mother made an appointment at the orthodontist's office. The first step was to find out exactly what kind of work Paul's teeth would need, so the orthodontist took special X-rays of Paul's teeth and gums. Then, she, Paul, and Paul's mom sat down to discuss what needed to be done. She explained that Paul's teeth were slightly crowded and that braces would help move and separate them. She also said that Paul had a slight overbite. That meant that his upper teeth overlapped his lower teeth a little. Both problems could easily be corrected with braces, so Paul and his mom decided to get started.

1. How does Paul find out that he needs braces?

Ⓐ His friend told him he needs braces.
Ⓑ His mom told him he needs braces.
Ⓒ His dad told him he needs braces.
Ⓓ His dentist told him he needs braces.

2. What does the orthodontist explain about Paul's teeth?

Ⓐ Paul's teeth are slightly crowded, and he has a slight overbite.
Ⓑ Paul's teeth are too small for his mouth.
Ⓒ Paul is missing several teeth.
Ⓓ Paul does not need braces after all.

3. What is an *orthodontist*?

Ⓐ a special kind of dentist who studies the heart and lungs
Ⓑ a special kind of dentist who creates overbites
Ⓒ a special kind of dentist who straightens teeth
Ⓓ a special kind of dentist who makes toothbrushes and toothpaste

4. Which part of speech is *work* in the phrase *kind of work*?

Ⓐ noun
Ⓑ verb
Ⓒ adjective
Ⓓ all of the above

5. Which word or phrase has the same meaning as the word *discuss*?

Ⓐ talk about
Ⓑ ignore
Ⓒ work on
Ⓓ purchase

NAME: ______________________ **DATE:** ______________

DIRECTIONS Read the text and then answer the questions.

Paul needed braces for his teeth, so he and his mother went to the orthodontist to get started. The orthodontist told them what to expect. She explained that everyone is different, so not everyone wears braces for the same amount of time. But she gave Paul and his mom a good idea of what would probably happen. After Paul got his braces, he would probably wear them for two years. Every couple of months, he would go to the orthodontist for a checkup. He would also get his braces adjusted. After about two years, Paul would get his braces removed. He would then get a retainer to help keep his teeth straightened. At first, Paul would need the retainer all the time, but gradually, he would wear it less often. After about another six months, he probably wouldn't need the retainer.

1. Which statement is **not** true?

- (A) Paul will wear his braces for about two years.
- (B) Paul will wear a retainer after his braces are removed.
- (C) Everyone wears braces for the same amount of time.
- (D) Paul will go to the orthodontist to get his braces adjusted.

2. Why will Paul need to go to the orthodontist every couple of months?

- (A) to get his hearing and vision checked
- (B) for checkups and to get his braces adjusted
- (C) to get his braces removed every few months
- (D) so his mom can get her braces checked

3. Which word is defined as *a device that helps keep teeth straightened*?

- (A) X-ray
- (B) dentist
- (C) checkup
- (D) retainer

4. What does the adverb *gradually* tell you about Paul's use of a retainer?

- (A) He would stop wearing his retainer little by little.
- (B) He would not wear a retainer at all.
- (C) He would suddenly stop wearing his retainer.
- (D) He would get his braces removed.

5. Which prefix can be added to *adjusted* to make a word meaning *badly adjusted*?

- (A) *hemo–*
- (B) *super–*
- (C) *pro–*
- (D) *mal–*

SCORE

1. Ⓨ Ⓝ

2. Ⓨ Ⓝ

3. Ⓨ Ⓝ

4. Ⓨ Ⓝ

5. Ⓨ Ⓝ

___ / 5
Total

NAME: ______________________ **DATE:** ______________

SMILE!

Paul was going to get braces on his teeth. He and his mother had talked to the orthodontist about what was going to happen, so he was prepared, but he was still a little nervous. Before Paul could have his braces put on, the orthodontist had to know the size and shape of his mouth and teeth so the braces would be the right size. So one day, Paul went to the orthodontist's office to get molds made of his teeth.

When he arrived for his appointment, Paul sat down in the orthodontist's chair. First, one of the technicians gave him a strip of wax to bite. That would show the size of his mouth. Then, the technician prepared two trays of what looked like clay. He explained that those trays were filled with a special kind of paste. He placed them in Paul's mouth and asked him to bite down. The paste didn't taste bad, but it did feel weird in Paul's mouth, and it felt strange to have to keep his tongue out of the way. The technician left the trays in Paul's mouth for a few minutes and then carefully removed them. He explained that the paste would harden into the same shape as Paul's mouth and teeth. When the molds were finished, the technician handed Paul a paper cup of water and showed him where to rinse out his mouth. Finally, another technician took photographs of Paul's teeth, mouth, and jaws. Then, the appointment was over. Paul was relieved to realize that it hadn't hurt at all.

Two weeks later, Paul's mother got a call to tell her that Paul's braces were ready. So they went to the orthodontist's office again to have the braces put on. Paul was surprised that it didn't hurt to have the braces put on. After the orthodontist was finished, though, Paul's teeth started to hurt. The orthodontist explained that Paul would be uncomfortable for a few days, but his teeth wouldn't hurt for long. And she was right! Within a few days, Paul was getting used to the braces, and before long, he often forgot he had them.

NAME: ____________________ **DATE:** ______________

DIRECTIONS Read "Smile!" and then answer the questions.

1. Which statement is supported by the illustration?

- (A) The story is about going to school.
- (B) The story is about taking pictures.
- (C) The story is about getting braces.
- (D) The story is about feeling scared.

2. Using context clues, what does *technician* mean?

- (A) a person who likes technology
- (B) a person who makes dental tools
- (C) a medical doctor
- (D) a child's dentist

3. Why do you think Paul is a little nervous before getting his braces?

- (A) He does not know what braces are.
- (B) He is afraid it will hurt to get braces.
- (C) His mom does not know Paul needs braces.
- (D) The orthodontist did not tell Paul what is going to happen.

4. Why does Paul need to rinse his mouth out?

- (A) He had paste in his mouth.
- (B) He is very thirsty.
- (C) He just ate something that tasted terrible.
- (D) He has just brushed his teeth.

5. This text is told in

- (A) third-person point of view.
- (B) first-person point of view.
- (C) second-person point of view.
- (D) There is no point of view.

6. What is a reasonable prediction?

- (A) Paul will visit the orthodontist for checkups.
- (B) Paul will not go to the orthodontist again.
- (C) Paul will have his braces removed tomorrow.
- (D) Paul will get braces again.

7. Why does the orthodontist need to know the size and shape of Paul's mouth and teeth?

- (A) to know how tall Paul has grown
- (B) so Paul will have his braces for a longer time
- (C) so Paul's braces will fit properly
- (D) so Paul's braces will be the right color

8. What might have happened if the orthodontist had **not** prepared Paul for getting braces?

- (A) Paul would know exactly what would happen.
- (B) Paul might be even more nervous about getting braces.
- (C) Paul would not need to get braces.
- (D) Paul's mom might need to get braces.

SCORE

1. Ⓨ Ⓝ
2. Ⓨ Ⓝ
3. Ⓨ Ⓝ
4. Ⓨ Ⓝ
5. Ⓨ Ⓝ
6. Ⓨ Ⓝ
7. Ⓨ Ⓝ
8. Ⓨ Ⓝ

___ / 8
Total

NAME: ______________________ DATE: ______________

SCORE

___ / 4

DIRECTIONS

Reread "Smile!" Then, read the prompt and respond on the lines below.

Do you have braces? What was it like to get them? If you do not have braces, does someone you know have braces? What do you think it would be like? Write about what it was like or what it would be like.

NAME: ______________________ **DATE:** ______________

DIRECTIONS Read the text and then answer the questions.

Track and field events are an important part of the Olympic Games. When many people think of the Olympics, they think about track and field events first. Track and field events involve running, jumping, and throwing and are usually held at a stadium with an oval running track. There are three kinds of running events: sprints, middle-distance races, and long-distance races. Sprints are short races. Runners win them by going as fast as possible. Sprinting events are very old; they have been around for thousands of years. Middle- and long-distance races require more stamina (STAM-min-uh), or endurance. In those races, it is more important to keep going for a long time than to go fast. Some running events are relay races. Those races are for teams of runners.

1. Which is **not** a kind of track and field event?

- Ⓐ running
- Ⓑ jumping
- Ⓒ throwing
- Ⓓ swimming

2. What do middle-distance and long-distance races require?

- Ⓐ speed
- Ⓑ stamina
- Ⓒ practice
- Ⓓ a team of runners

3. Which word is a synonym for *endurance*?

- Ⓐ stamina
- Ⓑ sprint
- Ⓒ relay
- Ⓓ oval

4. What type of race does a team of runners compete in?

- Ⓐ sprint
- Ⓑ stamina
- Ⓒ relay
- Ⓓ middle-distance

5. What is the tone of the text?

- Ⓐ informative
- Ⓑ silly
- Ⓒ persuasive
- Ⓓ serious

SCORE

1. Ⓨ Ⓝ
2. Ⓨ Ⓝ
3. Ⓨ Ⓝ
4. Ⓨ Ⓝ
5. Ⓨ Ⓝ

___ / 5
Total

NAME: ______________________ **DATE:** ______________

DIRECTIONS Read the text and then answer the questions.

SCORE

1. Ⓨ Ⓝ
2. Ⓨ Ⓝ
3. Ⓨ Ⓝ
4. Ⓨ Ⓝ
5. Ⓨ Ⓝ

___ / 5
Total

Running events are not the only track and field events. There are also several jumping events. In those events, the goal is to jump as high or as far as possible. For example, in the long jump, athletes run for a short distance to a jumping board and a sandpit. They use the jumping board to try to jump as far as they can. In the high jump, the idea is to get as much height as possible when the athlete jumps. In that event, athletes run for a short distance, and then they take off from one foot and jump over a raised bar. In the pole vault, athletes run along a runway holding a long pole. When they get to the end of the runway, they plant one end of the pole in a metal box and use the pole to jump over a very high bar.

1. What is true for both the high jump and the pole vault?

Ⓐ Athletes jump over a metal bar.
Ⓑ Athletes jump into a sandpit.
Ⓒ Athletes jump into water.
Ⓓ Athletes jump onto a horse.

2. Which is true of all three jumping events?

Ⓐ Athletes start by throwing something.
Ⓑ Athletes start by carrying a pole.
Ⓒ Athletes start by diving.
Ⓓ Athletes start by running for a short distance.

3. What does the word *plant* mean in this text?

Ⓐ to put a seed in the ground
Ⓑ a factory
Ⓒ to place firmly
Ⓓ to colonize

4. In which sentence below is the word *foot* used as a noun?

Ⓐ My mom does not want to foot the bill for dinner.
Ⓑ The child walked a foot or two before crying.
Ⓒ My favorite sport is football.
Ⓓ What time does the foot race start?

5. What does the phrase *take off* mean in this text?

Ⓐ remove
Ⓑ leave the ground
Ⓒ cut off
Ⓓ copy

NAME: ______________________________ **DATE:** ________________

DIRECTIONS Read the text and then answer the questions.

Some track and field events involve throwing things. For all of those events, the goal is to see how far the athlete can throw an object. One of the throwing events is called the shot put. Shot putters try to "put," or throw, the "shot," a 16-pound ball, as far as possible. In the javelin (JAV-lin) throw, athletes try to throw a javelin, which is a little like a spear, as far as possible. The discus throw is one of the oldest track and field events. It was one of the original Olympic events in the games held in ancient Greece. Discus throwers compete with a 4.4-pound disc, and each athlete tries to hurl the discus as far as possible. The final throwing event is the hammer throw. In this event, athletes compete using a heavy metal ball that is attached to a wire and a handle.

1. What is this text mostly about?

- (A) throwing the javelin
- (B) ancient Greece
- (C) track and field throwing events
- (D) hammers and other tools

2. How are javelin throwers and shot putters alike?

- (A) Neither are athletes.
- (B) Both throw something that looks like a spear.
- (C) Both throw a 16-pound ball.
- (D) Both try to throw something as far as possible.

3. Which word is a synonym for *throw*?

- (A) hurl
- (B) discus
- (C) compete
- (D) javelin

4. Which noun is similar in meaning to a spear?

- (A) discus
- (B) hammer
- (C) shot
- (D) javelin

5. What type of sentence is the following: *Discus throwers compete with a 4.4-pound disc, and each athlete tries to hurl the discus as far as possible.*

- (A) a simple sentence
- (B) a compound sentence
- (C) a complex sentence
- (D) an interrogatory sentence

SCORE

1. Ⓨ Ⓝ
2. Ⓨ Ⓝ
3. Ⓨ Ⓝ
4. Ⓨ Ⓝ
5. Ⓨ Ⓝ

___ / 5 **Total**

NAME:______________________________ **DATE:**__________________

ON YOUR MARK, GET SET, GO! THE STORY OF WILMA RUDOLPH

Many athletes start playing sports when they are little children. But nobody would have expected Wilma Rudolph to be an athlete. Wilma was born in 1940 near Clarksville, Tennessee. At the time she was born, there was only one doctor in town who would treat African Americans. Besides, the Rudolph family was very poor. So Wilma's mother had to help her daughter through many illnesses. Then, Wilma developed polio and lost the use of her leg. Today, there is a vaccine for polio, but there wasn't one then. So the doctor told Wilma's family that she would probably never walk. But everyone in the family worked very hard to help get Wilma on her feet. Wilma worked very hard, too. Eventually, she was able to walk and then, run.

Wilma liked sports, so when she was ready for high school, she decided to play basketball. Two years later, she was noticed. The head coach of the women's track team at Tennessee State University saw her play. She was such a good athlete that he wanted her to be on his track team. Wilma became a track and field star in college. Then, she headed for the Olympic Games. She won a bronze medal in the 1956 Olympic Games. Then, she won three gold medals in the 1960 Olympic Games.

After her Olympic career was over, Wilma did many other things. She coached at her old high school and at other schools, and worked on sports programs on television. She also worked for a group that helped poor children from the inner city to learn track and field skills. All of these things were done by a woman people said would never be able to walk! Wilma died in 1994, but she is still remembered as one of the fastest women in the world and as a reminder of what hard work can accomplish.

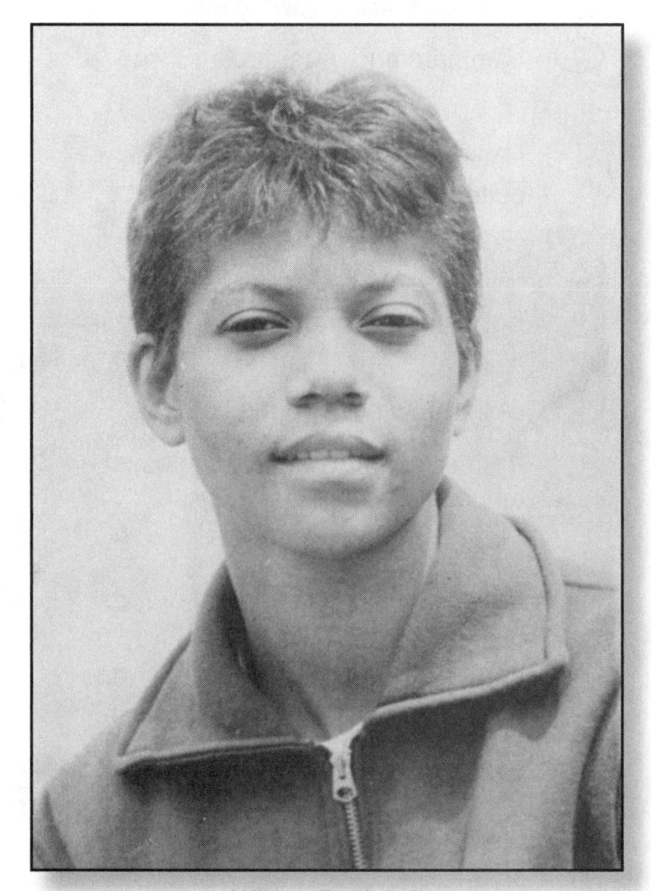

Wilma Rudolph

NAME: ______________________________ **DATE:** ________________

DIRECTIONS Read "On Your Mark, Get Set, Go! The Story of Wilma Rudolph" and then answer the questions.

1. What did Wilma do before she went to college?

- (A) worked on sports programs on television
- (B) taught at her old high school
- (C) went to the Olympics
- (D) played basketball in high school

2. What do you think might happen if Wilma were born today?

- (A) She would not have polio.
- (B) She would not be an athlete.
- (C) She would never be able to walk.
- (D) She would not go to high school.

3. How did Wilma's family likely feel when she won her Olympic medals?

- (A) excited and proud
- (B) frightened and anxious
- (C) angry and jealous
- (D) confused

4. Why would nobody have expected Wilma to be an athlete?

- (A) Her parents did not think playing sports was a good idea.
- (B) She was afraid to be active.
- (C) She hated sports.
- (D) She had polio and could not walk.

5. What is a reason for reading this text?

- (A) to read about the history of Tennessee
- (B) to try track and field events
- (C) to understand Wilma Rudolph's life
- (D) to learn how to run faster

6. Which is an accurate opinion of Wilma?

- (A) She is funny.
- (B) She is athletic.
- (C) She is artistic.
- (D) She is musical.

7. Which word from the text gives a good summary of Wilma's life?

- (A) Olympics
- (B) woman
- (C) accomplishment
- (D) polio

8. What is remarkable about Wilma's Olympic career?

- (A) Women usually did not compete in the Olympics at that time.
- (B) She did not enjoy sports.
- (C) She was born in 1940.
- (D) She had polio when she was young, and doctors said she probably would never walk.

SCORE

1. Ⓨ Ⓝ
2. Ⓨ Ⓝ
3. Ⓨ Ⓝ
4. Ⓨ Ⓝ
5. Ⓨ Ⓝ
6. Ⓨ Ⓝ
7. Ⓨ Ⓝ
8. Ⓨ Ⓝ

___ / 8
Total

NAME: ______________________ DATE: ______________

SCORE

___ / 4

DIRECTIONS

Reread "On Your Mark, Get Set, Go! The Story of Wilma Rudolph." Then, read the prompt and respond on the lines below.

Wilma Rudolph had to work very hard to learn to walk and run. What do you have to work very hard to do? Write about what you work very hard at doing and what you have accomplished.

NAME: ______________________ **DATE:** ______________

DIRECTIONS Read the text and then answer the questions.

Sara noticed the letter among the rest of the letters in the day's mail. She grabbed it excitedly and ripped it open. After hastily scanning its contents, she rushed into the kitchen waving it. "My information's here!" she yelled joyfully to her father. The letter was from the U.S. Space and Rocket Center; it contained information Sara would need for her upcoming Space Academy week. Sara had always enjoyed science, especially space science, so when she first learned about Space Academy, she was determined to go. She and her parents had checked the website, found out information, and planned her trip. She was thrilled to know she'd be among the students who would be going this year.

1. Why is Sara so excited?

- Ⓐ She is going to Space Academy.
- Ⓑ She has been accepted for band camp.
- Ⓒ She has won a prize.
- Ⓓ She has found a lot of money.

2. What does Sara like to study?

- Ⓐ social studies
- Ⓑ history
- Ⓒ art
- Ⓓ science

3. Which suffix could replace *–ful* in the word *joyful* to make its antonym?

- Ⓐ *–ous*
- Ⓑ *–less*
- Ⓒ *–ish*
- Ⓓ *–tion*

4. Which word is a synonym for *thrilled*?

- Ⓐ dejected
- Ⓑ delighted
- Ⓒ confused
- Ⓓ aware

5. What do the words *hastily scanning* tell you about Sara's actions?

- Ⓐ She does not understand the letter.
- Ⓑ She reads the letter very carefully.
- Ⓒ She glances at the letter very quickly.
- Ⓓ She does not receive the letter.

SCORE

1. Ⓨ Ⓝ
2. Ⓨ Ⓝ
3. Ⓨ Ⓝ
4. Ⓨ Ⓝ
5. Ⓨ Ⓝ

___ / 5

Total

NAME:______________________ DATE:______________

DIRECTIONS Read the text and then answer the questions.

SCORE

1. Ⓨ Ⓝ
2. Ⓨ Ⓝ
3. Ⓨ Ⓝ
4. Ⓨ Ⓝ
5. Ⓨ Ⓝ

___ / 5 Total

Sara would be leaving the next day for a week at Space Academy, so today, she was packing her things. She and her parents had discussed what she would need for the trip, and they had downloaded a guide from the Space Academy website. Now, Sara checked the guide as she looked at the things she planned to put into her suitcase. Her bed was heaped with things, and now she had to sort everything out and pack. The guide suggested bringing towels and a swimsuit as well as clothes. Sara would also need comfortable shoes, socks, sleepwear, and a jacket. She'd also be bringing her brush and comb, toothbrush, soap, and shampoo. Sara checked everything off on the guide and then put things into her suitcase. She wasn't sure everything would fit, but she managed to get everything into one bag. Sara was ready to go!

1. Where does this story take place?

Ⓐ Space Academy
Ⓑ school
Ⓒ Sara's room
Ⓓ the living room

2. Which of these is **not** something Sara will bring?

Ⓐ winter boots
Ⓑ a swimsuit
Ⓒ clothes
Ⓓ shoes and socks

3. Which word is a synonym for *heaped*?

Ⓐ lots
Ⓑ piled
Ⓒ messy
Ⓓ empty

4. Which of these sentences has a compound subject?

Ⓐ Sara was ready to go!
Ⓑ Now, Sara checked the guide as she looked at the things she planned to put into her suitcase.
Ⓒ Sara checked everything off on the guide and then put things into her suitcase.
Ⓓ She and her parents had discussed what she would need for the trip.

5. Which word or phrase has the same meaning as *as well as*?

Ⓐ along with
Ⓑ instead of
Ⓒ underneath
Ⓓ in place of

NAME: ____________________ **DATE:** ____________

DIRECTIONS Read the text and then answer the questions.

Sara was on her way to Space Academy for a week. She was a little nervous about traveling alone, but she was excited to be going. Her mom and dad drove her to the airport and made sure that she boarded the right airplane. Space Academy is in Huntsville, Alabama, so it would be a long flight. When Sara got on board the plane, she settled herself into her seat and prepared for takeoff. The flight left on time, and before she knew it, they were in the air. After a four-hour flight, the plane landed in Alabama. Sara got off the plane and looked around for the Space Academy staff who would take her to the training center. Soon, she spotted the person in the Space Academy uniform, just as the online guide had said she would. She and the other kids who were going to Space Academy got on a bus, and soon, they were on their way.

1. How is Sara getting to the training center?

- (A) by train
- (B) by air
- (C) her mom and dad are driving her
- (D) by boat

2. Why is Sara a little nervous?

- (A) The flight is very late.
- (B) Her parents are angry with her.
- (C) She does not want to go to space camp.
- (D) She is traveling alone.

3. What part of speech is *spotted* in this text?

- (A) noun
- (B) verb
- (C) pronoun
- (D) adjective

4. In the word *aboard*, what does the prefix *a–* mean?

- (A) over
- (B) not
- (C) on or in
- (D) under

5. What is the meaning of the phrase *before she knew it*?

- (A) Sara does not know the flight is leaving.
- (B) The flight takes off quickly.
- (C) Sara is afraid to fly.
- (D) The flight is delayed.

SCORE

1. Ⓨ Ⓝ
2. Ⓨ Ⓝ
3. Ⓨ Ⓝ
4. Ⓨ Ⓝ
5. Ⓨ Ⓝ

___ / 5

Total

NAME: ______________________ **DATE:** ______________

SARA BLASTS OFF

August 12, 2012

Dear Mom and Dad,

You have no idea what a busy week I'm having at Space Academy! Our schedule is full every day, but what we're doing is amazing and fun! We get up in the morning at 7:00 a.m. and have breakfast, and then it's time for our mission briefing. We work in teams, so each team has a mission to accomplish. Our team is making a two-stage rocket, and we're hoping it will launch. After our mission briefing and some work with the team, it's time for lunch.

When lunch is over, we do some other activities. Yesterday, I tried out the one-sixteenth Gravity Chair! It's a chair that makes you feel the way you'd feel if you were on the moon, where there's a lot less gravity than there is on Earth. Tomorrow, I want to try the Manned Maneuvering Unit—that's a special room that lets you feel what it's like to work without any friction. I hope I'll also get to experiment with the Five Degrees of Freedom Chair—they call it the 5DF. That's a special kind of chair that moves you back and forth—even upside down!

We do other kinds of things, too. For example, the training center has a rock climber and a mobility trainer. There's a pool, too, and we do water activities. It's a good thing I brought my swimsuit!

I'm really having an amazing time. I'm so glad I came, even though I was a little nervous at first. But I miss you guys, and I'll be glad to come home, too. Graduation from Space Academy will be on Friday afternoon—you'll be there, right? I want you to meet some of my friends and see the planetarium and the museum.

It's almost time for "lights out," so I'd better finish this. I'll call you on Thursday morning before our mission briefing.

Love,

Sara

NAME: ______________________________ **DATE:** ________________

DIRECTIONS Read "Sara Blasts Off" and then answer the questions.

1. What does a quick glance of this text explain to readers?

- Ⓐ The text is very descriptive.
- Ⓑ The text is too challenging.
- Ⓒ The text is long.
- Ⓓ The text is a letter.

2. What does Sara's use of exclamation marks tell readers?

- Ⓐ She is happy and writing with excitement.
- Ⓑ She is confused.
- Ⓒ She does not know how to feel.
- Ⓓ She is still nervous.

3. What do you predict Sara will do when she gets home?

- Ⓐ She will tell her friends what a good time she had.
- Ⓑ She will warn her friends not to go to Space Academy.
- Ⓒ She will be angry with her mom and dad.
- Ⓓ She will go to Space Academy for the first time.

4. What makes Sara feel less anxious about Space Academy?

- Ⓐ She is having a good time.
- Ⓑ She is lonely.
- Ⓒ Her mom and dad visit her.
- Ⓓ She is sick.

5. Who is the narrator?

- Ⓐ Mom
- Ⓑ Dad
- Ⓒ Sara's brother
- Ⓓ Sara

6. What inference can be made about how Sara feels about Space Academy?

- Ⓐ She is afraid of it.
- Ⓑ She loves it.
- Ⓒ She dislikes it.
- Ⓓ She has never been to it.

7. Which best summarizes Sara's letter?

- Ⓐ It is all about her first day at Space Academy.
- Ⓑ It is about the bus ride to Space Academy.
- Ⓒ It tells about the exciting activities and equipment at Space Academy.
- Ⓓ It describes what she wants to do when she gets home.

8. How do Sara's feelings about camp change?

- Ⓐ from sad to angry
- Ⓑ from happy to nervous
- Ⓒ from nervous to happy and enthusiastic
- Ⓓ from anxious to scared

SCORE

1. Ⓨ Ⓝ
2. Ⓨ Ⓝ
3. Ⓨ Ⓝ
4. Ⓨ Ⓝ
5. Ⓨ Ⓝ
6. Ⓨ Ⓝ
7. Ⓨ Ⓝ
8. Ⓨ Ⓝ

___ / 8
Total

NAME: ______________________ DATE: ______________

DIRECTIONS

Reread "Sara Blasts Off." Then, read the prompt and respond on the lines below.

SCORE

___ / 4

Imagine you are at Space Academy. What do you think a day there would be like? Describe your day.

NAME: ______________________ **DATE:** ________________

DIRECTIONS Read the text and then answer the questions.

SCORE

1. Ⓨ Ⓝ
2. Ⓨ Ⓝ
3. Ⓨ Ⓝ
4. Ⓨ Ⓝ
5. Ⓨ Ⓝ

___ / 5 Total

Today, we take airplane travel for granted, but that wasn't always the case. For thousands of years, people wanted to fly and were interested in flight. The ancient Greeks, for instance, had several myths about people who could fly. In real life, though, their experiments with flight failed. In the late 1400s, Leonardo da Vinci designed a machine that could help people fly. The machine was never created, but da Vinci's design was the inspiration for today's helicopter. Da Vinci was fascinated by flight, though. He drew over 100 pictures of his theories about flying. In 1783, the first hot air balloon took flight in France. Its first passengers were a sheep, a rooster, and a duck!

1. What is this text mostly about?

Ⓐ the history of flight
Ⓑ Leonardo da Vinci
Ⓒ the ancient Greeks
Ⓓ hot air balloons

2. Which feature would help readers best understand this topic?

Ⓐ a picture of da Vinci's design next to a hot air balloon
Ⓑ a time line showing how airplanes have changed in the 1900s
Ⓒ a photograph of a sheep, a rooster, and a duck
Ⓓ a graph showing how much today's planes cost

3. Which word is a synonym for *myths*?

Ⓐ theories
Ⓑ inventors
Ⓒ history
Ⓓ legends

4. Which word from the text is used as a verb?

Ⓐ drew
Ⓑ hot
Ⓒ thousands
Ⓓ late

5. What does the phrase *take airplane travel for granted* mean?

Ⓐ to be afraid to travel by airplane
Ⓑ to go somewhere by airplane
Ⓒ to be fascinated by airplanes
Ⓓ not think airplane travel is special

NAME: ______________________ **DATE:** ______________

DIRECTIONS Read the text and then answer the questions.

SCORE

1. Ⓨ Ⓝ
2. Ⓨ Ⓝ
3. Ⓨ Ⓝ
4. Ⓨ Ⓝ
5. Ⓨ Ⓝ

___ / 5 Total

Over the centuries, inventors had tried to find a way for people to fly. But they weren't successful until 1903. That was the year that brothers Wilbur and Orville Wright flew the first airplane. For years, the Wright brothers had been interested in flight. They tried to learn all they could about it. In 1902, they built a glider, which is a machine that flew without an engine. The glider used wind to power its flight. But the Wright brothers wanted a machine that could fly even without wind. So they created a glider with a small engine. They called it their flying machine. On December 14, 1903, Orville Wright flew the first gasoline-powered airplane at Kitty Hawk, North Carolina. The age of the airplane had begun!

1. What is this text mostly about?

Ⓐ Kitty Hawk, North Carolina
Ⓑ the Wright brothers' childhood
Ⓒ the invention of the airplane
Ⓓ how to make your own airplane

2. According to the sequence of events in this text, what did the Wright brothers do before they built a glider with an engine?

Ⓐ flew the first gasoline-powered airplane
Ⓑ learned all they could about flight
Ⓒ created a glider with a gasoline-powered engine
Ⓓ went to Kitty Hawk, North Carolina

3. What is the meaning of the word *age* in this text?

Ⓐ to get older
Ⓑ how old a person is
Ⓒ years
Ⓓ era

4. Which part of speech is the word *fly* in the first sentence?

Ⓐ a noun
Ⓑ a verb
Ⓒ an adverb
Ⓓ a noun and a verb

5. What is the tone of the text?

Ⓐ informative
Ⓑ silly
Ⓒ persuasive
Ⓓ manipulative

NAME: ______________________________ DATE: ________________

DIRECTIONS Read the text and then answer the questions.

The first airplanes were very fragile. They were made of light material such as bamboo, and their wings were made of fabric. That was so that they would be able to fly more easily. But those light materials were also easily broken and torn. There was another problem, too. An engine powerful enough to keep a plane flying was often too large and heavy for the plane's structure. An engine that was light enough and small enough for a plane was also not very powerful. But the people who developed and flew those planes kept working at it. Eventually, airplane design improved. Planes were slimmer and made better use of air currents. Motors got both smaller and more efficient. The people who designed and flew these first planes were called "birdmen." Their hard work led to the airplanes we know today.

1. Why were the first airplanes made of light materials?

- (A) so they would fit together better
- (B) so they would be able to fly more easily
- (C) so they would be less expensive
- (D) so they would be easier to make

2. Which is an example of a cause-and-effect relationship?

- (A) The first people to fly planes were called "birdmen."
- (B) Because airplanes were made of light materials, they easily broke and tore.
- (C) People worked hard at the airplane design.
- (D) Early planes were fragile.

3. Which word is a synonym for *fabric*?

- (A) fragile
- (B) motor
- (C) engine
- (D) cloth

4. Which adjective describes something that is easily torn or broken?

- (A) efficient
- (B) powerful
- (C) fragile
- (D) slim

5. Who were *birdmen*?

- (A) men who hunted birds
- (B) people who enjoyed watching birds
- (C) men who dressed up as birds
- (D) the people who worked on and flew the first airplanes

SCORE

1. Ⓨ Ⓝ
2. Ⓨ Ⓝ
3. Ⓨ Ⓝ
4. Ⓨ Ⓝ
5. Ⓨ Ⓝ

___ / 5
Total

NAME:______________________________ **DATE:**__________________

BARNSTORMING

In the early days of airplanes, a lot of people didn't think it was really possible for humans to fly. So at that time, airplanes were a novelty. They were something interesting that people hadn't seen before. Early pilots sometimes put on air shows for the public so people could see what airplanes were capable of doing. Those pilots were called *barnstormers*. Some barnstormers took people on plane rides. That was a very exciting and sometimes dangerous thing to do! Those barnstormers would borrow a farmer's field and offer rides. People would pay the pilot and take a plane ride.

Other barnstormers did stunts, or tricks, in the air. For example, some barnstormers flew upside down, and others flew their planes in a zigzag pattern. Sometimes, barnstormers flew in pairs. One person would fly the plane, and the other would walk on the plane's wing or do some other stunt. People loved to see these air shows—the fancier or more dangerous the stunts, the better they liked it.

Some barnstormers grew quite rich. They traveled around to different air shows. They were paid for their performances. But most barnstormers did not fly in order to get rich. They flew because they loved flying. Sometimes, they flew because they liked the danger. And flying was dangerous at that time. Many barnstormers got into accidents or crashed their planes. Several of them died.

After the 1920s, planes became much safer. They began to be used for regular travel. And people became more familiar with them. So by the late 1930s, barnstorming wasn't as popular anymore. But the barnstormers are still remembered as daring pilots.

barnstormers

NAME: ______________________ **DATE:** ______________

DIRECTIONS Read "Barnstorming," and then answer the questions.

1. What could a reader do to understand the word *novelty*?

- Ⓐ say the word aloud
- Ⓑ read the title and look at the picture
- Ⓒ reread the paragraph where you see the word
- Ⓓ read the last sentence

2. Which question is **not** answered in the text?

- Ⓐ What is a barnstormer?
- Ⓑ When did barnstorming stop being popular?
- Ⓒ How many barnstormers were there?
- Ⓓ What did barnstormers do?

3. How does the author likely feel about barnstormers?

- Ⓐ interested
- Ⓑ bored
- Ⓒ angry
- Ⓓ confused

4. What is the author's purpose?

- Ⓐ to persuade readers to become barnstormers
- Ⓑ to inform readers about barnstorming
- Ⓒ to entertain readers with a fictional story
- Ⓓ to make readers afraid to fly

5. According to the text, when did planes become much safer?

- Ⓐ after the 1930s
- Ⓑ after the 1920s
- Ⓒ before the 1920s
- Ⓓ they are not safe even today

6. Why do you think barnstormers did not do shows in the middle of a city?

- Ⓐ They were afraid of being in airplanes.
- Ⓑ They did not want to do tricks in the air.
- Ⓒ They did not know where cities were.
- Ⓓ They did not have room to take off and land.

7. Which is an accurate description of barnstormers?

- Ⓐ elderly
- Ⓑ clumsy
- Ⓒ timid
- Ⓓ brave

8. Why did barnstormers stop performing?

- Ⓐ Airplanes became safer, more familiar objects to the audiences.
- Ⓑ Barnstormers became scared to fly.
- Ⓒ It was made to be against the law.
- Ⓓ People became too nervous to watch the daring acts.

SCORE

1. Ⓨ Ⓝ
2. Ⓨ Ⓝ
3. Ⓨ Ⓝ
4. Ⓨ Ⓝ
5. Ⓨ Ⓝ
6. Ⓨ Ⓝ
7. Ⓨ Ⓝ
8. Ⓨ Ⓝ

___ / 8
Total

NAME: ______________________ **DATE:** ______________

SCORE

___ / 4

DIRECTIONS Reread "Barnstorming." Then, read the prompt and respond on the lines below.

What do you think it would be like to be a barnstormer? Would you want to be one? Why or why not? Write about what you think it would be like, and explain why you would or would not like the job.

NAME: ____________________ **DATE:** ____________

DIRECTIONS Read the text and then answer the questions.

Zach had liked soccer for a long time. In fact, he had been playing since he was six years old. But until now, he had only played in a neighborhood soccer league. That changed one day when he heard the morning announcements at school. The principal announced that the school would be starting a soccer team! Zach was so excited about it that he almost didn't listen closely to the details. But he did hear the most important information. There would be a meeting on Wednesday for everyone who was interested in being on the soccer team. Zach didn't want to miss out on that meeting, so he wrote down the time. He would have to talk to his parents about it, but he was sure they would let him join the team. After all, they hadn't had a problem letting him play in the neighborhood league.

1. Why is Zach excited?

- (A) His school is starting a baseball team.
- (B) He got a very good grade on a test.
- (C) His school is starting a soccer team.
- (D) He just won a big prize.

2. What makes Zach think his parents will let him join the team?

- (A) They let him play in the neighborhood team.
- (B) He already asked them if he could join.
- (C) Both his parents play soccer.
- (D) The principal asked them if he could join the team.

3. Which prefix could you add to *interested* to make an antonym for it?

- (A) *uni–*
- (B) *chrom–*
- (C) *sub–*
- (D) *un–*

4. Which word in the text is used as an adjective to describe a league?

- (A) soccer
- (B) team
- (C) Zach
- (D) played

5. What does the phrase *to miss out on* mean?

- (A) to leave out
- (B) to feel lonely for
- (C) to attend
- (D) to lose a chance for

SCORE

1. Ⓨ Ⓝ
2. Ⓨ Ⓝ
3. Ⓨ Ⓝ
4. Ⓨ Ⓝ
5. Ⓨ Ⓝ

___ / 5 Total

NAME: ____________________ **DATE:** ____________________

DIRECTIONS Read the text and then answer the questions.

SCORE

1. Ⓨ Ⓝ
2. Ⓨ Ⓝ
3. Ⓨ Ⓝ
4. Ⓨ Ⓝ
5. Ⓨ Ⓝ

___ / 5 Total

Zach's school was starting a soccer team, and he wanted to join it. Zach already played for a neighborhood soccer league. So when he asked his parents about trying out for the school team, they were concerned. They thought he might be so busy with soccer that he wouldn't have time for his schoolwork. But Zach explained that he would rather play for the school team. If he made that team, he would stop playing in the neighborhood league. The neighborhood league was for younger kids anyway, and Zach was getting too old for it. So his mom and dad said that he could try out for the school team. On tryout day, Zach got to the field early to practice—and so did a lot of other kids. But Zach was a good player, so when it was his turn to try out, the coach chose Zach immediately.

1. Where does the end of this story take place?

Ⓐ at home
Ⓑ on a soccer field
Ⓒ at a swimming pool
Ⓓ in a forest

2. Why does Zach want to play for the school team and **not** the neighborhood league?

Ⓐ Zach is getting too old for the neighborhood league.
Ⓑ Zach is too young for the neighborhood league.
Ⓒ Zach was not picked for the neighborhood team.
Ⓓ The neighborhood league has ended.

3. What does the word *already* tell you about what Zach was doing?

Ⓐ He wants to keep playing in the neighborhood league.
Ⓑ He does not want to play soccer.
Ⓒ He is not playing in the neighborhood league.
Ⓓ He was playing in the neighborhood league before the story starts.

4. What does the adverb *immediately* indicate to readers?

Ⓐ The coach chose Zach after a long time.
Ⓑ The coach chose Zach very quickly.
Ⓒ The coach chose Zach reluctantly.
Ⓓ The coach chose Zach last.

5. Which word or phrase holds the same meaning as the word *rather*?

Ⓐ object to
Ⓑ never
Ⓒ prefer to
Ⓓ sometimes

NAME: ____________________ **DATE:** ______________

DIRECTIONS Read the text and then answer the questions.

Zach played on his school's new soccer team, and he really enjoyed it. Practices were difficult, but he was learning a lot. Soon, the school's team started playing some other teams. At first, Zach's school didn't win very many games, and losing was very disappointing. But the coach told the team not to give up. He explained that every new team loses games while everyone learns to work together. He promised the team members that if they worked hard and helped one another, the team would begin to win, and after a few more games, it started to happen. Zach's team won the first one, and then another game, and it wasn't long until they started winning most of their games. Zach couldn't have been happier! Then came very good news: The team was going to play in this year's soccer tournament!

1. What good news does the team get?

- (A) There are some new people on the team.
- (B) Zach will play more often.
- (C) The team will play in this year's soccer tournament.
- (D) The team is getting new equipment.

2. Why does Zach's team start to win games?

- (A) The team has new uniforms and new soccer balls.
- (B) Zach is the best player on the team.
- (C) The other teams do not play very well.
- (D) The team members work hard and help one another.

3. Which word has the same meaning as *give up*?

- (A) begin
- (B) quit
- (C) complain
- (D) prevail

4. Which noun describes a series of games?

- (A) tournament
- (B) coach
- (C) team
- (D) game

5. Which word or phrase is an antonym of *disappointing*?

- (A) infuriating
- (B) saddening
- (C) pleasing
- (D) confusing

SCORE

1. Ⓨ Ⓝ
2. Ⓨ Ⓝ
3. Ⓨ Ⓝ
4. Ⓨ Ⓝ
5. Ⓨ Ⓝ

___ / 5 Total

NAME: ____________________ **DATE:** ______________

GOAL!

Zach's school now had a soccer team, and he was excited to be a part of it. The team practiced regularly, and everyone worked hard. The team members tried to help one another, and their hard work paid off with good results. Little by little, the team began to win their games. Then, they were invited to play in a soccer tournament. Zach wanted his team to win the tournament, and he was determined to do his best to see that they would.

On the day the tournament began, Zach and his team got to the soccer field early. They wanted to practice as much as they could before the tournament started. The coach told them to do their best and play as well as they could. He said that it wouldn't be easy because the other teams were very good. But he explained that even if the team didn't win the tournament, they should be proud they were there. Then, the first games began. Zach and the team played against some very good teams that day, and they almost lost a few times. But everybody kept working hard, and they managed to win. The more games they won, the harder the games got.

The final games in the tournament were held the next day. Zach and his team still had a chance to win the tournament, so they all played the best they could, and they beat several teams. Then, came the final game. This time, they were up against the best soccer team in the tournament. Zach and his team gave the game their best effort, but the other team won. Everyone was upset about losing, but the coach told them they'd done a fantastic job. He said he thought they'd done very well in the tournament considering they were a new team. That didn't make Zach any happier, but he knew the coach was right. And he knew that he and his team would be back next year.

NAME: ____________________ **DATE:** ______________

DIRECTIONS Read "Goal!" and then answer the questions.

1. Where would a reader find a text like this?

- (A) in a science textbook
- (B) in a recipe book
- (C) in a book of short stories
- (D) in a fishing magazine

2. What would readers who enjoy this text also like to read about?

- (A) sports
- (B) history
- (C) television
- (D) science

3. What might have happened if Zach and his team had **not** practiced and worked hard?

- (A) They would have won the tournament.
- (B) They would not have been in the tournament.
- (C) They would have been much better at soccer.
- (D) The coach would have been very proud of them.

4. Which statement is likely true about Zach and his team?

- (A) They will never play soccer again.
- (B) They will work very hard and try to win the tournament next year.
- (C) They will celebrate winning the soccer tournament.
- (D) They will go to a soccer tournament tomorrow.

5. From what point of view is this text told?

- (A) third person
- (B) first person
- (C) second person
- (D) there is no point of view

6. What does the author's word choice tell readers about Zach and his team?

- (A) They are lazy.
- (B) They are studious.
- (C) They are athletic.
- (D) They are clumsy.

7. Why do you think the games get harder as the tournament goes on?

- (A) Everyone gets too tired to play.
- (B) Only the best teams move on in the tournament.
- (C) Everyone is bored with soccer.
- (D) The very best teams leave the tournament early.

8. Why should Zach and his team be proud of themselves, even though they did not win?

- (A) They worked hard and improved a lot over the course of the season.
- (B) They do not play very well.
- (C) They have new uniforms.
- (D) The other team was rude and did not show good sportsmanship.

SCORE

1. Ⓨ Ⓝ
2. Ⓨ Ⓝ
3. Ⓨ Ⓝ
4. Ⓨ Ⓝ
5. Ⓨ Ⓝ
6. Ⓨ Ⓝ
7. Ⓨ Ⓝ
8. Ⓨ Ⓝ

___ / 8 **Total**

NAME: ______________________ **DATE:** ______________

DIRECTIONS Reread "Goal!" Then, read the prompt and respond on the lines below.

SCORE

___ / 4

Have you ever lost at something? What happened? What was it like? What did you do about it? Write about what happened, or how you will respond to a loss in the future.

NAME: ____________________ **DATE:** ____________

DIRECTIONS Read the text and then answer the questions.

Have you ever wanted to get a desk, a table, or a chair for your room? Maybe you've wanted to put shelves up. Making changes to your room can cost a lot of money if you go to a store and buy new furniture. But you don't have to do that. You can make some amazing changes in your room without spending a lot of money at all. Sometimes, people sell furniture they no longer want. They often do this when they are moving or when they are buying new things. You can frequently find that furniture at yard sales or garage sales. Flea markets are also good places to look for used desks, tables, or chairs. You can also go to swap meets, where people bring things that they want to sell and look for things they want to buy. If you know where to look, you can find some very nice things that aren't expensive.

1. What is this text mostly about?

Ⓐ how to find inexpensive furniture
Ⓑ how to make a new desk
Ⓒ how to hold a yard sale
Ⓓ where to find a good garage sale

2. Why might an author start a piece of text with a question?

Ⓐ to hook the reader
Ⓑ to explain what the author does not know
Ⓒ to share opinions
Ⓓ to state the main idea

3. Which two words are synonyms?

Ⓐ *frequently* and *find*
Ⓑ *often* and *frequently*
Ⓒ *often* and *rarely*
Ⓓ *costly* and *inexpensive*

4. Which is **not** a good place to look for used furniture?

Ⓐ a swap meet
Ⓑ a garage sale
Ⓒ a yard sale
Ⓓ a department store

5. What is *frequently find* an example of?

Ⓐ a simile
Ⓑ synonyms
Ⓒ alliteration
Ⓓ personification

SCORE

1. Ⓨ Ⓝ
2. Ⓨ Ⓝ
3. Ⓨ Ⓝ
4. Ⓨ Ⓝ
5. Ⓨ Ⓝ

___ / 5
Total

NAME: ____________________ DATE: ____________

DIRECTIONS Read the text and then answer the questions.

SCORE

1. Ⓨ Ⓝ

2. Ⓨ Ⓝ

3. Ⓨ Ⓝ

4. Ⓨ Ⓝ

5. Ⓨ Ⓝ

___ / 5

Total

What if you find the perfect desk, table, or chair, but you dislike the color? You can paint your new furniture exactly the color you want. To do that, though, you need to choose the kind of paint that will work best for your furniture. Different kinds of paint work best for different kinds of material, so the first step to painting is selecting the right kind of paint. If you have a metal desk, chair, or table, you may want latex paint. Latex paint has a water base. One of its ingredients is latex, a kind of rubber. You can also use enamel paint on metal. Enamel paint has an oil base. Enamel paint looks glossy when it dries. You can also use enamel paint to paint wooden furniture. You can also use wood stain, which is a kind of dye, on wooden furniture.

1. Which of these is true about painting furniture?

Ⓐ Different kinds of paint work best for different materials.

Ⓑ Latex paint is never a good choice for furniture.

Ⓒ It doesn't matter which paint you use on your furniture.

Ⓓ Furniture cannot be painted.

2. Which of these is a good title for this text?

Ⓐ Finding the Right Paint Store

Ⓑ How Latex Paint is Made

Ⓒ You Can Paint Your Furniture

Ⓓ The Story of Wood Stain

3. Which word is a synonym for *glossy*?

Ⓐ dull

Ⓑ green

Ⓒ sticky

Ⓓ shiny

4. Which word is used as an adjective to describe paint that has a water base and a kind of rubber as an ingredient?

Ⓐ enamel

Ⓑ latex

Ⓒ stain

Ⓓ oil

5. What is the tone of the text?

Ⓐ informational

Ⓑ silly

Ⓒ persuasive

Ⓓ serious

NAME: ______________________ **DATE:** ______________

DIRECTIONS Read the text and then answer the questions.

Suppose you've found exactly the desk, table, or chair you want. You've decided to paint it, and you've found exactly the color you want. Before you paint, you'll need to prepare your furniture. That way, your desk, table, or chair will look its best when you're finished. The way you prepare furniture depends on its material. For example, if your furniture is made of wood, you will want to make sure the wood is very smooth before you apply any paint. You will also want to get rid of old, flaky paint that may be there. If you are using wood stain, you will want to use sandpaper to smooth the wood first. If your furniture is made of metal, it may be rusty. You'll want to remove the rust before you paint it. A wire brush will scrape away the rust, and then you can wash the piece of furniture to remove dirt.

1. What does this text tell readers?

- Ⓐ where to find metal furniture
- Ⓑ how to prepare furniture for painting
- Ⓒ why you need to paint furniture
- Ⓓ the history of furniture

2. According to the text, which object helps a person to prepare wooden furniture for painting?

- Ⓐ a wire brush
- Ⓑ rust
- Ⓒ sandpaper
- Ⓓ wood

3. Which two words are antonyms?

- Ⓐ *ready* and *prepared*
- Ⓑ *remove* and *apply*
- Ⓒ *flaky* and *rusty*
- Ⓓ *smooth* and *stain*

4. What word or phrase has the same meaning as the verb *remove*?

- Ⓐ apply
- Ⓑ put on
- Ⓒ wash
- Ⓓ take away

5. What is the meaning of the word *apply* in this text?

- Ⓐ put on
- Ⓑ relate
- Ⓒ ask for
- Ⓓ refer

SCORE

1. Ⓨ Ⓝ
2. Ⓨ Ⓝ
3. Ⓨ Ⓝ
4. Ⓨ Ⓝ
5. Ⓨ Ⓝ

___ / 5 Total

NAME: ______________________ **DATE:** ______________

DO IT YOURSELF

Have you ever wanted to change the look of your room? Maybe you have wanted a new table, chair, or desk. Brand new furniture can be very expensive, though, so many kids don't think they can easily get new things. But you really don't have to spend a lot of money on furniture. You can find a terrific desk, table or chair that doesn't cost much and turn it into the perfect piece of furniture for your room.

Start by going to yard sales, garage sales, flea markets, and swap meets. All of those are good places to find furniture. If you don't find what you want at first, keep looking. Chances are you'll find exactly the kind of desk, chair, or table you want for your room. And you won't pay nearly as much for it as you would in a department store.

Once you find the furniture you want, it's time to make it your own. Choose the kind of paint that will work best for the furniture you've bought. Most stores offer latex and enamel paints in many colors. Choose a color that will match the rest of what you have in your room, and then get enough paint in that color to do the job. You will also want to get supplies to prepare your furniture for painting.

If your table, desk, or chair is wooden, you may choose to use wood stain. If you do, you'll want to smooth it with sandpaper first. If you will be painting it, you don't need sandpaper unless there are cuts or splinters in the wood. If your furniture is made of metal, you'll want a wire brush to get rid of rust and prepare it for painting.

Before you start painting or staining, be sure you're wearing old clothing. If you will be using wood stain, apply the stain carefully, and then let it dry. If you use paint, you may want to start with primer, which is an undercoat for paint. Primer covers up old paint. It also helps the new paint adhere, or stick to the furniture. After the primer is dry, paint your furniture. Now you've got an amazing new look for your room!

NAME: ______________________ **DATE:** ______________

DIRECTIONS Read "Do It Yourself" and then answer the questions.

1. What is the first step in finding great new furniture for your room?

- (A) Use primer to cover up old paint.
- (B) Check out flea markets, thrift shops, and swap meets.
- (C) Choose a paint color that will match your room.
- (D) Make sure you are wearing old clothing.

2. If a reader doesn't remember what *primer* is used for, what would likely help?

- (A) Read the word aloud.
- (B) Read the title again.
- (C) Read the paragraph again.
- (D) Read the first sentence again.

3. What is the author's purpose?

- (A) to tell a personal story
- (B) to tell how to change the look of a room without spending much money
- (C) to get readers to go to a furniture store
- (D) to show how to stay safe in an emergency

4. What is a reason for reading this text?

- (A) to find out how to paint furniture
- (B) to find a good furniture store
- (C) to learn how to paint portraits
- (D) to learn the history of furniture-making

5. What might people who are interested in this topic also like?

- (A) doing home projects
- (B) playing football
- (C) reading a lot
- (D) watching movies on TV

6. Why should you wear old clothes if you are painting or staining?

- (A) so you can easily find your old clothes
- (B) so you will be able to wear your new clothes
- (C) so you will not stain clothes you like
- (D) so you can make room in your closet

7. What are the facts in this text about?

- (A) buying furniture
- (B) making clothes
- (C) taking photographs
- (D) painting furniture

8. Why might kids think they can't get new furniture for their rooms?

- (A) New furniture is extremely hard to find.
- (B) Kids do not like to use furniture.
- (C) Most parents do not want kids to have rooms.
- (D) Brand new furniture can be expensive.

SCORE

1. Ⓨ Ⓝ
2. Ⓨ Ⓝ
3. Ⓨ Ⓝ
4. Ⓨ Ⓝ
5. Ⓨ Ⓝ
6. Ⓨ Ⓝ
7. Ⓨ Ⓝ
8. Ⓨ Ⓝ

___ / 8 Total

NAME: ______________________ DATE: ______________

SCORE

___ / 4

DIRECTIONS

Reread "Do It Yourself." Then, read the prompt and respond on the lines below.

What kind of furniture would you want for your room? Write about what you would do to find what you want, get it ready, and paint or stain it.

NAME: ______________________ **DATE:** ______________

DIRECTIONS Read the text and then answer the questions.

Crystal was a reporter for her school's newspaper, *The Real Story*. She liked interviewing people. She also liked getting new ideas for stories and special features. She enjoyed it so much that she wanted a career in news reporting. Every week, the kids who worked on the newspaper met with their advisor, Mr. Thorne. They put together the news stories for that week's edition of the paper. Then, they planned the next week's edition. During the week, the reporters would get their stories and write them up. Then, they would bring their stories to the next week's meeting. Crystal especially liked it when the newspaper was ready for publishing and she could see how her stories and interviews fit in with everyone else's work.

1. What does Crystal enjoy the most?

- (A) playing on her school's basketball team
- (B) writing news stories and interviews
- (C) playing video games
- (D) going to the movies

2. Which event does **not** happen at the newspaper meetings?

- (A) planning the next week's paper
- (B) putting together the stories for that week's paper
- (C) writing up stories
- (D) sharing stories with other reporters

3. What word means *a version of a newspaper*?

- (A) edition
- (B) advisor
- (C) interview
- (D) idea

4. Which prefix could you add to make an antonym for the verb *liked*?

- (A) *bi–*
- (B) *sub–*
- (C) *mega–*
- (D) *dis–*

5. What is the meaning of *feature* in this text?

- (A) part
- (B) element
- (C) trait
- (D) story

SCORE

1. Ⓨ Ⓝ

2. Ⓨ Ⓝ

3. Ⓨ Ⓝ

4. Ⓨ Ⓝ

5. Ⓨ Ⓝ

___ / 5 Total

NAME: ______________________ **DATE:** ______________

DIRECTIONS Read the text and then answer the questions.

SCORE

1. Ⓨ Ⓝ
2. Ⓨ Ⓝ
3. Ⓨ Ⓝ
4. Ⓨ Ⓝ
5. Ⓨ Ⓝ

___ / 5 **Total**

Crystal really enjoyed working on *The Real Story,* her school's newspaper, but one day she got a story assignment she was convinced she would hate. The newspaper's advisor, Mr. Thorne, asked her to interview the school nurse, Mrs. Curtis. Crystal was positive that an interview with the nurse would be a really boring story. Who wanted to read a feature about going to the nurse's office for hearing and vision testing and to take medicine? But Mr. Thorne insisted that Crystal do the interview. He reminded her that everyone has a story to tell. "You never know what you might learn," he told her. So, very reluctantly, Crystal agreed to do the story. She contacted Mrs. Curtis and asked if she could interview her for the school paper. Mrs. Curtis agreed willingly, and the two set up an appointment.

1. Why doesn't Crystal want to interview the nurse?

- Ⓐ She thinks the story will be boring.
- Ⓑ She does not like Mrs. Curtis.
- Ⓒ She does not know how to do an interview.
- Ⓓ She thinks the story will be too hard.

2. How does Mrs. Curtis feel about doing the interview?

- Ⓐ She is angry about it.
- Ⓑ She is nervous about it.
- Ⓒ She does not want to do it.
- Ⓓ She is happy about it.

3. Which two words are synonyms?

- Ⓐ *positive* and *unsure*
- Ⓑ *convinced* and *certain*
- Ⓒ *boring* and *convinced*
- Ⓓ *really* and *willingly*

4. What does the verb *insisted* tell readers about Mr. Thorne?

- Ⓐ He does not know Crystal will do the interview.
- Ⓑ He wants to do the interview.
- Ⓒ He feels strongly about Crystal doing the interview.
- Ⓓ He does not care if Crystal does the interview.

5. Which two words are antonyms?

- Ⓐ *reluctantly* and *willingly*
- Ⓑ *insisted* and *agreed*
- Ⓒ *newspaper* and *advisor*
- Ⓓ *feature* and *interview*

NAME: ____________________ **DATE:** ____________________

DIRECTIONS Read the text and then answer the questions.

Crystal had been assigned to interview the school nurse, Mrs. Curtis, for her school's newspaper. Although she wasn't enthusiastic about the idea, Crystal kept the appointment for the interview. After the two greeted each other, Crystal thanked Mrs. Curtis for being willing to do the interview. Mrs. Curtis responded, "Oh, it's no problem at all. I remember doing some stories for the newspaper years ago when I was a student here."

That got Crystal's interest immediately, and she asked in surprise, "You were a student here?"

"Sure was," Mrs. Curtis answered proudly. "In fact," she lowered her voice and continued, "did you ever hear about the secret basement here at the school?"

Now, Crystal was really interested. Who knew what might be stashed in a secret basement? This was going to be a real story!

1. Where does this text take place?

Ⓐ the supermarket
Ⓑ the mall
Ⓒ Crystal's home
Ⓓ the nurse's office

2. What does Mrs. Curtis tell Crystal?

Ⓐ The school has a secret basement.
Ⓑ The school is 300 years old.
Ⓒ The school is about to be closed.
Ⓓ The school is about to get a new set of computers.

3. Which word is an antonym for *enthusiastic*?

Ⓐ willing
Ⓑ proud
Ⓒ reluctant
Ⓓ secret

4. What part of speech is the word *greeted*?

Ⓐ verb
Ⓑ noun
Ⓒ adverb
Ⓓ adjective

5. What is the tone of the story?

Ⓐ informative
Ⓑ silly
Ⓒ engaging
Ⓓ serious

SCORE

1. Ⓨ Ⓝ
2. Ⓨ Ⓝ
3. Ⓨ Ⓝ
4. Ⓨ Ⓝ
5. Ⓨ Ⓝ

___ / 5
Total

NAME: ______________________ **DATE:** ______________

CRYSTAL GETS THE SCOOP

Crystal was a reporter for her school's newspaper, *The Real Story*. She'd done several different kinds of stories before, but never anything like the story she was about to do. During an interview, the school nurse, Mrs. Curtis, had told Crystal that the school had a secret basement. Crystal couldn't resist the opportunity to find out what was in the basement. It could be just about anything! So on the day she turned in her interview with Mrs. Curtis, Crystal asked the newspaper's advisor, Mr. Thorne, if she could do a feature on the school's basement. He agreed with her that the basement might be a fascinating story, especially since a lot of people weren't even aware that it existed.

Crystal got permission from the principal to go down into the basement as long as some teachers went with her. So Mr. Thorne and Mrs. Curtis accompanied Crystal when she went to explore the basement. The janitor unlocked the basement door, and Crystal and the two teachers slowly descended the narrow staircase. When they reached the bottom of the stairs, Mrs. Curtis turned on the light, and she, Mr. Thorne, and Crystal began to look around.

Crystal soon discovered a large set of bookshelves with a collection of old dusty books on them. "What are those?" she wondered aloud. Neither of the two teachers knew, so Crystal made her way over to look more closely at the books. They turned out to be yearbooks from every year since the school opened. For almost an hour, Crystal, Mr. Thorne, and Mrs. Curtis paged slowly through the yearbooks. They joked about the old-fashioned clothes and hair in the oldest books, and they commented on some of the people they recognized. All of a sudden, Crystal knew the next feature she wanted to write. These books were the school's story just waiting to be told.

NAME: ______________________ **DATE:** ______________

DIRECTIONS Read "Crystal Gets the Scoop" and then answer the questions.

1. Which prediction based on the title of the text is most accurate?

Ⓐ This text is about ice cream.
Ⓑ This text is about picking something up.
Ⓒ This text is about a famous journalist.
Ⓓ This text is about a reporter getting a story.

2. What do context clues indicate about the relevant meaning of the word *descended*?

Ⓐ went down
Ⓑ sloped
Ⓒ was related to
Ⓓ arrived suddenly

3. Which statement is likely true about the yearbooks?

Ⓐ They are sold in bookstores.
Ⓑ They are very popular.
Ⓒ They are brand-new.
Ⓓ They have been there for a long time.

4. Which word describes Crystal?

Ⓐ timid
Ⓑ curious
Ⓒ disrespectful
Ⓓ athletic

5. Why do Mr. Thorne and Mrs. Curtis go to the basement with Crystal?

Ⓐ They want to stop Crystal from going.
Ⓑ They are afraid to go alone.
Ⓒ Crystal is too afraid to go by herself.
Ⓓ The principal says that some teachers must go to the basement with Crystal.

6. What can you infer about the basement?

Ⓐ It is not used very often.
Ⓑ Everyone goes there.
Ⓒ It is the largest room in the building.
Ⓓ Many groups hold meetings there.

7. How does Crystal feel about her experience?

Ⓐ happy and inspired
Ⓑ upset and nervous
Ⓒ afraid
Ⓓ jealous and unhappy

8. Why does Crystal want her next story to be about the old yearbooks?

Ⓐ She wants to tell the school about old friends.
Ⓑ Mr. Thorne wants her to write about the yearbooks.
Ⓒ She believes the old yearbooks have stories that should be told.
Ⓓ She is tired of the stories she usually writes.

SCORE

1. Ⓨ Ⓝ
2. Ⓨ Ⓝ
3. Ⓨ Ⓝ
4. Ⓨ Ⓝ
5. Ⓨ Ⓝ
6. Ⓨ Ⓝ
7. Ⓨ Ⓝ
8. Ⓨ Ⓝ

___ / 8
Total

NAME: ____________________ **DATE:** ____________

DIRECTIONS Reread "Crystal Gets the Scoop." Then, read the prompt and respond on the lines below.

SCORE

___ / 4

What story would you want to write about your school? Explain the story you would write about.

NAME: ____________________ **DATE:** ______________

DIRECTIONS Read the text and then answer the questions.

You probably write all the time without even thinking about it. Writing is a very important part of daily life. It serves several important purposes. One purpose of writing is to communicate. In fact, before there were telephones, writing was just about the only way people could stay in contact. That was especially true if they did not live in the same town. Writing also helps us to remember things and keep records. That's one reason you take notes in class. It's also why people make shopping lists and write down telephone numbers. Imagine what it would be like if your teacher did not keep records of your assignments and exam scores. It would be difficult to recall what work you had completed. It would also be hard to know how you were doing in class.

1. What is this text mostly about?

- Ⓐ why people make shopping lists
- Ⓑ why people write
- Ⓒ what life was like before telephones
- Ⓓ how to get a better exam score

2. Which is **not** a reason people write?

- Ⓐ to keep records
- Ⓑ to remember things
- Ⓒ to communicate
- Ⓓ to follow rules

3. Which word is a synonym for *recall*?

- Ⓐ remember
- Ⓑ write
- Ⓒ discuss
- Ⓓ complete

4. What part of speech is the word *true*?

- Ⓐ noun
- Ⓑ adverb
- Ⓒ adjective
- Ⓓ verb

5. What is the meaning of the word *record* in this text?

- Ⓐ a musical release
- Ⓑ a top performance
- Ⓒ an exam
- Ⓓ written proof

SCORE

1. Ⓨ Ⓝ
2. Ⓨ Ⓝ
3. Ⓨ Ⓝ
4. Ⓨ Ⓝ
5. Ⓨ Ⓝ

___ / 5 Total

NAME:______________________ DATE:______________

DIRECTIONS Read the text and then answer the questions.

SCORE

1. Ⓨ Ⓝ
2. Ⓨ Ⓝ
3. Ⓨ Ⓝ
4. Ⓨ Ⓝ
5. Ⓨ Ⓝ

___ / 5
Total

The alphabet you use is a very important tool for writing, but it is not the only one. There are many kinds of alphabets. Children in Japan learn to write with *kanji* (KAHN-gee). *Kanji* are small drawings, or characters. They do not represent letters, the way the alphabet you know does. Instead, they represent a whole meaning. For instance, there is a *kanji* for *water* and one for *big*. Russian children learn another kind of alphabet called the *Cyrillic* (si-RIL-ik) alphabet. Some Cyrillic letters, such as *O* and *T*, sound like the letters you know. But there are many Cyrillic letters that sound different from the letters you know. Hebrew and Arabic also use alphabets that are different from the one you know. So does Hindi. Hindi is a language spoken in India.

1. Which of these is the topic sentence for this text?

- Ⓐ There are many kinds of alphabets.
- Ⓑ Hindi is a language spoken in India.
- Ⓒ They do not represent letters, the way the alphabet you know does.
- Ⓓ Children in Japan learn to write with *kanji*.

2. Which statement is **not** true about alphabets?

- Ⓐ There are many kinds of alphabets.
- Ⓑ *Kanji* represent whole meanings.
- Ⓒ Everyone around the world uses the same alphabet.
- Ⓓ Some Cyrillic letters sound like the letters you know.

3. Which word is defined as *drawings, or characters, that represent whole meanings*?

- Ⓐ Cyrillic letters
- Ⓑ *kanji*
- Ⓒ alphabets
- Ⓓ languages

4. Which word from the text can be both a noun and a verb?

- Ⓐ writing
- Ⓑ one
- Ⓒ letters
- Ⓓ learn

5. What is the meaning of the word *tool* as it is used in the first sentence?

- Ⓐ somebody manipulated by another
- Ⓑ way to get something
- Ⓒ hammer
- Ⓓ instrument

NAME: ______________________ **DATE:** ______________

DIRECTIONS Read the text and then answer the questions.

There are several languages that do not have a written alphabet. One example is American Sign Language. It is a language used by many people who are deaf. This language uses hand signs and facial expressions. It has an alphabet, but it is not a written alphabet. Instead, each letter is made with a special hand shape. Many American Indian languages did not have written languages at first. So people created alphabets for them. For instance, the Cherokee did not have a written alphabet. So a Cherokee named Sequoyah (si-KWOI-uh) created one. There are also some other languages that do not have written alphabets. *Ainu* is an example. Ainu is a very old language spoken in Japan.

1. Which of these is the main idea of this text?

- Ⓐ Ainu is a very old language.
- Ⓑ American Sign Language is used by people with deafness.
- Ⓒ The Cherokee did not used to have a written alphabet.
- Ⓓ Several languages do not have a written alphabet.

2. How are American Sign Language letters made?

- Ⓐ with characters
- Ⓑ with a written alphabet
- Ⓒ with special hand shapes
- Ⓓ with pictures

3. Which is **not** an example of a *facial expression*?

- Ⓐ a slap
- Ⓑ a scowl
- Ⓒ a smile
- Ⓓ a look of surprise

4. What does the pronoun *it* in the third sentence refer to?

- Ⓐ Ainu
- Ⓑ American Sign Language
- Ⓒ American Indians
- Ⓓ people

5. What is the meaning of the phrase *for instance*?

- Ⓐ for that matter
- Ⓑ for what it's worth
- Ⓒ for example
- Ⓓ for a start

SCORE

1. Ⓨ Ⓝ
2. Ⓨ Ⓝ
3. Ⓨ Ⓝ
4. Ⓨ Ⓝ
5. Ⓨ Ⓝ

___ / 5 Total

NAME: ______________________ **DATE:** ______________

ALPHABET SOUP

Alphabets are very important tools. Without them, we wouldn't be able to write. How did alphabets get started in the first place? When and why did people start to write?

The first people were hunter-gatherers who didn't really need a writing system. They left behind beautiful paintings, but they didn't leave anything written. Then, people learned to grow crops and domesticate animals. Now, people needed some sort of system to record what they grew and keep track of their animals. They needed a writing system to help them keep records.

The first writing systems developed in two places, Egypt and Mesopotamia, at about the same time. Both systems used pictograms, which are pictures that represent things. For instance, a picture of a bull might represent a real bull. For a while, those systems were very successful.

But as cities began to grow, people needed more than a system of pictures. People needed to be able to represent new ideas. So the Sumerians developed a system of wedge-shaped marks. That system is called *cuneiform* (kyoo-NEE-uh-fawrm). At first, those marks represented things. Later, they represented sounds. A similar thing happened in Egypt. At first, Egyptian *hieroglyphics* (hahy-er-uh-GLIF-iks) were pictures of things. Later, they came to represent sounds, and still later, the symbols for those sounds became letters.

The alphabet you know developed from those symbols. Even the word *alphabet* itself comes from those ancient symbols. The first letter of the Hebrew alphabet is *alef*, which is the Hebrew word for "ox." The original Hebrew letter looks a little like a symbol for an ox's head—that is how that letter got its name. The second letter of the Hebrew alphabet is *bet*, which is also the Hebrew word for "house." The Hebrew letter *bet* looks a little like a symbol for a house, and that is how that letter got its name.

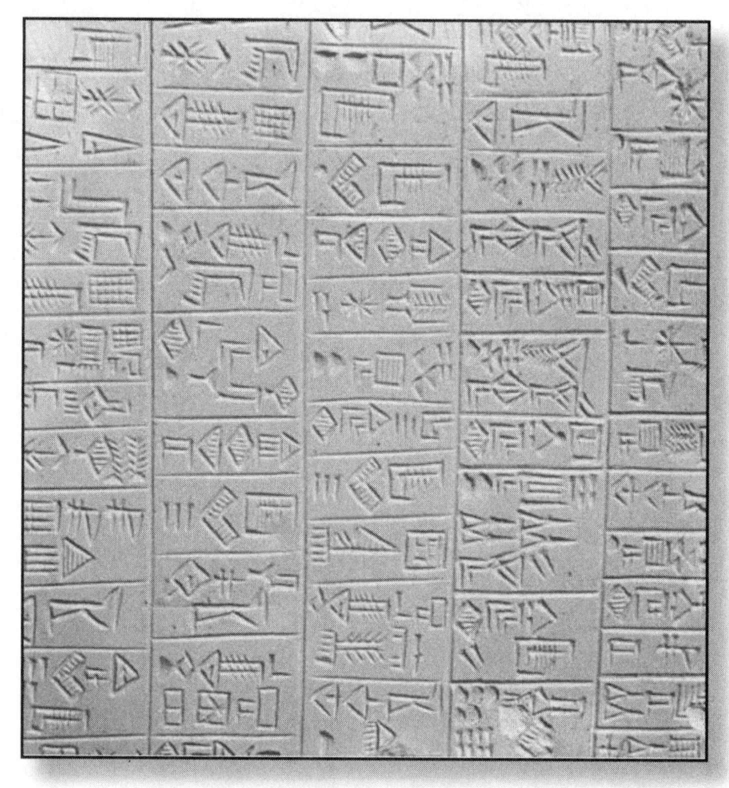

cuneiform writing

NAME: ______________________________ **DATE:** ________________

DIRECTIONS Read "Alphabet Soup" and then answer the questions.

1. Why did hunter-gatherers **not** need an alphabet?

Ⓐ They lived in Mesopotamia.
Ⓑ They lived in large cities.
Ⓒ They didn't need to keep track of things.
Ⓓ They used hieroglyphics.

2. If readers forget what *cuneiform* means, what can they do?

Ⓐ Write the word.
Ⓑ Read the last sentence again.
Ⓒ Read the title and look at the pictures.
Ⓓ Read the fourth paragraph again.

3. Which statement reflects an appropriate purpose for reading this?

Ⓐ I want to learn the recipe for alphabet soup.
Ⓑ I want to know the history of alphabets and how they came to be.
Ⓒ I want to memorize a new alphabet.
Ⓓ I want to alphabetize words.

4. Why did pictograms stop being successful?

Ⓐ Pictograms took too long to write.
Ⓑ Pictograms were too small.
Ⓒ People were bored with pictograms.
Ⓓ People needed to represent new ideas.

5. What happened as a result of the Sumerians developing cuneiform writing?

Ⓐ Today's alphabet was developed.
Ⓑ Hunter-gatherers left paintings behind.
Ⓒ People began to live in cities.
Ⓓ People used pictograms.

6. Which topic is the author interested in?

Ⓐ science
Ⓑ language
Ⓒ music
Ⓓ soccer

7. Why did the first writing systems develop in Egypt and Mesopotamia?

Ⓐ The first humans hunted there.
Ⓑ Those places had a lot of animals.
Ⓒ The first cities were located there.
Ⓓ Those places had very cold climates.

8. What do all the alphabets discussed in the text have in common?

Ⓐ They were all established in the same era.
Ⓑ They are important tools that allow people to write and communicate.
Ⓒ They all share some symbols and letters.
Ⓓ The alphabets in the text do not have anything in common.

SCORE

1. Ⓨ Ⓝ
2. Ⓨ Ⓝ
3. Ⓨ Ⓝ
4. Ⓨ Ⓝ
5. Ⓨ Ⓝ
6. Ⓨ Ⓝ
7. Ⓨ Ⓝ
8. Ⓨ Ⓝ

___ / 8
Total

NAME: ______________________________ **DATE:** ____________________

SCORE

___ / 4

DIRECTIONS

Reread "Alphabet Soup." Then, read the prompt and respond on the lines below.

Imagine you lived in Mesopotamia. What sort of writing would you invent? Create five or six symbols. Draw the symbols and explain what they mean.

NAME: ____________________ **DATE:** ______________

DIRECTIONS Read the text and then answer the questions.

Tyler enjoyed riding his bike almost more than anything else. Most of all, he liked the feeling of freedom it gave him. He didn't have to ask his parents for rides every time he wanted to go somewhere, and if he wanted to spend time with his friends after school, he didn't have to worry about missing the school bus. In fact, Tyler was riding his bike home from school one day when he got into an accident. He was two blocks from home when a car came out of a side street without stopping and knocked Tyler and his bicycle to the ground. The driver immediately stopped and rushed back to see if Tyler was hurt. Tyler was wearing his helmet, so the accident could have been much worse. But he broke his arm. There would be no bike riding for Tyler for several weeks to come.

1. How does Tyler break his arm?

Ⓐ Tyler runs his bike into a curb.

Ⓑ A car comes out of a side street and knocks Tyler over.

Ⓒ A bus pulls out of a parking space and knocks Tyler over.

Ⓓ Tyler tries a trick on his bike and falls off.

2. What does Tyler like most about riding his bike?

Ⓐ the time it saves him

Ⓑ the fact that his friends want a bike like his

Ⓒ the exercise he gets

Ⓓ the feeling of freedom it gives him

3. Which word tells you that the driver is in a hurry to see if Tyler is hurt?

Ⓐ back

Ⓑ stopped

Ⓒ rushed

Ⓓ driver

4. What does the adjective *side* tell readers about the street?

Ⓐ a small, less busy street

Ⓑ a major highway

Ⓒ the largest street in the area

Ⓓ very famous

5. Which expression means the same thing as *most of all*?

Ⓐ more than anything else

Ⓑ without stopping

Ⓒ could have been much worse

Ⓓ worry about

SCORE

1. Ⓨ Ⓝ

2. Ⓨ Ⓝ

3. Ⓨ Ⓝ

4. Ⓨ Ⓝ

5. Ⓨ Ⓝ

___ / 5
Total

NAME: ____________________ DATE: ____________

DIRECTIONS Read the text and then answer the questions.

SCORE

1. Ⓨ Ⓝ
2. Ⓨ Ⓝ
3. Ⓨ Ⓝ
4. Ⓨ Ⓝ
5. Ⓨ Ⓝ

___ / 5 Total

Tyler had gotten into an accident while riding his bicycle. He was going to be fine, but he'd broken his arm, so he wasn't going to be riding his bicycle any time soon. Tyler was a careful bike rider. He always wore his helmet—even on summer days when it made his scalp itch—and he always watched where he was going. That was part of what made him curious about how the accident had happened. He knew he'd been careful, and the driver of the car that struck him wasn't driving recklessly. So one afternoon, Tyler decided to try to figure out what had happened. He walked to the corner where the accident had occurred. All of a sudden, he realized the problem: there were no stop signs at that corner. The driver hadn't known that Tyler was coming and hadn't stopped because there was no stop sign.

1. What does Tyler want to know?

- (A) when he can ride his bike again
- (B) where to get a new bike
- (C) how his bike accident happened
- (D) who has a bike that he can borrow

2. According to Tyler, what caused the accident?

- (A) There is no stop sign at the corner where the accident happened.
- (B) Tyler was not watching where he was going.
- (C) The driver of the car was driving recklessly.
- (D) Tyler was not wearing his helmet.

3. Which word is an antonym for *reckless*?

- (A) careless
- (B) cautious
- (C) happy
- (D) curious

4. Which two words are synonyms?

- (A) *accident* and *happened*
- (B) *curious* and *careful*
- (C) *recklessly* and *carefully*
- (D) *happened* and *occurred*

5. What is the meaning of the phrase *figure out*?

- (A) request
- (B) hide
- (C) discover
- (D) refuse

NAME: ______________________ **DATE:** ______________

DIRECTIONS Read the text and then answer the questions.

Tyler had broken his arm in a bicycle accident at a corner near his home. A car had pulled out of a side street without stopping and knocked Tyler off of his bike. Tyler had discovered that there was no stop sign at that corner, and that was why the driver hadn't stopped. Tyler thought that if there had been a stop sign at the corner, the driver would have stopped and wouldn't have hit him. Tyler decided that he was going to do something about it. He was going to see if there could be a stop sign put up at that corner. That would make it safer for neighborhood kids to ride their bikes in that area. Tyler talked to his parents about his idea. He went online for information, too. He found out what he needed to do to get the city to put up a stop sign, and he got started.

1. What is the problem that Tyler wants to solve?

- (A) There is no place for cars to park in his neighborhood.
- (B) The drivers in his neighborhood drive too fast.
- (C) There are too many stop signs in his neighborhood.
- (D) It is not safe enough for kids to ride their bikes in his neighborhood.

2. How does Tyler plan to solve the problem?

- (A) He will try to get the city to put up a stop sign.
- (B) He will try to get drivers to stay away from his street.
- (C) He will stop riding his bike.
- (D) He will stop taking walks near his home.

3. Which prefix can be added to *safe* to make its antonym?

- (A) *sub–*
- (B) *un–*
- (C) *hyper–*
- (D) *–less*

4. What part of speech is the word *safer* in this text?

- (A) noun
- (B) verb
- (C) adjective
- (D) pronoun

5. What does the phrase *pulled out of* mean in this text?

- (A) removed
- (B) came from
- (C) added to
- (D) quit

SCORE

1. Ⓨ Ⓝ
2. Ⓨ Ⓝ
3. Ⓨ Ⓝ
4. Ⓨ Ⓝ
5. Ⓨ Ⓝ

___ / 5 Total

NAME: ______________________ **DATE:** ______________

STOPPING FOR SAFETY

Tyler had broken his arm in a bicycle accident. The accident happened when a car came out of a side street without stopping and knocked Tyler down. Tyler figured out that the reason the car didn't stop was that there was no stop sign at the corner where the accident happened. So he decided to try to get the city to put up a stop sign.

First, Tyler's parents helped him to write a petition to have a stop sign put up. Then, Tyler and his parents asked everyone they knew to sign the petition. They got their neighbors and friends to sign and asked those people to talk to other people. Tyler asked everyone at school to sign and to ask their parents to sign. He asked his teachers to sign the petition, too. Soon, there were hundreds of names on the petition.

Tyler also got some information about other accidents at the same corner where he'd had his own accident. If he could show the city that it was a dangerous corner, they might put up a stop sign there. He hoped that this information and his petition would work.

When the petition was ready, Tyler and his parents went to a meeting of the city council. They brought along the petition. They also brought the other information. After a long wait, Tyler got a chance to tell what had happened to him. He told the story of the bicycle accident. Then, he explained his idea. If there were a stop sign at the corner where the accident happened, other kids would be safer. After that, Tyler read the petition out loud. Then, he handed it and the other information to the council. The city council agreed to consider the request and make a decision before their next meeting.

The next month, there was another meeting of the city council. Tyler and his parents attended this meeting, too. The head of the city council announced that the city had decided to agree to the petition! There would be a stop sign on the corner where Tyler had his accident. Now other kids would be safer when they rode their bikes.

NAME: ____________________ **DATE:** ______________

DIRECTIONS Read "Stopping for Safety" and then answer the questions.

1. What is the first thing Tyler does to get a stop sign at the corner?

(A) He finds out about other accidents.
(B) He writes a petition for the stop sign.
(C) He and his parents give the petition to the members of the city council.
(D) He puts the stop sign on the corner.

2. Which words signal that this text is written in sequential order?

(A) *now* and *when*
(B) *first* and *then*
(C) *if* and *they might*
(D) *after* and *long wait*

3. What might have happened if Tyler had **not** had his accident?

(A) He would have broken his leg, too.
(B) He would not live in the same neighborhood.
(C) He would never learn to ride a bike.
(D) He would not have noticed the need for a stop sign.

4. Which is a reasonable purpose for reading this text?

(A) to find out how to get the city to put up a stop sign
(B) to find out how to stop safely on my bicycle
(C) to find out about speed limits
(D) to find out about safety stops for emergency vehicles

5. How will the other kids likely feel when the new stop sign is put up?

(A) confused
(B) angry
(C) jealous
(D) grateful

6. Which inference makes the most sense?

(A) Tyler's parents agree with him.
(B) Tyler's mom and dad do not want the new stop sign.
(C) Tyler's parents do not know about Tyler's idea.
(D) Tyler's mom and dad think kids should not ride bikes.

7. What does the information about other accidents on that corner show?

(A) that the corner does not need a stop sign
(B) that it is a dangerous corner
(C) that Tyler does not ride his bike safely
(D) that the city needs a new street

8. What does the text tell a reader?

(A) Stop signs should be put on every corner.
(B) Adults are the only ones who can change anything.
(C) Kids can make a positive change in their neighborhoods.
(D) Kids should not ride their bikes.

SCORE

1. Ⓨ Ⓝ
2. Ⓨ Ⓝ
3. Ⓨ Ⓝ
4. Ⓨ Ⓝ
5. Ⓨ Ⓝ
6. Ⓨ Ⓝ
7. Ⓨ Ⓝ
8. Ⓨ Ⓝ

___ / 8
Total

NAME: ______________________ DATE: ______________

SCORE

___ / 4

DIRECTIONS

Reread "Stopping for Safety." Then, read the prompt and respond on the lines below.

What change would you like to see in your town or city? Write about the change you want and why it is important.

NAME: ______________________ **DATE:** ______________

DIRECTIONS Read the text and then answer the questions.

Hundreds of years ago, people from Europe explored North America. They thought they had found a new land. They thought nobody else lived in North America. But they were wrong. Many people already lived in North America. We call those native people American Indians. Different groups of American Indians lived in different places. Each group had its own language and its own way of life. Each group was a little different from the other groups. Today, there are still several groups of American Indians called *nations*. They live in different regions of the United States. Each American Indian nation still has its own ways of life and its own language. Some nations have their own schools, too, where kids learn the language of their nation.

1. Which of these sentences is a fact?

Ⓐ There are several different American Indian nations.

Ⓑ American Indians do not live in the United States.

Ⓒ Nobody lived in North America hundreds of years ago.

Ⓓ All American Indians speak the same language.

2. Which title would be a good fit for this text?

Ⓐ Facts About American Indians

Ⓑ Groupings in America

Ⓒ New Lands

Ⓓ Countries

3. Which word is a synonym for *region*?

Ⓐ city

Ⓑ house

Ⓒ area

Ⓓ country

4. What does the adjective *native* mean?

Ⓐ explorer

Ⓑ born in a place

Ⓒ region

Ⓓ a small nation

5. Which phrases indicate that this text describes both the present and the past?

Ⓐ *own language* and *own way of life*

Ⓑ *different groups* and *different places*

Ⓒ *hundreds of years ago* and *today*

Ⓓ *some* and *too*

SCORE

1. Ⓨ Ⓝ

2. Ⓨ Ⓝ

3. Ⓨ Ⓝ

4. Ⓨ Ⓝ

5. Ⓨ Ⓝ

___ / 5
Total

NAME: ____________________ DATE: ______________

DIRECTIONS Read the text and then answer the questions.

SCORE

1. Ⓨ Ⓝ
2. Ⓨ Ⓝ
3. Ⓨ Ⓝ
4. Ⓨ Ⓝ
5. Ⓨ Ⓝ

___ / 5 Total

One American Indian nation is called the *Navajo Nation*. Most Navajo live in the Southwest. One part of the Navajo reservation is in Arizona and another part is in New Mexico. There are also parts in Colorado and in Utah. Some Navajo live in cities, and some live on the reservation. Some Navajo live in houses called *hogans*. Hogans are usually round, but they can also be square. The door of a hogan faces east. Navajo believe that a house should face the rising sun. Many Navajo speak their own language. It is a very different language from English. Some Navajo kids go to Navajo schools. In those schools, they learn the same things you are learning, but they learn other things, too. They also learn their own language and they learn Navajo ways of life.

1. According to this text, where do most Navajo live?

- Ⓐ the Northwest
- Ⓑ the Southwest
- Ⓒ Florida
- Ⓓ New York City

2. Which is **not** a subject that kids learn in Navajo schools?

- Ⓐ nursing
- Ⓑ the Navajo language
- Ⓒ math
- Ⓓ Navajo ways of life

3. Which word is defined as a *Navajo house*?

- Ⓐ nation
- Ⓑ reservation
- Ⓒ hogan
- Ⓓ Navajo

4. What part of speech is the word *Navajo*?

- Ⓐ an adjective
- Ⓑ a proper noun
- Ⓒ a pronoun
- Ⓓ a verb

5. What does it mean for a door to *face* a certain direction?

- Ⓐ It points in that direction.
- Ⓑ It has a face on it.
- Ⓒ It is in the front of a structure.
- Ⓓ It is in the back of a structure.

NAME: ____________________ **DATE:** ____________

DIRECTIONS Read the text and then answer the questions.

The Navajo people call themselves the *Diné* (dee-NEH). That means "the people" in Navajo. Nobody knows just when the Navajo came to the Southwest. But they have been there for hundreds of years. After they arrived, the Navajo learned several skills. They learned to tend sheep—in fact, they have become expert shepherds. They learned to weave, too. Many Navajo still practice this traditional skill. The Navajo also became skilled at riding. They got involved in rodeos, too. Some of today's Navajo still take part in rodeo riding, and they are experts at rodeo skills. In 1864, the Navajo were forced to leave their homes and travel to Fort Sumner, New Mexico. The Navajo call that terrible trip *The Long Walk*. They were kept at Fort Sumner for four years. In 1868, the Navajo who were still alive returned to their homes.

1. What is this text mostly about?

Ⓐ the Southwest
Ⓑ The Long Walk
Ⓒ weaving
Ⓓ the Navajo people

2. What is *The Long Walk*?

Ⓐ the forced move of the Navajo to Fort Sumner, New Mexico
Ⓑ the coming of the Navajo to the Southwest
Ⓒ the way the Navajo learned to tend sheep
Ⓓ the way the Navajo built their homes

3. What is the Navajo word for *the people*?

Ⓐ Fort Sumner
Ⓑ Navajo
Ⓒ Diné
Ⓓ Mexico

4. Which two words are synonyms?

Ⓐ *expert* and *skilled*
Ⓑ *expert* and *shepherds*
Ⓒ *rodeo* and *riding*
Ⓓ *tend* and *weave*

5. What makes a skill *traditional*?

Ⓐ It is handed down by ancestors.
Ⓑ It is challenging.
Ⓒ It has to do with sheep.
Ⓓ It is performed at the rodeo.

SCORE

1. Ⓨ Ⓝ
2. Ⓨ Ⓝ
3. Ⓨ Ⓝ
4. Ⓨ Ⓝ
5. Ⓨ Ⓝ

___ / 5 Total

NAME: ______________________________ **DATE:** ________________

CODE TALKERS

Have you ever made up a secret code? Codes let people communicate in a special way. The only people who can understand messages in code are people who know that code. During World War II, America needed a special code. Soldiers needed to send messages, but they did not want the enemy to know what those messages were. So America needed a secret code. American soldiers would know the code, but enemy soldiers would not. The Navajo people turned out to be the solution.

The Navajo language is not easy to understand, and not many people speak that language. So 29 Navajo soldiers used their language to make up a special code using Navajo words. When the code was ready, they used it and taught it to other soldiers. People who knew the code could understand messages that were in that code, but people who didn't know the code would not know what the messages meant. This group of people who used the code had a special name: they were called Code Talkers. Code Talkers were able to send important messages that had to be secret. For example, they could let everyone know when there would be an attack. They could let others know where the enemy was hiding. That was important information, and it helped America during the war. In fact, this code remains the only unbroken code in modern history.

When the war ended, the Code Talkers returned to their homes. They were welcomed home as heroes. But most people did not know about them because the code was so secret that nobody could know about it. It wasn't until the 1960s that anybody knew about the Code Talkers. Today, we know how important they were. We even know some of the code they used. Here is an example: The Navajo word for *turtle* is *ch'ééh digháhii* (ch-AY da-GAH-hee). A tank looks a little like a turtle, so when the Code Talkers wanted to send a message about tanks, they said *ch'ééh-digháhii*. Now you know some of the code, too!

Navajo Code Talkers

NAME: ______________________ DATE: ______________

DIRECTIONS Read "Code Talkers" and then answer the questions.

1. Why was Navajo a good choice for a code language?

- (A) It has more words than any other language.
- (B) It has very few words in it.
- (C) It is one of the most popular languages.
- (D) It is hard to learn, and not many people speak it.

2. Why does the author include the pronunciation for *ch'ééh digháhii*?

- (A) It is just like English.
- (B) It is a difficult word to pronounce.
- (C) It is not an important word.
- (D) It is a nonsense word.

3. If you made up a code, what would you have to do?

- (A) Tell everybody about it.
- (B) Tell people about it only if you wanted them to know.
- (C) Make a code that everyone could not understand.
- (D) Make a code that you would forget easily.

4. How did the Code Talkers likely feel about what they did during the war?

- (A) jealous
- (B) angry
- (C) unsure
- (D) proud

5. What is a reasonable purpose for reading this?

- (A) to read a personal story
- (B) to learn the Navajo language
- (C) to learn about the Code Talkers
- (D) to learn the story of World War II

6. What is the author's likely opinion about Code Talkers?

- (A) They were very brave.
- (B) They were boring.
- (C) They were not important.
- (D) They were not very helpful.

7. Why were Code Talkers effective in the war?

- (A) Very few people knew the code.
- (B) The Code Talkers told everybody they knew what the code was.
- (C) The code was very easy to learn.
- (D) The Code Talkers did not speak much Navajo.

8. Which description of Code Talkers makes the most sense?

- (A) heroes who helped their countries
- (B) traitors who gave away secrets
- (C) people who were difficult to understand
- (D) smart people who could speak to anyone

SCORE

1. Ⓨ Ⓝ
2. Ⓨ Ⓝ
3. Ⓨ Ⓝ
4. Ⓨ Ⓝ
5. Ⓨ Ⓝ
6. Ⓨ Ⓝ
7. Ⓨ Ⓝ
8. Ⓨ Ⓝ

___ / 8
Total

NAME: ______________________________ DATE: ____________________

DIRECTIONS

Reread "Code Talkers." Then, read the prompt and respond on the lines below.

SCORE

___ / 4

If you wanted to send a message in code, how would you do it? Make up your own code and write a word or two in that code. Then, explain how the code works.

NAME: ______________________ **DATE:** ______________

DIRECTIONS Read the text and then answer the questions.

Naomi took a long, critical look at herself in the mirror. This was going to be her first day at her new school, and she wanted to make the perfect first impression. She finally decided she was satisfied with her appearance and got her things together for school. She loaded up her backpack, carried it downstairs, and dropped it by the front door. Then, she went into the kitchen to get some breakfast. There was her mom, sipping her coffee, wearing those boring old clothes. Naomi wished her mom wasn't going to drop her off at school, but she had insisted on driving Naomi for her first day. Well, at least she wasn't going to get out of the car. It was embarrassing enough that she was even going to be there.

1. What is Naomi's problem?

- (A) She does not have a backpack.
- (B) There is nothing to eat for breakfast.
- (C) Her mom will not drive her to school.
- (D) Her mom insists on driving her to school.

2. Why doesn't Naomi want her mom to drop her off?

- (A) She is embarrassed.
- (B) Naomi's mom does not know the way to school.
- (C) Naomi is very angry with her mom.
- (D) Naomi's mom does not want to drive her.

3. Which prefix can be added to the word *satisfied* to make its antonym?

- (A) *–less*
- (B) *sub–*
- (C) *dis–*
- (D) *hyper–*

4. What does the verb *sipping* tell the reader?

- (A) Naomi's mom is not drinking anything.
- (B) Naomi's mom is drinking her coffee quickly.
- (C) Naomi's mom is drinking her coffee slowly.
- (D) Naomi's mom is not at home.

5. What is the meaning of the word *impression* in this story?

- (A) idea
- (B) impact or effect
- (C) dent or mark
- (D) imitation

SCORE

1. Ⓨ Ⓝ
2. Ⓨ Ⓝ
3. Ⓨ Ⓝ
4. Ⓨ Ⓝ
5. Ⓨ Ⓝ

___ / 5 Total

NAME: ______________________________ **DATE:** ________________

DIRECTIONS Read the text and then answer the questions.

SCORE

1. Ⓨ Ⓝ

2. Ⓨ Ⓝ

3. Ⓨ Ⓝ

4. Ⓨ Ⓝ

5. Ⓨ Ⓝ

___ / 5
Total

Naomi and her mom slowly pulled up to Naomi's new school. Naomi looked around her anxiously and then glanced over at her mom out of the corner of her eye. Why did her mom have to wear that stupid sweater and those jeans? Couldn't she wear something at least a *little* less embarrassing? Naomi hunched down in her seat and muttered, "This is fine, Mom. Just stop here." She grabbed her backpack and hurtled out of the car as quickly as she could, not noticing that a notebook had fallen out of her backpack. She quickly headed toward the door of the school without looking behind her. She hadn't even responded to her mother's "Hope it goes well!" Nervously, Naomi looked around her. Nobody seemed to have noticed her getting out of the car. Maybe she'd survive her first day at this school after all.

1. Where does most of this text take place?

Ⓐ in the supermarket
Ⓑ outside Naomi's house
Ⓒ in the car
Ⓓ at the library

2. How does Naomi feel about her mom driving her to school?

Ⓐ proud
Ⓑ embarrassed
Ⓒ curious
Ⓓ excited

3. What tone of voice is used by someone who *mutters*?

Ⓐ excited
Ⓑ happy
Ⓒ very loud
Ⓓ low

4. Which part of speech is the word *slowly*?

Ⓐ verb
Ⓑ noun
Ⓒ adverb
Ⓓ adjective

5. Which is **not** an example of alliteration?

Ⓐ little less
Ⓑ stupid sweater
Ⓒ not noticing
Ⓓ slowly pulled

NAME: ______________________________ **DATE:** ________________

DIRECTIONS Read the text and then answer the questions.

It was Naomi's first day in her new school, and so far, it wasn't going too terribly. She had only gotten lost once, and she had gotten out of that situation without having to ask anyone for help. Then, everything fell apart. Naomi was on her way from math class to lunch when she heard a familiar voice calling her name. What was her mom doing here? Naomi wanted more than anything to ignore her mother, but she knew she couldn't. So she rushed up to her mother and hissed, "What are you doing here?"

Her mom answered evenly, "I wanted to give you your notebook. You left it in the car." Everyone seemed to be staring at Naomi as she silently took the notebook. She wished the floor would swallow her up. She turned away without saying anything and fled to the cafeteria.

1. Why is Naomi's mom at her school?

- (A) She wants to talk to Naomi's teacher.
- (B) She forgot something at the school.
- (C) She is lost and needs directions.
- (D) She wants to give Naomi her notebook.

2. How does Naomi feel about her mom bringing her notebook?

- (A) embarrassed
- (B) grateful
- (C) excited
- (D) jealous

3. What does the word *hissed* tell readers about Naomi's tone of voice?

- (A) It is very loud.
- (B) It is happy.
- (C) It is low and angry.
- (D) It is musical.

4. Which verb means the same as the word *fled*?

- (A) crawled
- (B) skipped
- (C) escaped
- (D) slept

5. What is the following sentence an example of: *She wished the floor would swallow her up.*

- (A) simile
- (B) personification
- (C) alliteration
- (D) metaphor

SCORE

1. Ⓨ Ⓝ
2. Ⓨ Ⓝ
3. Ⓨ Ⓝ
4. Ⓨ Ⓝ
5. Ⓨ Ⓝ

___ / 5 Total

NAME:_______________ DATE:_______________

WHAT REALLY MATTERS

Naomi was more embarrassed than she had ever been before. It was her first day in a new school, and already her mom had completely ruined it by coming to the school. Not only had she come into the school, but she was also wearing that stupid sweater and those ridiculous jeans. How could she do that to Naomi? Didn't she know that Naomi was nervous enough about starting in a new school? This was so unfair! Naomi sat miserably in the cafeteria. Nobody came near her, and it was easy to see why: Everyone was probably already laughing at her.

Just when Naomi thought things couldn't get any more humiliating, a girl came up to her and said, "You're new here, aren't you?"

"Yeah," Naomi murmured, "I am."

"I didn't think I recognized you when I saw you in math class before. I'm Emily, by the way."

"I'm Naomi," Naomi responded almost in disbelief. This girl was actually talking to her! After a moment of stunned silence, Naomi haltingly invited Emily to sit down.

Emily plopped down at the table and then continued, "I saw you in the hall just now, too. Was that your mom with you?"

Naomi cringed with embarrassment at that question. Of all the things Emily could have noticed, it had to be that. Unable to say anything, she just nodded.

"You're so amazingly lucky," Emily responded. "My mom doesn't even live with me. I haven't talked to her in forever."

Suddenly everything seemed different to Naomi. Not see your mom every day? Not have her there when you get home from school? That would be even more horrible than having your mom embarrass you publicly. "I'm sorry," she finally said quietly.

For the rest of lunch, the two girls chatted, and by the time lunch was over, they had decided they liked each other. On her way to her next class, Naomi promised Emily she would have lunch with her again tomorrow. And she promised herself she would apologize to her mom later, too.

NAME: ______________________ **DATE:** ______________

DIRECTIONS Read "What Really Matters" and then answer the questions.

1. How does Naomi feel about her new school when she first arrives?

- (A) nervous
- (B) happy
- (C) confused
- (D) exhausted

2. Why does Emily say that Naomi is lucky?

- (A) Naomi's mom lets her do whatever she wants.
- (B) Naomi has a lot of money.
- (C) Naomi doesn't live with her mother.
- (D) Naomi gets to live with her mom.

3. What might happen when Naomi gets home from school?

- (A) She will not speak to her mom.
- (B) She will apologize to her mom.
- (C) She will go to school.
- (D) She will beg to stay home from school.

4. What is a reason for reading this text?

- (A) to find out how to prioritize things
- (B) to learn about science topics
- (C) to consider important priorities in life
- (D) to find out important business ideas

5. From what point of view is this story told?

- (A) third person
- (B) first person
- (C) second person
- (D) There is no point of view.

6. How does Naomi probably feel when Emily says that she is lucky?

- (A) She is furious.
- (B) She is jealous.
- (C) She is surprised.
- (D) She is exhausted.

7. Why does everything seem different to Naomi when she talks to Emily?

- (A) She learns that Emily did not notice her mom.
- (B) She realizes that some people don't get to live with their mothers.
- (C) She finds out that Emily won't speak to her.
- (D) She finds out that she is going to the wrong school.

8. Why is Naomi so surprised at what Emily says to her?

- (A) She and Emily are having a fight.
- (B) She is sitting with her mom.
- (C) She thinks Emily will embarrass her about her mom, but Emily doesn't.
- (D) She thinks Emily is too shy to talk to her.

SCORE

1. Ⓨ Ⓝ
2. Ⓨ Ⓝ
3. Ⓨ Ⓝ
4. Ⓨ Ⓝ
5. Ⓨ Ⓝ
6. Ⓨ Ⓝ
7. Ⓨ Ⓝ
8. Ⓨ Ⓝ

___ / 8
Total

NAME: ______________________ DATE: ______________

DIRECTIONS Reread "What Really Matters." Then, read the prompt and respond on the lines below.

SCORE
___ / 4

Describe a time when something embarrassing happened to you. How did you deal with it? Write about how you coped with being embarrassed.

NAME: ______________________ **DATE:** ______________

DIRECTIONS Read the text and then answer the questions.

No matter where on Earth you live, you have day and night. That happens because of a movement of Earth called *rotation*. Earth rotates, or turns, on an imaginary line called an *axis*. Imagine a line that starts at the North Pole and goes straight through Earth to the South Pole. That is Earth's axis. About every 24 hours, Earth rotates around that axis. To get an idea of how the Earth rotates, try this. Spin a basketball around, and you will see that it spins around in a circle. The basketball is rotating around its axis, just as Earth rotates around its axis. You see daylight when your part of Earth is facing the sun. You see darkness when Earth has turned so that your part of Earth faces away from the sun.

1. What is this text mostly about?

- (A) the North Pole
- (B) what it is like at night
- (C) how Earth turns on its axis
- (D) basketball

2. According to the facts in this text, when do people see daylight?

- (A) when part of Earth is facing the sun
- (B) when people see darkness
- (C) when part of Earth is facing away from the sun
- (D) when people see the South Pole

3. Which word is a synonym for *rotate*?

- (A) imaginary
- (B) the North Pole
- (C) axis
- (D) turn

4. What verb is used to describe Earth's movement around its axis?

- (A) the South Pole
- (B) an axis
- (C) rotation
- (D) darkness

5. What does the phrase *to get an idea* mean in this text?

- (A) to visualize something
- (B) to speak something
- (C) to try something
- (D) to learn something

SCORE

1. (Y)(N)

2. (Y)(N)

3. (Y)(N)

4. (Y)(N)

5. (Y)(N)

___ / 5
Total

NAME: ____________________ **DATE:** ______________

DIRECTIONS Read the text and then answer the questions.

SCORE

1. Ⓨ Ⓝ
2. Ⓨ Ⓝ
3. Ⓨ Ⓝ
4. Ⓨ Ⓝ
5. Ⓨ Ⓝ

___ / 5 Total

Our Earth does not just rotate on its axis. It also revolves, or turns, around the sun. Earth revolves around the sun because of the sun's gravity. That gravity pulls Earth toward the sun. But Earth is far away from the sun—it is about 93 million miles away. So Earth's revolutions do not happen quickly. Each revolution of Earth around the sun takes about 365 days, or one year. The path that Earth takes around the sun is called its *orbit*. You might think of that path as a circle, but actually, it isn't a perfect circle. Earth's orbit is oval, much like the shape of an egg. Earth rotates and revolves, but you do not feel that motion because you rotate and revolve with the planet.

1. What is this text mostly about?

Ⓐ how Earth was formed
Ⓑ how Earth moves around the sun
Ⓒ what an axis is
Ⓓ where the planets are located

2. Why do we **not** feel Earth's motion?

Ⓐ because we are not moving
Ⓑ because Earth does not move
Ⓒ because Earth takes many years to revolve around the sun
Ⓓ because we are moving at the same speed as Earth

3. Which word is defined as *Earth's path around the sun*?

Ⓐ axis
Ⓑ rotation
Ⓒ orbit
Ⓓ gravity

4. Which verb means the same as *turns*?

Ⓐ revolves
Ⓑ axis
Ⓒ pulls
Ⓓ gravity

5. Which word means *the force that pulls Earth toward the sun*?

Ⓐ gravity
Ⓑ axis
Ⓒ rotation
Ⓓ revolution

NAME: ______________________ **DATE:** ______________

DIRECTIONS Read the text and then answer the questions.

Our Earth has seasons because of the tilt of Earth's axis. Remember that Earth rotates on its axis, and that is why we have day and night. But that axis does not go straight up and down; it is slightly tilted. So as Earth revolves around the sun, different parts of Earth are tilted toward the sun and get more sunlight. For example, in June, July, and August, the Northern Hemisphere is tilted toward the sun. So people who live there have longer days and warmer weather—it is summer there. But people in the Southern Hemisphere have winter at that time. During December, January, and February, the opposite happens—the Southern Hemisphere is tilted toward the sun. So it gets longer days and warmer weather. Those are summer months there. But people in the Northern Hemisphere have winter at that time.

1. According to this text, what causes seasons?

Ⓐ the Southern Hemisphere
Ⓑ Earth's revolution
Ⓒ the Northern Hemisphere
Ⓓ the tilt of Earth's axis

2. What is true about December, January, and February?

Ⓐ It is summer in the Southern Hemisphere.
Ⓑ It is winter in the Southern Hemisphere.
Ⓒ There is more sunlight in the Northern Hemisphere.
Ⓓ There is no sunlight at all anywhere on Earth.

3. What is the definition of *tilted*?

Ⓐ straight
Ⓑ slanted
Ⓒ tiny
Ⓓ important

4. Which of the following words is used as a verb in the text?

Ⓐ sunlight
Ⓑ people
Ⓒ tilted
Ⓓ warmer

5. What meaning do both *revolution* and *rotation* share?

Ⓐ warms
Ⓑ grows
Ⓒ turns
Ⓓ cools

SCORE

1. Ⓨ Ⓝ
2. Ⓨ Ⓝ
3. Ⓨ Ⓝ
4. Ⓨ Ⓝ
5. Ⓨ Ⓝ

___ / 5
Total

NAME: ______________________ **DATE:** ______________

THE PLANETS GET MOVING

the Solar System

Earth is not the only planet in the solar system that moves. All of the planets do that. The sun's gravity is very strong, so it pulls all of the planets toward it. That is why all of the planets revolve around the sun. And each planet rotates on its own axis, too. But there are many differences in the way the planets rotate and revolve.

Each planet takes a different amount of time to travel around the sun. The chart tells you how long it takes each planet to do that. Look at the amount of time each planet needs to go around the sun. Do you notice any pattern in those times? Here is a hint: Mercury is the closest planet to the sun, and Neptune is the most distant planet. The closer a planet is to the sun, the less time it takes to travel around the sun. Each planet also takes a different amount of time to rotate on its axis. The chart shows you that information.

Here are a few interesting things about the planets. Uranus and Venus are the only two planets that rotate backward. Every other planet, including Earth, rotates in the other direction. Also, Uranus does not have a vertical axis the way Earth does. Its axis is horizontal. So it rotates on its side! Venus has the slowest rotation. A rotation takes longer than a revolution does. Why don't Venus and Uranus move the way the other planets do? Many scientists have a theory about that. They think that a large asteroid might have hit those planets millions of years ago. A hit like that could change a planet's rotation. Then, the planet might rotate in the other direction. It could also make a planet rotate on its side.

Planet	Revolution in Earth Time	Rotation
Mercury	88 days	59 days
Venus	225 days	243 days
Earth	365 days	24 hours
Mars	687 days	26 hours
Jupiter	12 years	10 hours
Saturn	29 years	10 hours
Uranus	84 years	18 hours
Neptune	164 years	19 hours

NAME: ______________________ DATE: ______________

DIRECTIONS Read "The Planets Get Moving" and then answer the questions.

1. The chart shows which planets have the same rotation time?

- Ⓐ Jupiter and Venus
- Ⓑ Earth and Venus
- Ⓒ Saturn and Mercury
- Ⓓ Jupiter and Saturn

2. Which of these planets has the shortest rotation time?

- Ⓐ Jupiter
- Ⓑ Venus
- Ⓒ Mercury
- Ⓓ Uranus

3. If there were a planet closer to the sun than Mercury, it would likely

- Ⓐ be much bigger than Mercury.
- Ⓑ take more time to travel around the sun than Mercury does.
- Ⓒ be the same size as Mercury.
- Ⓓ take less time to travel around the sun than Mercury does.

4. Why do scientists think Venus and Uranus move differently than the other planets do?

- Ⓐ They are the largest planets in our solar system.
- Ⓑ They are both very small planets.
- Ⓒ They may have been hit by an asteroid.
- Ⓓ They are very close together.

5. What is a reason for reading this text?

- Ⓐ to learn how the planets move
- Ⓑ to decide to become a scientist
- Ⓒ to read a personal story
- Ⓓ to learn how asteroids are formed

6. Why does Neptune take longer to go around the sun than Earth does?

- Ⓐ It is farther from the sun than Earth.
- Ⓑ It is much larger than Earth.
- Ⓒ It is closer to the sun than Earth.
- Ⓓ It is much smaller than Earth.

7. How are all the planets in the solar system alike?

- Ⓐ They all revolve around the sun.
- Ⓑ They rotate on a horizontal axis.
- Ⓒ They all rotate at the same speed.
- Ⓓ They all have a vertical axis.

8. What does it mean for a planet to be farther from the sun?

- Ⓐ It takes a planet longer to travel around the sun.
- Ⓑ It takes a planet a shorter time to travel around the sun.
- Ⓒ It takes a planet the same time as closer planets to travel around the sun.
- Ⓓ The planet is unable to travel around the sun.

SCORE

1. Ⓨ Ⓝ
2. Ⓨ Ⓝ
3. Ⓨ Ⓝ
4. Ⓨ Ⓝ
5. Ⓨ Ⓝ
6. Ⓨ Ⓝ
7. Ⓨ Ⓝ
8. Ⓨ Ⓝ

___ / 8 Total

NAME: ______________________ DATE: ______________

SCORE

___ /4

DIRECTIONS Reread "The Planets Get Moving." Then, read the prompt and respond on the lines below.

What do you think it would be like if Earth were as far away from the sun as Jupiter is? What would happen to its revolution? Would its rotation change? Explain your answer.

NAME: ____________________ **DATE:** ______________

DIRECTIONS Read the text and then answer the questions.

There I was one afternoon, getting ready to play my new video game. I was really excited about it. I had saved my allowance for a month, and yesterday, I finally had enough money to buy it. I put the game into the game system, and at first, the game looked as though it was loading up. All of a sudden, though, everything stopped! I pushed a few buttons, but the game system stared stubbornly at me, daring me to make it work. I managed to unload the game itself, but that didn't help very much. My game system seemed to be completely dead. I yelled for my big brother, Cody, to come and help me, but he took one look at the game system and said, "Justin, you're out of luck. This system is gone. You'll have to get another one."

1. Who is the narrator in this text?

Ⓐ Dad
Ⓑ Cody
Ⓒ Justin
Ⓓ Mom

2. What is the main problem?

Ⓐ Justin cannot get a new game.
Ⓑ Justin's game system is broken.
Ⓒ Cody takes Justin's game system.
Ⓓ Justin takes Cody's game system.

3. What does Cody mean when he says Justin is *out of luck*?

Ⓐ Justin cannot use his game system.
Ⓑ He wishes he had Justin's game system.
Ⓒ He will fix Justin's game system.
Ⓓ Justin is lucky to have his game system.

4. In this text, what does the adjective *gone* mean?

Ⓐ broken
Ⓑ disappeared
Ⓒ difficult
Ⓓ interesting

5. What is this phrase an example of: *The game system stared stubbornly at me, daring me to make it work.*

Ⓐ simile
Ⓑ rhyming
Ⓒ metaphor
Ⓓ personification

SCORE

1. Ⓨ Ⓝ
2. Ⓨ Ⓝ
3. Ⓨ Ⓝ
4. Ⓨ Ⓝ
5. Ⓨ Ⓝ

___ / 5 Total

NAME: ______________________ **DATE:** ______________

DIRECTIONS Read the text and then answer the questions.

SCORE

1. Ⓨ Ⓝ
2. Ⓨ Ⓝ
3. Ⓨ Ⓝ
4. Ⓨ Ⓝ
5. Ⓨ Ⓝ

___ / 5 Total

My game system was completely broken and wouldn't work at all. I couldn't remember exactly when I'd bought it, but I didn't think it was very long ago, so Dad suggested I try to get it replaced. He said it might still be under warranty, and if it were, then I could exchange it for a new game system. I was hoping Dad was right—good game systems are expensive, and I didn't want to have to save up my money for months. So I took my system back to the store where I'd bought it. The manager looked up my purchase. He said, "I'm sorry, Justin, but you actually bought this 14 months ago, and the warranty only lasted for 12 months. So you won't be able to get a replacement system unless you purchase a new one." I was running out of options fast!

1. What does Justin's dad suggest?

Ⓐ He suggests that Justin save up his money and buy a new system.

Ⓑ He suggests that Justin try to exchange his broken game system.

Ⓒ He suggests that Justin stop playing video games.

Ⓓ He suggests that Justin look for new video games to try.

2. What does Justin find out when he goes to the store?

Ⓐ He will not be able to shop at that store any more.

Ⓑ He will be able to get a free replacement system.

Ⓒ He will have to buy three new video games.

Ⓓ He cannot get a replacement system unless he buys a new one.

3. Which word describes a promise that if something breaks, it will be replaced?

Ⓐ warranty

Ⓑ game system

Ⓒ replacement

Ⓓ exchange

4. Which two words are synonyms and the same parts of speech?

Ⓐ replacement, warranty

Ⓑ warranty, system

Ⓒ bought, purchased

Ⓓ purchase, option

5. What is the tone of the text?

Ⓐ informational

Ⓑ anxious

Ⓒ persuasive

Ⓓ passive

NAME: ______________________ **DATE:** ______________

DIRECTIONS Read the text and then answer the questions.

My game system was broken and couldn't be repaired. I had also found out that the warranty on it ended, so I couldn't get it replaced unless I bought a new one. But that was the problem—I didn't have the money for a new one. Mom and Dad gave me an allowance every week, but I would have to save for a few months if I were going to get the kind of system I wanted. I didn't want to wait that long, and I knew Mom and Dad wouldn't just buy me a new game system—not unless it was my birthday, which it wasn't. I complained about it all to my brother Cody—maybe he would have an idea. Cody suggested, "You could get some kind of job, Justin. That way, you could earn the money for the game system."

1. What is Justin's problem?

- (A) He doesn't have the money for a new game system.
- (B) Cody took his game system.
- (C) His mom and dad will not let him have a game system.
- (D) He does not want to use his game system.

2. What suggestion does Cody make?

- (A) Justin should ask his mom and dad for a new game system.
- (B) Justin should stop playing video games.
- (C) Justin should get a job to earn money for a game system.
- (D) Justin should ask his friends to let him use their game systems.

3. Which word is a synonym for *repaired*?

- (A) purchased
- (B) replaced
- (C) destroyed
- (D) fixed

4. Which noun has the same meaning as *allowance*?

- (A) meals
- (B) direction
- (C) pocket money
- (D) special permission

5. What does the word *complained* reveal about Justin?

- (A) He is excited.
- (B) He is unhappy.
- (C) He is proud.
- (D) He is hopeful.

SCORE

1. Ⓨ Ⓝ
2. Ⓨ Ⓝ
3. Ⓨ Ⓝ
4. Ⓨ Ⓝ
5. Ⓨ Ⓝ

___ / 5
Total

NAME: ______________________ **DATE:** ______________

GETTING INTO THE GAME

My game system was broken and couldn't be repaired, and I didn't have enough money to buy a new one. The only solution I could think of was to earn some extra money. I tried to come up with some good ideas for a job—that was what my brother Cody had suggested. One morning, I was staring out my window wondering what sort of job a kid my age could get, when something I noticed gave me an inspiration.

My neighbor, Mr. Drummond, was wheeling his garbage barrel out to the curb. Mr. Drummond was elderly, and I could tell he was struggling to move his garbage barrel. I sprinted downstairs and outside, dashed across the street, and offered to move Mr. Drummond's trash to the curb. He was very grateful. After he thanked me, I decided to discuss my inspiration with him. "I'm trying to earn some extra money," I explained, "and I'm just wondering whether people would be interested in having me do chores."

"Well, I certainly would, Justin," Mr. Drummond answered. "There are several things that are more difficult for me now that I'm getting on in years, and it'd be helpful to have a young person around to do those jobs. I wouldn't be surprised if there are other people my age in the same situation."

I decided to take Mr. Drummond's suggestion about helping elderly people, and I visited some of my other neighbors. It turned out that Mr. Drummond was right. A lot of them were interested in having someone come around to do chores. I made up a schedule of people to visit and chores they wanted me to do, and started working. At first, it was exhausting, but before long, I got accustomed to it. Within a month, I'd earned enough money to get my new game system, and that made me very happy. And a lot of people in the neighborhood were getting the help they needed. That made me happy, too. I guess having a broken game system wasn't so awful.

NAME: ____________________ DATE: ____________

DIRECTIONS Read "Getting Into the Game" and then answer the questions.

1. Which prediction about the text is most relevant?

Ⓐ Justin will stop talking to his neighbors.
Ⓑ Justin will stop playing video games.
Ⓒ Justin will never speak to Mr. Drummond again.
Ⓓ Justin will keep doing chores for people.

2. Why does Justin want to earn money?

Ⓐ Mr. Drummond needs help with his trash.
Ⓑ He wants to help people who need someone to do chores.
Ⓒ He wants to buy a new bicycle.
Ⓓ His game system is broken, and he wants to buy a new one.

3. What do you think Mr. Drummond will do the next time he needs someone to do a chore?

Ⓐ He will hire Justin to do the work.
Ⓑ He will do the chore himself.
Ⓒ He will not know what he should do.
Ⓓ He will call a friend his age for help.

4. What can be inferred about Mr. Drummond's garbage barrel?

Ⓐ It is heavy.
Ⓑ It is very light.
Ⓒ It is easy to move.
Ⓓ It is brand-new.

5. Which point of view does this text use?

Ⓐ first person
Ⓑ second person
Ⓒ third person
Ⓓ There is no point of view.

6. How do Justin's parents likely feel about the solution to his problem?

Ⓐ worried
Ⓑ pleased
Ⓒ unhappy
Ⓓ angry

7. How does Justin solve the problem of his broken game system?

Ⓐ He fixes the game system.
Ⓑ He asks his parents for the money to buy a new game system.
Ⓒ He does chores for people in the neighborhood to earn money.
Ⓓ He decides he doesn't want a game system after all.

8. What is the theme of this text?

Ⓐ Money is the best reward.
Ⓑ Video games are very fun and entertaining.
Ⓒ Hard work and helping others can be very rewarding.
Ⓓ Justin's parents gave him the money for the new system.

SCORE

1. Ⓨ Ⓝ
2. Ⓨ Ⓝ
3. Ⓨ Ⓝ
4. Ⓨ Ⓝ
5. Ⓨ Ⓝ
6. Ⓨ Ⓝ
7. Ⓨ Ⓝ
8. Ⓨ Ⓝ

___ / 8
Total

NAME: ______________________ **DATE:** ______________

DIRECTIONS Reread "Getting Into the Game." Then, read the prompt and respond on the lines below.

SCORE

___ / 4

If you wanted to earn extra money for something, what would you do to earn it? Write about what you would want to buy and how you would earn the money.

NAME: ____________________ **DATE:** ____________

DIRECTIONS Read the text and then answer the questions.

SCORE

1. Ⓨ Ⓝ
2. Ⓨ Ⓝ
3. Ⓨ Ⓝ
4. Ⓨ Ⓝ
5. Ⓨ Ⓝ

___ / 5 **Total**

You know where North America is, and you might also know where South America is. But there is an important place between them that you might not know about. That place is called *Central America*. There are seven countries in Central America. In most of them, the people speak Spanish. That is because long ago, people from Spain explored there. And for many years, Central America belonged to Spain. But after many years of Spanish rule, those countries did not want to belong to Spain anymore. They saw that Mexico and the United States were free. They wanted the same thing for themselves. So in the early 1800s, those countries declared their independence. Today, each of those seven countries has its own government.

1. Why do most people in Central America speak Spanish?

- (A) Many years ago, people from England explored there.
- (B) Central America does not have many people.
- (C) Central America is very close to Spain.
- (D) For many years, Central America belonged to Spain.

2. Which is a good title for this text?

- (A) All About Spain
- (B) The History of Central America
- (C) Where to Go in Mexico
- (D) Let's Visit the United States

3. Which word is a synonym for *independent*?

- (A) free
- (B) Spanish
- (C) government
- (D) central

4. What part of the adjective *independent* could be taken away to make its antonym?

- (A) *–endent*
- (B) *indep–*
- (C) *in–*
- (D) *–ent*

5. What is the meaning of *declare*?

- (A) ask
- (B) state
- (C) grow
- (D) run

NAME: ______________________ **DATE:** ______________

DIRECTIONS Read the text and then answer the questions.

SCORE

1. Ⓨ Ⓝ

2. Ⓨ Ⓝ

3. Ⓨ Ⓝ

4. Ⓨ Ⓝ

5. Ⓨ Ⓝ

___ / 5
Total

Explorers from Spain were not the first people to live in Central America. Another group of people was already living there when the Spanish came. They were the Mayans. The Mayans are a group of American Indians. They have lived in Central America for thousands of years. For a very long time, they had a strong empire. It stretched from southern Mexico to northern Colombia. The Mayans were the first American Indians to have their own written language. They were also very skilled at math. And they were especially skilled at astronomy. There is no longer a Mayan empire. But you can still see the ruins of many Mayan buildings, and there are still many Mayan people. They live in several places in Central America. They have their own language and their own culture.

1. Which statement is **not** true about the Mayans?

Ⓐ There are no more Mayans.
Ⓑ They are a group of American Indians.
Ⓒ They live in several places in Central America.
Ⓓ They have their own language and culture.

2. Which event happened first?

Ⓐ The Spanish came to Central America.
Ⓑ You can see ruins of Mayan buildings.
Ⓒ The Mayans created a strong empire.
Ⓓ The Mayan empire disappeared.

3. Which word is a synonym for *skilled*?

Ⓐ afraid
Ⓑ unable
Ⓒ unknown
Ⓓ talented

4. What does the noun *ruins* tell readers?

Ⓐ There are no ruins of Mayan buildings.
Ⓑ People still live in those Mayan buildings.
Ⓒ People no longer live in those Mayan buildings.
Ⓓ Mayan buildings are brand new.

5. What is the tone of the text?

Ⓐ informative
Ⓑ humorous
Ⓒ persuasive
Ⓓ inspirational

NAME: ______________________ **DATE:** ______________

DIRECTIONS Read the text and then answer the questions.

Because Central America is close to the equator, it has a tropical climate. Most of Central America has two seasons, a rainy season and a dry season. The rainy season usually lasts from May to November. Central America has two coasts. On the east are the Caribbean Sea and the Atlantic Ocean. On the west is the Pacific Ocean. Some parts are so narrow that going from coast to coast takes very little time. For example, Panama is one country in Central America. In some parts of Panama, there are only 30 miles between coasts! There isn't much flat land in Central America. Most of the land is hilly, and there are many mountains. In fact, Central America has several active volcanoes. The weather is sometimes very hot and humid on the coasts. But in the mountains, it is cooler. Central America has several rainforests. Many animals and plants live there.

1. Why does Central America have a tropical climate?

- (A) It is very narrow.
- (B) It is very far from the equator.
- (C) It is very large.
- (D) It is near the equator.

2. Which statement is true about Central America?

- (A) It has very few animals or plants.
- (B) It is mostly a large desert.
- (C) It is very hilly, and there are many mountains.
- (D) The weather is very cold most of the year.

3. Which word is an antonym of *narrow*?

- (A) wide
- (B) watery
- (C) wild
- (D) windy

4. The adjective *tropical* describes which word?

- (A) Central America's climate
- (B) time
- (C) miles
- (D) volcanoes

5. What is the tone of the text?

- (A) informative
- (B) silly
- (C) persuasive
- (D) serious

SCORE

1. (Y) (N)

2. (Y) (N)

3. (Y) (N)

4. (Y) (N)

5. (Y) (N)

___ / 5

Total

NAME: ______________________ **DATE:** ______________

WELCOME TO HONDURAS!

Do you enjoy seeing all kinds of different animals? Would you like to visit a place where you can swim in the sea and hike in the mountains? Then, you would probably enjoy a trip to Honduras. The country of Honduras is located in the middle of Central America. Many years ago, it was part of the Mayan empire. Then, it belonged to Spain until 1821. It was even a part of Mexico for a time. That is why the people of Honduras speak Spanish. But since 1838, Honduras has been an independent country. Most of the country is mountainous, so the climate tends to be cooler. But along the Caribbean coast, the land is flat; there, the climate is warm and humid and the beaches are beautiful.

There are many things to do and see in Honduras. You can visit beautiful Mayan ruins and see how the people lived thousands of years ago. You can take a hike through a rainforest. There, you will see hundreds of different kinds of plants and animals. You can even go diving from a coral reef off the Caribbean coast. You can take a beach vacation, and go swimming and snorkeling. You can see a professional soccer game, too. Hondurans love soccer, and there are many teams.

Honduras has several cities. Its capital is Tegucigalpa (tay-goo-see-GAL-pah). That city is in the mountains. Another very popular city is La Ceiba (la SAY-bah). La Ceiba is on the beach. It is a very popular vacation place. Every year in May, the people of La Ceiba have a carnival with parades, dances, and lots of good food. During the carnival, the city also holds a Milk Fair, which is a lot like a farmer's market. People from rural areas bring in their animals and crops to the Milk Fair to show and sell.

No matter what you decide to do in Honduras, you won't be bored!

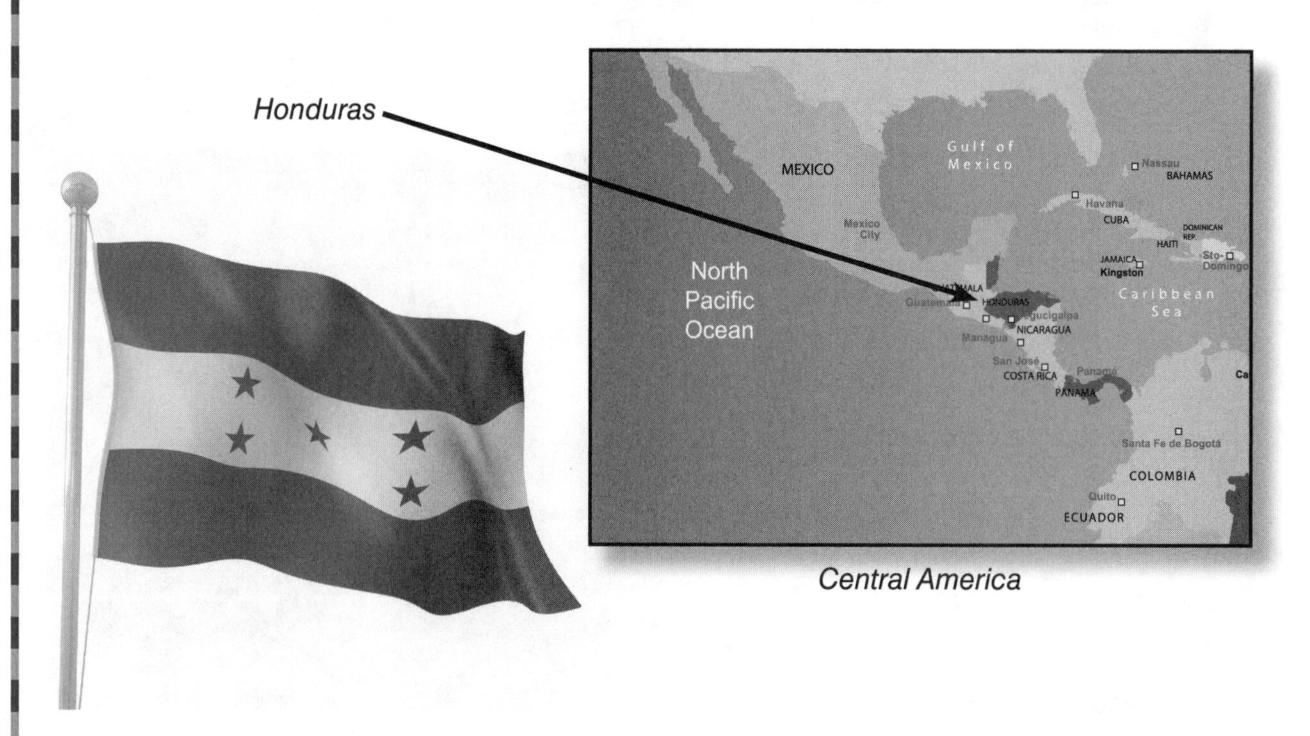

Central America

NAME:______________________ DATE:________________

DIRECTIONS Read "Welcome to Honduras!" and then answer the questions.

1. Who might be interested in reading this text?

(A) a person who likes mountain ranges
(B) a person who wants to travel to Honduras
(C) a person who likes plants
(D) a person who speaks Spanish

2. Knowing where Central America is located helps the reader understand

(A) where to find Honduras.
(B) what the Milk Fair is.
(C) how to go snorkeling.
(D) how to play soccer.

3. How does the author likely feel about Honduras?

(A) The author does not know about it.
(B) The author dislikes it.
(C) The author is afraid of it.
(D) The author likes it.

4. How does the climate of Tegucigalpa likely compare to the climate of La Ceiba?

(A) It is much warmer.
(B) It is cooler.
(C) It is the same.
(D) It is much drier.

5. If Honduras belonged to France instead of Spain, which language would people probably speak?

(A) English
(B) Spanish
(C) French
(D) Dutch

6. Why might La Ceiba be popular for vacations?

(A) It has a very cool, rainy climate.
(B) It has beautiful beaches.
(C) It is high up in the mountains.
(D) It is very close to New York City.

7. Where is the country of Honduras located?

(A) the western part of Central America
(B) the middle of Central America
(C) the eastern part of Central America
(D) the southern part of Central America

8. What is a word or phrase that summarizes the author's opinion about Honduras?

(A) small
(B) very cold
(C) fun for visitors
(D) remote

SCORE

1. (Y)(N)
2. (Y)(N)
3. (Y)(N)
4. (Y)(N)
5. (Y)(N)
6. (Y)(N)
7. (Y)(N)
8. (Y)(N)

___ / 8
Total

NAME: ____________________ DATE: ____________

DIRECTIONS Reread "Welcome to Honduras!" Then, read the prompt and respond on the lines below.

SCORE

___ / 4

Imagine you are going to Honduras. What kind of vacation would you want? Write about your Honduras vacation.

NAME: ____________________ **DATE:** ____________________

DIRECTIONS Read the text and then answer the questions.

SCORE

1. Ⓨ Ⓝ
2. Ⓨ Ⓝ
3. Ⓨ Ⓝ
4. Ⓨ Ⓝ
5. Ⓨ Ⓝ

___ / 5 Total

Scented candles were one of Heather's favorite things. She particularly liked fruit-scented candles like cherry and strawberry. But she liked lots of other scents, too. She wasn't allowed to light her candles very often. Her mom and dad were afraid that her little sister, Sophia, would get too close to them and burn herself. But Heather lit her candles whenever she could. She enjoyed the way her candles made her room smell—it was as warm and comforting as a fuzzy favorite blanket. The candles helped Heather relax. She even swore that they helped her focus better when she was doing homework. One day, Heather's friend Brittany gave Heather an idea she had never considered before. "I'll bet candles wouldn't be hard to make," Brittany said. "You should learn to make your own."

1. Who is the main character?

Ⓐ Sophia
Ⓑ Heather
Ⓒ Dad
Ⓓ Brittany

2. What does Brittany think about Heather?

Ⓐ Heather should light her candles all the time.
Ⓑ Heather should buy a lot of candles.
Ⓒ Heather should get rid of her scented candles.
Ⓓ Heather should learn to make her own candles.

3. Which word is a synonym for *focus?*

Ⓐ compose
Ⓑ imagine
Ⓒ read
Ⓓ concentrate

4. Which adverb has a similar meaning as *particularly*?

Ⓐ frequently
Ⓑ hardly
Ⓒ especially
Ⓓ carefully

5. What is the phrase *as warm and comforting as a fuzzy favorite blanket* an example of?

Ⓐ a simile
Ⓑ personification
Ⓒ a metaphor
Ⓓ hyperbole

NAME: ______________________ **DATE:** ______________

DIRECTIONS Read the text and then answer the questions.

SCORE

1. Ⓨ Ⓝ
2. Ⓨ Ⓝ
3. Ⓨ Ⓝ
4. Ⓨ Ⓝ
5. Ⓨ Ⓝ

___ / 5 Total

Heather's friend Brittany had suggested that she learn to make candles. That idea made a lot of sense to Heather because she loved scented candles, and it might be fun to learn to make them. So Heather asked her mom and dad about candle making. Neither of them knew how to do it, but her dad suggested that Heather think about getting a candle-making kit. A few craft stores in town sold them. Maybe one of the people who worked in the stores would have some good ideas. Heather liked her dad's idea, so one Saturday afternoon, her mom drove her and Brittany to a few craft stores. The first one they visited didn't sell candle-making kits. But at the second store, they saw several. One of the salespeople helped Heather choose the right kit for a beginner. Heather couldn't wait to start.

1. Where does most of this text take place?

Ⓐ craft stores
Ⓑ school
Ⓒ Brittany's house
Ⓓ the supermarket

2. How will Heather learn to make candles?

Ⓐ She will work with a candle maker.
Ⓑ She will take lessons.
Ⓒ She will use a candle-making kit.
Ⓓ Her mom and dad will teach her.

3. Which word is an antonym of *beginner*?

Ⓐ seller
Ⓑ learner
Ⓒ novice
Ⓓ expert

4. In this text, what part of speech is the word *candle-making*?

Ⓐ noun
Ⓑ adjective
Ⓒ adverb
Ⓓ verb

5. What is the meaning of *kit* in this text?

Ⓐ a baby animal
Ⓑ a set of supplies for making something
Ⓒ a collection of clothes
Ⓓ a container

NAME: ______________________ **DATE:** ______________

DIRECTIONS Read the text and then answer the questions.

Heather was very excited to get started making her own candles. Heather's mom and dad had gotten her a candle-making kit, and she was eager to begin using it. The kit contained everything she would need: wax, wicks, molds, scented oil, and coloring. Heather's kit came with enough supplies for two kinds of candles: pillar candles and container candles. Pillar candles were tall and straight, and container candles were shorter and wider. The kit came with round, silver boxes for the container candles. Heather invited Brittany over to help make candles, and the two girls began. They decided to start with a pillar candle. Heather's mom helped them melt the wax, and Heather put the wick in the mold. When the wax was ready, Heather and Brittany carefully poured it into the mold. They added some red coloring and some strawberry scent. Soon, Heather had her own strawberry candle!

1. What is the first step in making Heather's candle?

- (A) melting the wax
- (B) adding red coloring and strawberry scent
- (C) putting the wick in the mold
- (D) pouring the wax into the mold

2. Which object does **not** come in the candle-making kit?

- (A) molds
- (B) wax
- (C) scented oil
- (D) matches

3. Which word is a synonym for *supplies*?

- (A) wax
- (B) materials
- (C) boxes
- (D) candles

4. Which word from the text is a verb?

- (A) container
- (B) scented
- (C) poured
- (D) own

5. What is the meaning of *mold* in this text?

- (A) soft, loose earth
- (B) a furry growth
- (C) a hollow form that gives shape
- (D) a frame

SCORE

1. (Y)(N)

2. (Y)(N)

3. (Y)(N)

4. (Y)(N)

5. (Y)(N)

___ / 5 Total

NAME: ______________________ **DATE:** ______________

LIGHTING THINGS UP

Heather's friend Brittany had suggested that Heather learn to make candles. Heather was really grateful to Brittany for that idea. Heather's mom and dad had gotten her a candle-making kit, and she was really enjoying it. She had already made two pillar candles—one was a strawberry candle and the other one had a vanilla scent. That weekend, Heather was planning to make a container candle. This one would be lavender. Heather invited Brittany over to spend the night on Friday to help her. When Brittany got to Heather's house, she tossed her backpack on Heather's bed, and the two girls got started.

Heather's dad saw them a few minutes later and teased Heather about spending all her time making candles. "You just wait—you'll thank me!" Heather teased back, and the girls returned to what they were doing. By the time they were finished preparing the container candle, it was almost time for dinner. Heather's mom had ordered pizza, and everyone crowded to feast on the pizza when it arrived. Then suddenly, the lights went out!

"I guess it's a neighborhood blackout," her dad said, glancing out the window, "It's dark all over the street."

All of a sudden, Heather and Brittany looked at each other. They both had the same idea. They ran up to Heather's room and got some candles, including the two that Heather had made. Then, they brought them downstairs to the living room. Heather's dad found a lighter and lit the candles, and in no time at all, there was plenty of light to eat dinner.

"You see?" Heather said triumphantly. "I was right! My candles saved the day." Her dad admitted that Heather was right and promised not to tease her again about the candles.

About two hours after everyone finished eating, the power was restored. Everyone was relieved, even though it had been sort of fun to eat by candlelight. Heather and Brittany returned to making candles. They would be handy to have around next time there was a blackout.

NAME: ______________________ DATE: ______________

DIRECTIONS Read "Lighting Things Up" and then answer the questions.

1. When is the power restored?

Ⓐ before the blackout
Ⓑ after dinner is over
Ⓒ before Heather and Brittany get home from school
Ⓓ after Heather and Brittany go to bed

2. Which prediction makes the most sense?

Ⓐ Heather's parents will stop making candles.
Ⓑ Heather's dad will tell her to stop making candles.
Ⓒ Heather's dad will not tease her again about making candles.
Ⓓ Heather's dad will tease her the next time she makes a candle.

3. At the end of the text, how do Heather's parents likely feel about her making candles?

Ⓐ grateful
Ⓑ worried
Ⓒ angry
Ⓓ jealous

4. What can be inferred about the setting of this text?

Ⓐ It takes place during school.
Ⓑ It takes place early in the morning.
Ⓒ It takes place in the middle of the night.
Ⓓ It takes place in the evening.

5. Which of these books would Heather likely want to read?

Ⓐ *A Biography of Thomas Edison*
Ⓑ *You Can Sew Your Own Clothes*
Ⓒ *The Best New Candle Designs!*
Ⓓ *How to Win at Computer Games*

6. Why is the street so dark during the blackout?

Ⓐ The other houses on the street do not have power.
Ⓑ There are no other houses.
Ⓒ The other houses are hidden behind trees.
Ⓓ The street is very long and narrow.

7. Which is the best summary?

Ⓐ This text is about making lights work.
Ⓑ This text is about making candles.
Ⓒ This text is about stars.
Ⓓ This text is about night lights.

8. What does it mean that Heather's candles *saved the day*?

Ⓐ She is sad about being teased.
Ⓑ The candles helped the family have light during the blackout.
Ⓒ Her candles were made in one day.
Ⓓ Heather wants to save the candles to use another day.

SCORE

1. Ⓨ Ⓝ
2. Ⓨ Ⓝ
3. Ⓨ Ⓝ
4. Ⓨ Ⓝ
5. Ⓨ Ⓝ
6. Ⓨ Ⓝ
7. Ⓨ Ⓝ
8. Ⓨ Ⓝ

___ / 8
Total

NAME: ______________________ **DATE:** ______________

DIRECTIONS Reread "Lighting Things Up." Then, read the prompt and respond on the lines below.

SCORE

___ / 4

In this story, Heather learns to make candles. What would you like to learn to make? How would you learn? Write about what you would like to learn to make and how you would learn it.

NAME: ____________________ **DATE:** ____________

DIRECTIONS Read the text and then answer the questions.

What kinds of rights do you think people should have? For example, you probably think that people have the right to be safe from burglars. There are a lot of other rights that many people think we should have, too. That is why we need to have a government. Governments are there to protect the rights of citizens. In return, citizens support the government by paying taxes and obeying laws, and some serve in the armed forces. There are many different kinds of governments. One of them is the republic, which is the kind of government the United States has. In a republic, citizens elect people to represent them. Those representatives make laws that protect the citizens. In a republic, citizens do not vote on laws, but elect people to make and vote on laws.

1. According to this text, why do we need to have a government?

- (A) to protect the rights of citizens
- (B) to pay taxes and obey laws
- (C) to serve in the military
- (D) to give people what they want

2. Which is **not** something citizens do to support the government?

- (A) pay taxes
- (B) obey laws
- (C) serve in the military
- (D) make laws

3. Which word is defined as *a person who lives in a state or country*?

- (A) representative
- (B) republic
- (C) law
- (D) citizen

4. Which noun below can also be used as a verb?

- (A) government
- (B) republic
- (C) support
- (D) citizens

5. What is the meaning of the phrase *in return*?

- (A) as a favor
- (B) instead of
- (C) in exchange
- (D) most of the time

SCORE

1. Ⓨ Ⓝ
2. Ⓨ Ⓝ
3. Ⓨ Ⓝ
4. Ⓨ Ⓝ
5. Ⓨ Ⓝ

___ / 5
Total

NAME: ______________________ DATE: ______________

DIRECTIONS Read the text and then answer the questions.

SCORE

1. Ⓨ Ⓝ
2. Ⓨ Ⓝ
3. Ⓨ Ⓝ
4. Ⓨ Ⓝ
5. Ⓨ Ⓝ

___ / 5
Total

There are many other kinds of governments besides republics. One of them is the monarchy. A monarchy is a government that is run by a ruler, often a king or a queen. The monarchy is one of the oldest forms of government. Many ancient people were ruled by monarchs. For example, in ancient Egypt, the monarch was called the Pharaoh (FAIR-oh). China and Japan had monarchs for a very long time, too. Some monarchies still exist today. For example, both England and Spain have monarchs. For many centuries, monarchs made all the decisions, and they could do whatever they wanted. But that is not true today. Today's monarchs usually do not have the last word when it comes to making decisions. The decisions are made by a group of representatives. The monarch still has some power, but it is shared with others.

1. What is this text mostly about?

- Ⓐ China
- Ⓑ representatives
- Ⓒ Japan
- Ⓓ monarchies

2. Which statement is true about monarchies?

- Ⓐ In a monarchy, the government is run by a ruler.
- Ⓑ There are no more monarchies.
- Ⓒ The monarchy is a brand-new form of government.
- Ⓓ Monarchies were not common in ancient times.

3. Which word is a synonym for *monarch*?

- Ⓐ country
- Ⓑ government
- Ⓒ ruler
- Ⓓ power

4. The root *cent* means 100. The noun *centuries* probably means

- Ⓐ hundreds of days
- Ⓑ hundreds of years
- Ⓒ thousands of days
- Ⓓ thousands of years

5. What does the phrase *to have the last word* mean?

- Ⓐ to make the decision
- Ⓑ to say something last
- Ⓒ to have no power
- Ⓓ to stand behind everyone else

NAME: ______________________________ **DATE:** ________________

DIRECTIONS Read the text and then answer the questions.

Sometimes, a government is run by a small group of people. That form of government is called an *oligarchy.* The people who run an oligarchy are all members of the same group. They are not elected to office. Instead, they hold power because they belong to that particular group. Some oligarchies are run by the very wealthy. Some are run by the members of a ruling family. Sometimes, they are run by members of one political party. There have been many oligarchies in history. For example, the kingdom of Sparta was a city-state in ancient Greece. It was run by an oligarchy. The ruling class of Sparta had all of the power and made all of the decisions. Ordinary people did not vote. The Soviet Union lasted from 1917 to 1991; it was also an oligarchy. Only members of the Communist Party could hold office. There have been other oligarchies, too.

1. Why are the people who run an oligarchy in charge?

- (A) The people elect them.
- (B) They are members of the same group.
- (C) They do not want to be in charge.
- (D) They know how to run a government.

2. Which is a fact about an oligarchy?

- (A) A king or queen makes all of the decisions.
- (B) Anyone may be elected.
- (C) Ordinary people do not vote.
- (D) There is no government.

3. The root *arch* means *chief* in *oligarchy*. What does the root *oli–* mean?

- (A) many
- (B) few
- (C) the study of
- (D) universe

4. Which word from the text is an adjective?

- (A) wealthy
- (B) party
- (C) oligarchy
- (D) member

5. What is the tone of the text?

- (A) informative
- (B) silly
- (C) persuasive
- (D) serious

SCORE

1. Ⓨ Ⓝ
2. Ⓨ Ⓝ
3. Ⓨ Ⓝ
4. Ⓨ Ⓝ
5. Ⓨ Ⓝ

___ / 5
Total

NAME: ______________________ **DATE:** ______________

WHO'S IN CHARGE?

For as long as people have lived in groups, they have had leaders. And when people began to live in cities, they began to create governments. Governments do several things for people. A government helps to protect people's rights and keep the peace. Governments also protect the borders of the countries they serve. They also provide things such as education, highways, and mail service. People cannot easily provide those things for themselves. So the government provides them. In return, people pay taxes, obey laws, and support the government.

People have tried many different forms of government. For example, one of the earliest forms of government was the *monarchy*. In a monarchy, a ruler, usually a king or queen, is in charge. For many years, monarchs had all of the power. They made all of the decisions. Those monarchies are called *absolute monarchies*. There are still monarchies today. But the rulers cannot do whatever they want. Today, most monarchs share power. They work with a group of elected representatives. The people vote for the members of that group. These monarchies are called *constitutional monarchies*. England and Spain are constitutional monarchies.

People have also been ruled by *oligarchies*. In an oligarchy, the government is run by a small group. Some are run by the wealthy, and others are run by members of a ruling family. Still others are run by members of the same political party. In many oligarchies, the people do not vote. The people who run the government are in charge because they are members of a particular group.

Queen Elizabeth II of England

Today, people want a voice in their government, and they want to be able to vote. So many governments are run by people who are elected to office. For example, many governments are republics. In a republic, the people vote, but they do not directly vote on laws. They vote for representatives. Then, those representatives make laws and vote on those laws. The United States is a republic. France, Israel, and Ireland are also republics.

As you can see, there are many different kinds of governments. Which government do you think works best?

NAME:____________________ **DATE:**______________

DIRECTIONS Read "Who's In Charge?" and then answer the questions.

1. If a reader doesn't remember what an *oligarchy* is, what could he or she do?

- (A) Review the title and the picture.
- (B) Reread the paragraph that has that word in it.
- (C) Say the word out loud.
- (D) Write the word a few times.

2. How is an absolute monarchy different from an oligarchy?

- (A) An absolute monarchy is run by a small group.
- (B) An absolute monarchy is very large.
- (C) An absolute monarchy is run by one ruler.
- (D) An absolute monarchy is elected by the people.

3. What might happen if there were no government?

- (A) People would pay taxes.
- (B) People would not be as safe.
- (C) There would be new highways.
- (D) People would vote in elections.

4. People who like to vote would like what form of government?

- (A) a republic
- (B) an oligarchy
- (C) an absolute monarchy
- (D) a king or queen

5. What is a purpose for reading this text?

- (A) to learn about different kinds of government
- (B) to learn how to vote
- (C) to read a personal story
- (D) to learn about a visit to England

6. How do absolute monarchs most likely feel about people who vote?

- (A) They want to teach them to vote.
- (B) They want them to vote.
- (C) They do not want them to vote.
- (D) They encourage them to vote.

7. What is something that the many different types of government have in common?

- (A) They have a queen or king.
- (B) All the citizens can vote.
- (C) They have nothing in common.
- (D) They protect their citizens and keep peace.

8. Why do you think many monarchies are now constitutional monarchies?

- (A) The people want a king or a queen.
- (B) Rulers do not want to share power.
- (C) Rulers want to share power.
- (D) The people want a voice.

SCORE

1. (Y)(N)
2. (Y)(N)
3. (Y)(N)
4. (Y)(N)
5. (Y)(N)
6. (Y)(N)
7. (Y)(N)
8. (Y)(N)

___ / 8
Total

NAME: ______________________________ **DATE:** ________________

SCORE

___ / 4

DIRECTIONS Reread "Who's In Charge?" Then, read the prompt and respond on the lines below.

If you could design a government, what would it be like? Write about the government you would have.

NAME: ______________________ **DATE:** ______________

DIRECTIONS Read the text and then answer the questions.

SCORE

Austin liked to spend time at his friend Devin's house. One of the greatest things about Devin's family was that Devin's older brother, Jacob, had his own band. Jacob and his band practiced in Devin's garage, and Austin really liked to hear them play. One day, Austin and Devin were talking about the band, and Austin suggested they should start a band of their own. Devin wasn't in the least bit interested in being in a band, but he said Austin ought to learn to play the guitar. "Who knows?" Devin said, "You might get really famous." Austin thought about what his friend had said. Maybe it would be a good idea to learn to play the guitar—the electric guitar. Then, when he was good enough at it, he could have a band like Jacob's even if Devin didn't want to join.

1. Who is the main character?

Ⓐ Devin
Ⓑ Austin
Ⓒ Jacob
Ⓓ Dad

2. What is Devin's suggestion for Austin?

Ⓐ He suggests that Austin not come to the house.
Ⓑ He suggests that Austin forget about music.
Ⓒ He suggests that Austin play in Jacob's band.
Ⓓ He suggests that Austin learn to play the guitar.

3. Which prefix could you add to *interested* to make a word that means "not in the least bit interested?"

Ⓐ *hyper–*
Ⓑ *semi–*
Ⓒ *un–*
Ⓓ *sub–*

4. Which word from the text can be both a noun and a verb?

Ⓐ idea
Ⓑ interested
Ⓒ band
Ⓓ talking

5. Which word has the same meaning as the phrase *ought to*?

Ⓐ should
Ⓑ cannot
Ⓒ might
Ⓓ could

1. Ⓨ Ⓝ
2. Ⓨ Ⓝ
3. Ⓨ Ⓝ
4. Ⓨ Ⓝ
5. Ⓨ Ⓝ

___ / 5
Total

NAME: ______________________ DATE: ______________

DIRECTIONS Read the text and then answer the questions.

SCORE

1. Ⓨ Ⓝ
2. Ⓨ Ⓝ
3. Ⓨ Ⓝ
4. Ⓨ Ⓝ
5. Ⓨ Ⓝ

___ / 5
Total

Austin had decided he wanted to learn to play the electric guitar. It was originally his friend Devin's idea, but the more he thought about it, the more Austin liked the idea of being a guitarist in a band. So he asked his parents if he could have a guitar. His mom and dad liked the idea, too, but they thought that an electric guitar might be really expensive. Austin thought so himself. Then one day, he stopped into a music-supply store to look at prices. He noticed a few ads at the store for used guitars. He asked the manager about the ads. "Oh, sure," the manager said. "People are always selling used guitars. That's really the best way for a beginner to get an inexpensive instrument." Now Austin knew how he could get a guitar without spending a lot of money.

1. What do Austin's mom and dad believe?

Ⓐ A guitar might be really expensive.
Ⓑ Austin should not play the guitar.
Ⓒ Austin can use their guitar.
Ⓓ A guitar will probably be very cheap.

2. How will Austin get a guitar without spending a lot of money?

Ⓐ The manager will give him a guitar.
Ⓑ His mom and dad will give him a guitar.
Ⓒ He will buy a used guitar.
Ⓓ He will not get a guitar.

3. Which prefix can be added to *expensive* to make its antonym?

Ⓐ *in–*
Ⓑ *hypo–*
Ⓒ *mal–*
Ⓓ *super–*

4. What does the suffix *–ist* in the noun *guitarist* mean?

Ⓐ very small
Ⓑ brand new
Ⓒ special kind
Ⓓ someone who does something

5. What is *inexpensive instrument* an example of?

Ⓐ personification
Ⓑ alliteration
Ⓒ simile
Ⓓ metaphor

NAME: ______________________ **DATE:** ______________

DIRECTIONS Read the text and then answer the questions.

Austin wanted to learn to play the electric guitar. His mom and dad thought it was a good idea, too, but they were concerned about the cost, and so was Austin. The solution to the problem turned out to be a used guitar. Austin had discovered that many musicians sell inexpensive, used electric guitars. So he returned to the music supply store where he had seen ads for guitars. He wrote down the names and telephone numbers listed on the ads. He didn't recognize any of the names he saw on the ads. So his mom and dad insisted on going with him when he went to look at the guitars. The first two guitars he wanted to see had already been sold, but the third one was still for sale, and Austin liked it. In a very short time, Austin had his electric guitar.

1. What is this text mostly about?

- (A) the history of the electric guitar
- (B) how Austin learns to play the guitar
- (C) how Austin gets an electric guitar
- (D) where to find an electric guitar

2. What happens before Austin's mom and dad go with him to look at guitars?

- (A) Austin buys the guitar he wants.
- (B) Austin writes down the names and numbers listed on the ads.
- (C) Austin and his parents look at guitars.
- (D) Austin finds out that two of the guitars have already been sold.

3. Which prefix can be added to *sold* to make a word that means "still for sale"?

- (A) *sub–*
- (B) *ambi–*
- (C) *bi–*
- (D) *un–*

4. What does the verb *returned* tell you about Austin?

- (A) He has never been to the music-supply store.
- (B) He has been to the music-supply store before.
- (C) He does not know where the music-supply store is.
- (D) He will never go to the music-supply store.

5. What is the tone of the text?

- (A) sarcastic
- (B) informal
- (C) persuasive
- (D) guilty

SCORE

1. Ⓨ Ⓝ
2. Ⓨ Ⓝ
3. Ⓨ Ⓝ
4. Ⓨ Ⓝ
5. Ⓨ Ⓝ

___ / 5 Total

NAME: ______________________ **DATE:** ______________

PLAYING IN THE BAND

Austin wanted to play the electric guitar. His friend, Devin, had first suggested the idea, and Austin thought it was a great one. Someday, he wanted to be in a band, but first he had to learn to play. So he bought a used electric guitar from a musician who was selling it. At first, Austin thought it would be easy to learn how to play. Devin's brother, Jacob, played electric guitar, and it looked easy when Austin watched him. But as soon as Austin tried to play his own guitar, he realized how mistaken he was.

Austin tried to play the same songs he heard Jacob and his band play, but he couldn't make his guitar sound the same at all. It wasn't long before he decided he was going to need lessons. Austin's mom and dad had thought of that, too, and together, the three of them found a guitar teacher. Austin attended the first few lessons, but he began to get bored. His teacher kept giving him little songs and music exercises to do, not real songs like Jacob played. When Austin complained to his mom and dad about it, his mother advised him, "Be patient. You need to learn the basics first so you can sound good later when you play harder songs." Austin didn't believe her, but he wasn't a quitter, either. So he kept going for lessons and practicing.

After a while, Austin started to sound good when he played, and he began to be able to play harder songs. One day, Jacob and his band even let Austin play a song with them. Austin didn't know if he was ever going to be famous, but it was going to be fun finding out!

NAME: ______________________ **DATE:** ______________

DIRECTIONS Read "Playing in the Band" and then answer the questions.

1. Why does Austin try to play his new guitar as soon as he gets it?

- (A) He starts to sound better.
- (B) He takes guitar lessons.
- (C) He thinks it will be easy to play.
- (D) He realizes that playing the guitar is not easy.

2. Why do Jacob and his band sound better than Austin does at first?

- (A) They have practiced more and played longer.
- (B) They have newer guitars.
- (C) They do not practice.
- (D) They have a bigger place to play.

3. Which reflects a reasonable purpose for reading this story?

- (A) to learn how to play an instrument in a band
- (B) to sign up to be in the school band
- (C) to read about a character who likes music
- (D) to read about a famous musician who plays in a band

4. Which would be a good gift for Austin?

- (A) a basketball
- (B) a science kit
- (C) a guitar songbook
- (D) a cookbook

5. What does Austin most likely hope will happen in the future?

- (A) He will have his own band someday.
- (B) He will stop playing the guitar.
- (C) He will never visit Devin and Jacob.
- (D) He will play only easy songs.

6. What inference can be made about Austin's mom and dad?

- (A) They do not know Austin wants guitar lessons.
- (B) They want to play the guitar.
- (C) They wish Austin would not take guitar lessons.
- (D) They are glad Austin is taking guitar lessons.

7. At the end of the text, what is Austin's attitude towards playing the guitar?

- (A) bored
- (B) confused and frustrated
- (C) jealous of Jacob's band
- (D) proud and pleased with his hard work

8. Why doesn't Austin like his music lessons at first?

- (A) His teacher doesn't give him real songs to play.
- (B) His music teacher is rude to him.
- (C) He can't understand what his music teacher says.
- (D) He doesn't want to be in a band.

SCORE

1. Ⓨ Ⓝ
2. Ⓨ Ⓝ
3. Ⓨ Ⓝ
4. Ⓨ Ⓝ
5. Ⓨ Ⓝ
6. Ⓨ Ⓝ
7. Ⓨ Ⓝ
8. Ⓨ Ⓝ

___ / 8 **Total**

NAME: ______________________ **DATE:** ______________

DIRECTIONS Reread "Playing in the Band." Then, read the prompt and respond on the lines below.

SCORE

___ / 4

What have you learned to do well? Did it take a lot of practice? Write about what you have learned to do well and how you learned it.

ANSWER KEY

Week 1

Day 1
1. A
2. C
3. B
4. B
5. A

Day 2
1. D
2. C
3. B
4. A
5. B

Day 3
1. A
2. A
3. B
4. D
5. C

Day 4
1. D
2. D
3. B
4. A
5. C
6. A
7. C
8. B

Day 5
Responses will vary.

Week 2

Day 1
1. C
2. B
3. D
4. C
5. A

Day 2
1. B
2. A
3. D
4. D
5. C

Day 3
1. D
2. C
3. A
4. C
5. D

Day 4
1. B
2. B
3. D
4. B
5. A
6. B
7. D
8. A

Day 5
Responses will vary.

Week 3

Day 1
1. B
2. C
3. A
4. D
5. D

Day 2
1. C
2. D
3. C
4. D
5. A

Day 3
1. A
2. C
3. B
4. D
5. B

Day 4
1. B
2. A
3. D
4. D
5. C
6. C
7. B
8. A

Day 5
Responses will vary.

Week 4

Day 1
1. A
2. A
3. C
4. B
5. C

Day 2
1. A
2. D
3. C
4. D
5. C

Day 3
1. C
2. C
3. A
4. A
5. D

Day 4
1. C
2. D
3. B
4. B
5. D
6. D
7. B
8. A

Day 5
Responses will vary.

Week 5

Day 1
1. C
2. B
3. A
4. C
5. D

Day 2
1. A
2. B
3. D
4. C
5. C

Day 3
1. B
2. C
3. C
4. D
5. A

Day 4
1. A
2. C
3. C
4. A
5. D
6. A
7. B
8. D

Day 5
Responses will vary.

Week 6

Day 1
1. B
2. A
3. D
4. A
5. A

Day 2
1. D
2. B
3. D
4. A
5. C

Day 3
1. B
2. A
3. D
4. B
5. C

ANSWER KEY *(cont.)*

Week 6 *(cont.)*

Day 4
1. D
2. C
3. C
4. A
5. C
6. C
7. D
8. B

Day 5
Responses will vary.

Week 7

Day 1
1. D
2. C
3. A
4. A
5. B

Day 2
1. C
2. B
3. C
4. A
5. D

Day 3
1. A
2. D
3. D
4. C
5. B

Day 4
1. A
2. D
3. D
4. B
5. D
6. A
7. B
8. C

Day 5
Responses will vary.

Week 8

Day 1
1. D
2. B
3. C
4. B
5. B

Day 2
1. C
2. A
3. D
4. B
5. A

Day 3
1. D
2. C
3. C
4. A
5. B

Day 4
1. B
2. C
3. D
4. A
5. C
6. C
7. B
8. A

Day 5
Responses will vary.

Week 9

Day 1
1. A
2. C
3. B
4. B
5. C

Day 2
1. B
2. D
3. B
4. D
5. A

Day 3
1. D
2. B
3. C
4. B
5. C

Day 4
1. C
2. B
3. D
4. B
5. D
6. B
7. A
8. C

Day 5
Responses will vary.

Week 10

Day 1
1. C
2. A
3. D
4. B
5. B

Day 2
1. A
2. C
3. A
4. B
5. D

Day 3
1. B
2. A
3. C
4. C
5. C

Day 4
1. D
2. C
3. D
4. B
5. B
6. A
7. B
8. C

Day 5
Responses will vary.

Week 11

Day 1
1. C
2. C
3. D
4. D
5. B

Day 2
1. B
2. C
3. A
4. B
5. C

Day 3
1. A
2. D
3. C
4. C
5. C

Day 4
1. A
2. D
3. B
4. D
5. A
6. D
7. A
8. C

Day 5
Responses will vary.

Week 12

Day 1
1. C
2. B
3. D
4. A
5. A

ANSWER KEY *(cont.)*

Week 12 *(cont.)*

Day 2
1. C
2. B
3. C
4. C
5. D

Day 3
1. D
2. C
3. B
4. A
5. C

Day 4
1. A
2. B
3. B
4. A
5. A
6. A
7. D
8. C

Day 5
Responses will vary.

Week 13

Day 1
1. C
2. B
3. A
4. B
5. D

Day 2
1. C
2. B
3. A
4. D
5. C

Day 3
1. A
2. D
3. D
4. C
5. D

Day 4
1. B
2. A
3. A
4. B
5. D
6. D
7. C
8. D

Day 5
Responses will vary.

Week 14

Day 1
1. A
2. A
3. B
4. C
5. D

Day 2
1. C
2. B
3. A
4. C
5. D

Day 3
1. B
2. A
3. D
4. A
5. C

Day 4
1. D
2. B
3. D
4. B
5. A
6. A
7. C
8. A

Day 5
Responses will vary.

Week 15

Day 1
1. A
2. C
3. C
4. D
5. A

Day 2
1. B
2. D
3. D
4. A
5. A

Day 3
1. B
2. D
3. A
4. A
5. A

Day 4
1. D
2. D
3. C
4. B
5. B
6. B
7. A
8. B

Day 5
Responses will vary.

Week 16

Day 1
1. A
2. B
3. C
4. C
5. C

Day 2
1. A
2. B
3. B
4. D
5. A

Day 3
1. C
2. A
3. D
4. B
5. D

Day 4
1. B
2. A
3. D
4. C
5. A
6. B
7. C
8. D

Day 5
Responses will vary.

Week 17

Day 1
1. D
2. A
3. B
4. A
5. C

Day 2
1. C
2. B
3. A
4. C
5. D

Day 3
1. A
2. A
3. D
4. C
5. C

Day 4
1. C
2. A
3. C
4. D
5. B
6. D
7. B
8. A

ANSWER KEY *(cont.)*

Week 17 *(cont.)*

Day 5

Responses will vary.

Week 18

Day 1

1. C
2. D
3. A
4. C
5. B

Day 2

1. D
2. B
3. B
4. A
5. C

Day 3

1. C
2. A
3. D
4. B
5. C

Day 4

1. D
2. C
3. A
4. B
5. B
6. D
7. A
8. C

Day 5

Responses will vary.

Week 19

Day 1

1. C
2. B
3. A
4. D
5. D

Day 2

1. A
2. C
3. B
4. C
5. B

Day 3

1. B
2. C
3. A
4. D
5. A

Day 4

1. C
2. D
3. B
4. B
5. B
6. D
7. A
8. C

Day 5

Responses will vary.

Week 20

Day 1

1. D
2. B
3. A
4. C
5. B

Day 2

1. D
2. A
3. C
4. A
5. A

Day 3

1. C
2. B
3. D
4. A
5. D

Day 4

1. C
2. B
3. B
4. A
5. A
6. A
7. C
8. B

Day 5

Responses will vary.

Week 21

Day 1

1. D
2. B
3. A
4. C
5. A

Day 2

1. A
2. D
3. C
4. B
5. B

Day 3

1. C
2. D
3. A
4. D
5. B

Day 4

1. D
2. A
3. A
4. D
5. C
6. B
7. C
8. D

Day 5

Responses will vary.

Week 22

Day 1

1. A
2. D
3. B
4. B
5. C

Day 2

1. C
2. A
3. B
4. D
5. A

Day 3

1. B
2. D
3. B
4. C
5. B

Day 4

1. D
2. A
3. A
4. A
5. D
6. B
7. C
8. C

Day 5

Responses will vary.

Week 23

Day 1

1. A
2. A
3. D
4. A
5. D

Day 2

1. C
2. B
3. D
4. B
5. A

ANSWER KEY *(cont.)*

Week 23 *(cont.)*

Day 3
1. B
2. B
3. D
4. C
5. D

Day 4
1. C
2. C
3. A
4. B
5. B
6. D
7. D
8. A

Day 5
Responses will vary.

Week 24

Day 1
1. C
2. A
3. D
4. A
5. D

Day 2
1. B
2. A
3. D
4. B
5. C

Day 3
1. C
2. D
3. B
4. A
5. C

Day 4
1. C
2. A
3. B
4. B
5. A
6. C
7. B
8. A

Day 5
Responses will vary.

Week 25

Day 1
1. A
2. A
3. B
4. D
5. C

Day 2
1. A
2. C
3. D
4. B
5. A

Day 3
1. B
2. C
3. B
4. D
5. A

Day 4
1. B
2. C
3. B
4. A
5. A
6. C
7. D
8. D

Day 5
Responses will vary.

Week 26

Day 1
1. B
2. C
3. A
4. D
5. D

Day 2
1. A
2. D
3. B
4. C
5. A

Day 3
1. D
2. A
3. C
4. A
5. C

Day 4
1. D
2. A
3. D
4. B
5. D
6. A
7. A
8. C

Day 5
Responses will vary.

Week 27

Day 1
1. B
2. D
3. A
4. C
5. D

Day 2
1. A
2. C
3. B
4. A
5. D

Day 3
1. D
2. C
3. A
4. B
5. C

Day 4
1. C
2. D
3. B
4. D
5. A
6. B
7. C
8. B

Day 5
Responses will vary.

Week 28

Day 1
1. B
2. D
3. C
4. A
5. A

Day 2
1. C
2. A
3. B
4. D
5. C

Day 3
1. D
2. A
3. B
4. C
5. B

Day 4
1. B
2. B
3. D
4. A
5. D
6. A
7. B
8. C

Day 5
Responses will vary.

ANSWER KEY *(cont.)*

Week 29

Day 1
1. A
2. A
3. C
4. B
5. C

Day 2
1. B
2. A
3. C
4. B
5. A

Day 3
1. D
2. A
3. C
4. A
5. A

Day 4
1. D
2. B
3. B
4. D
5. C
6. A
7. A
8. A

Day 5
Responses will vary.

Week 30

Day 1
1. D
2. A
3. C
4. C
5. B

Day 2
1. C
2. B
3. D
4. C
5. D

Day 3
1. D
2. A
3. C
4. C
5. B

Day 4
1. A
2. D
3. B
4. C
5. A
6. C
7. B
8. C

Day 5
Responses will vary.

Week 31

Day 1
1. C
2. A
3. D
4. C
5. A

Day 2
1. B
2. D
3. C
4. A
5. A

Day 3
1. D
2. A
3. B
4. C
5. C

Day 4
1. D
2. A
3. D
4. C
5. A
6. A
7. A
8. A

Day 5
Responses will vary.

Week 32

Day 1
1. C
2. B
3. A
4. A
5. D

Day 2
1. B
2. D
3. A
4. C
5. B

Day 3
1. A
2. C
3. D
4. C
5. B

Day 4
1. D
2. D
3. A
4. A
5. A
6. B
7. C
8. C

Day 5
Responses will vary.

Week 33

Day 1
1. D
2. B
3. A
4. C
5. B

Day 2
1. A
2. C
3. D
4. C
5. A

Day 3
1. D
2. C
3. A
4. A
5. A

Day 4
1. B
2. A
3. D
4. B
5. C
6. B
7. B
8. C

Day 5
Responses will vary.

Week 34

Day 1
1. B
2. D
3. D
4. C
5. A

Day 2
1. A
2. C
3. D
4. B
5. B

ANSWER KEY *(cont.)*

Week 34 *(cont.)*

Day 3

1. A
2. D
3. B
4. C
5. C

Day 4

1. B
2. C
3. A
4. D
5. C
6. A
7. B
8. B

Day 5

Responses will vary.

Week 35

Day 1

1. A
2. D
3. D
4. C
5. C

Day 2

1. D
2. A
3. C
4. B
5. A

Day 3

1. B
2. C
3. B
4. A
5. A

Day 4

1. B
2. C
3. B
4. A
5. A
6. C
7. D
8. D

Day 5

Responses will vary.

Week 36

Day 1

1. B
2. D
3. C
4. C
5. A

Day 2

1. A
2. C
3. A
4. D
5. B

Day 3

1. C
2. B
3. D
4. B
5. B

Day 4

1. C
2. A
3. C
4. C
5. A
6. D
7. D
8. A

Day 5

Responses will vary.

REFERENCES CITED

Marzano, Robert. 2010. When Practice Makes Perfect...Sense. *Educational Leadership* 68 (3): 81–83.

National Reading Panel. 2000. Report of the National Reading Panel. *Teaching Children to Read: An Evidence-Based Assessment of the Scientific Research Literature on Reading and its Implication for Reading Instruction* (NIH Publication No. 00-4769). Washington, DC: U.S. Government Printing Office.

Rasinski, Timothy V. 2003. *The Fluent Reader: Oral Reading Strategies for Building Word Recognition, Fluency, and Comprehension.* New York: Scholastic.

———. 2006. Fluency: An Oft-Neglected Goal of the Reading Program. In *Understanding and Implementing Reading First Initiatives,* ed. C. Cummins, 60–71. Newark, DE: International Reading Association.

Wolf, Maryanne. 2005. *What is Fluency? Fluency Development: As the Bird Learns to Fly.* Scholastic professional paper. New York: ReadAbout. http://teacher.scholastic.com /products/fluencyformula/pdfs/What_is_Fluency.pdf (accessed June 8, 2007).

DIGITAL RESOURCES

Accessing the Digital Resources

The digital resources can be downloaded by following these steps:

1. Go to **www.tcmpub.com/digital**
2. Sign in or create an account.
3. Click **Redeem Content** and enter the ISBN number, located on page 2 and the back cover, into the appropriate field on the website.
4. Respond to the prompts using the book to view your account and available digital content.
5. Choose the digital resources you would like to download. You can download all the files at once, or you can download a specific group of files.

ISBN:
9781425809270

Please note: Some files provided for download have large file sizes. Download times for these larger files will vary based on your download speed.

CONTENTS OF THE DIGITAL RESOURCES

Teacher Resources

- Assessing Fluency
- Writing Rubric
- Practice Page Item Analysis Chart
- Student Item Analysis Chart

Student Resources

- Practice Pages

NOTES